Wakefield Press

Mary Thomas: Founding Mother

Elizabeth (Beth) Duncan was born at Glenelg, South Australia, a descendant of emigrants who reached the colony in 1839. After completing her schooling in South Australia she worked on a Northern Territory cattle station as a governess for two years, before undertaking nursing training at the Royal Adelaide Hospital. Following the completion of a Diploma in Social Studies at the University of Adelaide she worked as a social worker in Adelaide, Darwin and Brisbane, later gaining her Bachelor of Social Work from the University of Queensland.

After returning to Adelaide, Beth and her architect husband lived and worked on a small farm in the Adelaide Hills, before retiring in 1989. Since then Beth has followed her interests in writing and history, completing the Advanced Diploma of Arts (Professional Writing) at Adelaide TAFE in 2003. This is her first book.

Mary Thomas

Founding Mother

The life and times of a South Australian pioneer

BETH DUNCAN

Wakefield
Press

Wakefield Press
16 Rose Street
Mile End
South Australia 5031
www.wakefieldpress.com.au

First published 2007
Reprinted 2011, 2020

Copyright © Elizabeth (Beth) Duncan, 2007

All rights reserved. This book is copyright. Apart from any fair dealing for the purposes of private study, research, criticism or review, as permitted under the Copyright Act, no part may be reproduced without written permission. Enquiries should be addressed to the publisher.

Edited by Kathy Sharrad and Bethany Clark, Wakefield Press
Cover designed by Liz Nicholson, designBITE
Designed and typeset by Clinton Ellicott, Wakefield Press

National Library of Australia Cataloguing-in-publication entry

Author:	Duncan, Beth.
Title:	Mary Thomas: founding mother: the life and times of a South Australian pioneer / author, Beth Duncan.
ISBN:	978 1 86254 783 4 (pbk.)
Notes:	Includes index.
	Bibliography.
Subjects:	Thomas, Mary, 1787–1875.
	Pioneers – South Australia – History.
	Women pioneers – South Australia – Biography.
	Frontier and pioneer life – South Australia.
Dewey Number:	994.23031092

*To my husband, George Duncan,
who helped me stay the course.*

Contents

Equivalent monetary values · viii
Preface · 1

Part 1

Chapter 1 · Early years, marriage and London · 7
Chapter 2 · The decision to emigrate · 14
Chapter 3 · To the Antipodes · 27
Chapter 4 · A tent village · 41

Part 2

Chapter 5 · Makeshift dwellings in a forest city · 59
Chapter 6 · 'A tree transplanted whole' · 76
Chapter 7 · A wedding celebration in a new home · 90
Chapter 8 · Prosperity · 99

Part 3

Chapter 9 · An ongoing crisis · 117
Chapter 10 · A battle for survival · 130
Chapter 11 · Financial failure · 142
Chapter 12 · After the fall · 155

Part 4

Chapter 13 · Endurance · 173
Chapter 14 · Consolidation and renaissance · 192
Chapter 15 · A new prosperity · 215
Chapter 16 · Last years and requiem · 234

Acknowledgements · 252
Appendix A: Descendants of Robert and Mary Thomas to 1875 · 255
Appendix B: Serious Poems · 258
Notes · 266
Bibliography · 292
Index · 299

Equivalent monetary values

An approximate rate for the conversion of 19th-century prices, expressed in pounds sterling, has been based on the House of Commons Library Research Paper 99/20, Inflation: The Value of the Pound 1750–1998.

The further conversion to Australian dollars has been derived from the list of historical exchange rates published by the Reserve Bank of Australia.

From the House of Commons Research Paper the variation between 1838 and 1878 is within 10 per cent, which justifies the adoption of a single conversion rate throughout this period.

One pound sterling during Mary's years in South Australia approximates to AU$200 in 2007. Changes in the prices of goods and services have not been uniform, however. Some items, very expensive in Mary's time, have now become cheap everyday commodities, particularly those which were handmade and are now mass-produced, for example most footwear and clothing.

A pound was divided into 20 shillings, and a shilling was divided into 12 pennies. One guinea was equal to 21 shillings or £1 and 1 shilling. A sovereign was a gold coin valued at £1.

Preface

The pivotal point, and coincidentally virtually the mid point, of Mary Thomas's long life of 87 years (1787–1875) was the decision taken with her husband, Robert, to be among the first emigrants to make the long, arduous journey, in 1836, to the new colony of South Australia.

Apart from this decision Mary's life before emigration was unremarkable. Neither in Southampton as the daughter of a moderately prosperous merchant and innkeeper, nor as the wife of a successful London Fleet Street law stationer and publisher and the mother of six children, was she markedly different from others of her gender and position. Even the loss of her sixth and youngest child as an infant was not unusual for the times.

She differed in only two significant ways from the majority of her contemporaries who came from a similar social background: her age when she married – at 30 she was older than the average – and her publication of a book of poems (*Serious Poems*, 1831). Mary's poems demonstrate not so much her skill as a poet, but her levels of education and intelligence. Both were considerable.

Her poems also indicate that Mary had liberal views regarding individual rights and freedoms. The founding of South Australia, based upon E.G. Wakefield's theories of emigration, was surrounded by a reformist aura and involved both Dissenters and republicans. The Thomas family's emigration, however, was motivated not only by their desire for an improved society but, as much, by the opportunity emigration offered for economic advancement, especially for their two sons.

Mary in particular emigrated in the belief that she would spend some years in the colony and 'obtain a competence' sufficient to make retirement in England possible for herself, her husband and their three daughters; perhaps in an idyllic village on the outskirts of her native Southampton. This was not a unique view of emigration to the new colony and many of the first settlers had similar ambitions. For Mary, this dream remained unfulfilled. She became, almost against her will, something else – an esteemed South Australian pioneer. Following the economic crises that beset the colony in 1842 with tragic consequences, not only for Mary and her family but for many others, she became her family's strength and mainstay, the support that enabled them to prevail.

In June 1836, just prior to his emigration, Robert Thomas, in partnership with George Stevenson as R. Thomas and Co., published in London the inaugural issue of what was to become the colony's first newspaper, the *South Australian Gazette and Colonial Register*. It marked the beginning of a free press in South Australia, a crucial element in the liberal reformist society promoted through Wakefield's theories of emigration. With almost continuous shortages of skilled staff, Mary became involved in the paper's production during its first years and thus a family engagement with the *Register* newspaper was begun. It was taken up later by Mary's second son, William, then by his sons and continued for almost 100 years. Subsequently, the Thomas's involvement with newspapers was maintained in two further generations through an association with Melbourne's *Herald and Weekly Times* and the Adelaide *Advertiser*.

Mary's eldest son, Robert George, emigrated in 1836 as the 16-year-old apprentice of the deputy surveyor-general, George Kingston; and, as Colonel Light's assistant, he drafted Light's City of Adelaide plan. Ten years later he left the colony for England to qualify as an architect. He eventually returned to Adelaide and after a period in private practice was appointed architect-in-chief for the colony. A number of his buildings still survive and are now listed on South Australia's heritage register.

Both of Mary's sons were significant figures in the colony: through the *Register* in the ideas, values and attitudes the paper espoused; and through architecture in the forging of Adelaide's enduring physical form.

Mary's family, both as individuals and as a group, feature strongly in her narrative – the domestic sphere was the focus of her life. Although she utilised the resources of Adelaide town acre 56 in Hindley Street to make a living and was for a time her family's sole breadwinner, she did not have a public life or a public profile. Most women of her era and social class did not engage in paid employment and, as a rule, those few who did, except for teachers, did not do so away from home. Neither did they join societies nor organisations, as in most instances, they would not have been entitled to membership, even had they sought it. Organisations for women, the Women's Christian Temperance Union and the Women's Suffrage League, did not emerge until the 1880s.

Virginia Woolf's biographer, Hermione Lee, quotes Virginia: 'My memoirs . . . are always private' and Lee comments:

> so were most women's . . . she [Virginia] is acutely aware that the sort of life-writing that might be appropriate for a public figure cannot 'fit' her . . . Virginia Woolf's curriculum vitae is in public terms full of gaps. She did not go to school. She did not work in an office. She did not belong to any institution. With rare exceptions she did not give public lectures or join committees or give interviews.

This lack of a public profile has militated against the writing of biographies of 'private' women. As far as I have been able to discover, the present biography of Mary is one of only two full biographies of a 'private' South Australian woman of this pioneering era. The other, of Mrs Agnes Hay by Anthony Laube, narrates the interaction with the public sphere of a society hostess. And there are only two biographies of others of the same period who might be considered 'public' women: that of Catherine Helen Spence, novelist, journalist and social reformer, by Susan Magarey; and of Matilda Evans, novelist and teacher, by Barbara Wall.

In coinciding with the first four decades of the colony, Mary's story is inextricably linked to the development of South Australia and Adelaide in particular. Mary spent all of her years in the colony in Adelaide, which during this span evolved from a clearing in the bush to a city whose liberal press supported legislative change in promoting the rights of women, and whose public buildings enhanced its planned streets and squares. This development is so closely intertwined with Mary's narrative that the village, then town, then city almost becomes a character in its own right.

Many other pioneer women who shared these early years were less articulate and less heard than Mary, whose diary of the voyage out and whose letters describing the first years of settlement were published posthumously and became very well known. With these women Mary braved the arduous living conditions and privations of the first settlement; worked alongside her husband at the printing press as they did alongside the plough; nursed family members through severe illnesses; and endured. With them she transcended economic disaster and somehow managed to hold her family together. And throughout it all, like many pioneer women, Mary experienced the acute pain of extreme homesickness.

This is not only Mary's story; she shares much of it with all women who reached South Australia during the first years of settlement.

Part 1

Chapter 1
Early years, marriage and London

> *Adieu, fair Southampton! I quit thee forever,*
> *Take leave of thy prospects, this beautiful shore;*
> *Ah, yes! My heart tells me that this time I sever*
> *From my dearly loved birthplace to see it no more.*[1]

Mary Thomas wrote her farewell to her childhood home when she was there in July 1831 to attend her father's funeral. This visit to Southampton was to be her last before she and her husband, with their children, embarked for South Australia. Her verse is prescient – seemingly emigration had always been in the back of her mind. And even at the age of 46, the prospect of emigration did not seem unrealistic or daunting. In about 1833, 14-year-old Frances, Mary's eldest daughter, painted a portrait of her mother, which Mary considered a 'fair likeness'.[2] Frances depicted Mary as youthful-looking and in vibrant good health.

Mary was born in Southampton in 1787, only a few months after the First Fleet left Portsmouth bound for Botany Bay. She was a contemporary of the novelist, Jane Austen (1775–1817); both were born and raised in Hampshire, and when the Austens made their home in Southampton between 1805 and 1808 it was in the same neighbourhood as Mary's, in the vicinity of the Dolphin Hotel.[3] Jane Austen attended balls at the Dolphin and patronised Southampton's theatres[4] – as Mary almost certainly did – and Mary shared many aspects of the social and domestic life that Austen described in her novels.

Mary's parents, George Harris and Mary Batchelor, were in their mid thirties when they married in November 1786.[5] At about the same time George became the proprietor of the Royal George[6], a High Street inn located near the wharves.[7] Mary was born 10 months later, on the 30th August, and was baptised in Southampton's Anglican Holy Rood Church. Her three siblings, Sarah, who lived for only a day or so, Ann, born in 1789, and George, in 1790, were also baptised there.[8] Their mother died[9] a few weeks before Mary's 12th birthday, and in September 1801 her father married Elizabeth Davies, a widow with no children.[10] By year's end George had given up the inn and moved his young family away from the wharves to other High Street premises alongside Holy Rood Church and not far from the Dolphin Hotel, the town's premier inn.[11] From there he sold glassware and the new porcelain tableware,[12] probably to wealthy newcomers who were building fine Georgian houses during an upsurge in Southampton's popularity as a seaside resort town.

During summer the town was crowded and gay. Its role as a strategic port in the wars with France – with the frequent movement of troops throughout the town – imbued a sense of feverish urgency. The High Street overflowed with stagecoaches and carriages carrying ladies dressed in the height of fashion and gentlemen resplendent in regimental uniforms. Visitors and residents graced race meetings, took the air of an evening along the beach promenades, and enhanced the elegance of balls and soirees held at the Assembly Rooms and in the long room of the Dolphin. Theatres, circulating libraries and coffee houses competed for custom, while the wharves offered daily excursion services to the Isle of Wight and other destinations along the coast.[13] The town was in an almost constant state of restless activity, providing an exciting and colourful environment for Mary and her siblings to grow up in.

In selecting a school for his daughters, George Harris had no shortage of choice among the many operating in Southampton.

During the late 18th and early 19th centuries the works of Southampton-born and educated female novelists were popular locally. This may have stimulated a particular interest in writing in Southampton girls' schools. Writing, especially poetry, became Mary's recreation and one of her greatest pleasures.[14]

When Mary was about 21 her father retired from his business but retained an interest in the High Street premises[15] through a lease and a mortgage.[16] He moved his family to a new home, Ashfield Lodge, near the small town of Romsey, in the Test Valley, about 13 kilometres from Southampton.[17] The surrounding countryside was arcadian. Mary and her family took walks and drives in the fine parks of the landed gentry to enjoy the serene vistas of the valley – meadows dotted with grazing cattle and sheep and in summer reapers bringing in the corn. The New Forest with its great trees, its deer and ponies, was only a short trip by carriage from Mary's home.[18]

Mary shared her father's home with her stepmother and her sister Ann. There is nothing to suggest that her relationship with her stepmother was other than amicable, but Mary and Ann did not get on – the sisters' relationship probably during these years, and certainly later, was acrimonious. Ann married Benjamin Self, a publican from Hursley, a hamlet near the Harris home, c. 1816, shortly before Mary's own marriage.[19]

On 8 January 1818, six months after her 30th birthday, Mary married Robert Thomas in Southampton's Holy Rood Church. Robert, six years Mary's senior, was a self-employed, modestly prosperous London law stationer and publisher. He was one of three sons and six daughters and grew up on his family's farm, Rhantregwnwyn, near the border of the then Welsh county of Montgomeryshire and England's Shropshire. Robert's forebears had owned land in the district for many generations and were probably successful yeoman farmers.[20]

As an aspiring younger son, by the age of 21 Robert was living in London,[21] where he would later establish his career and business at 203 Fleet Street, serving customers drawn from law firms in the vicinity of the nearby courts.[22] Mary and Robert set up home above the business, only a short walk from Temple Bar and the Strand, in a building with a Georgian-style shopfront and an apartment of three upper floors plus an attic.[23]

In November 1818, 11 months after their marriage, their first child, Frances Amelia, was born. Frances was followed by Robert George in 1820, and then William Kyffin 18 months later. Mary had two more girls, Mary Jnr, who was born on her mother's birthday in 1823, and Helen in 1825. Alfred completed her family in 1827. All of Mary and Robert's children were baptised in the Anglican parish of St Dustan's in the West.[24] This crumbling medieval church, located in Fleet Street, was demolished in 1830,[25] and Mary commemorated the consecration of the new St Dunstan's in 1833 with a hymn[26] – an indication that members of the Thomas family were regular worshippers there.

From the upper windows of her apartment Mary looked out on sights utterly unlike the tranquil beauty of the Test Valley – London's sheer size, noise and pollution had demanded many adjustments of her. Its population had doubled during the 18th century and had reached one million by 1800, making it the largest city in the world. The capital continued to swell during the new century, doubling its rate of growth again to reach two million by 1850.[27] Inevitably, services were overwhelmed by this ever-increasing demand as people, like the Thomases, left rural life and flocked to the city hoping to enhance their prospects.[28] By 1841 less than two thirds of its population had been born in London.[29] The rapidly expanding population caused serious problems – drinking water, described as 'offensive and destructive to health', was drawn from the Thames, which was virtually an open sewer.[30] Foetid, congested courts at the end of squalid, airless alleys to the back of Fleet Street, particularly around Fetter Lane, were only a short walk from Mary's home. Alfred, Mary's last born, succumbed to these unhealthy conditions at the age of 16 months; in some districts during these years one child in three died in their first year of life.[31] Mary attempted to assuage her grief in verse:

> Memory still unwilling
> To relinquish holds thee fast, and oft
> In fancy paints thy smiling image
> With its little hands held forth for aid.³²

Despite London's serious detractions it could, nevertheless, engage and enthral. By the late 1820s, inspired by the vision of King George IV, it was becoming a magnificent capital. All around her Mary watched the development of beautiful thoroughfares, like Regent Street, and the creation of splendid buildings to house great institutions, such as the British Museum and the National Gallery.³³ Across from her home and just beyond Fleet Street, in the relative peace of Middle Temple Gardens on the bank of the Thames, Mary could survey the river's sweep and the panorama of its traffic from the Houses of Parliament to the Tower. Directly beneath her windows was the hubbub of Fleet Street, and immediately opposite, in Dick's Coffee House, the arguing and debating of London's literati.³⁴

Mary and Robert paid to have water connected to their home,³⁵ probably to the kitchen. It was a luxury, which suggests a modest prosperity, even though Mary managed with only one live-in servant.³⁶ In many homes meals were frequently brought in from nearby coffee houses or cookshops, particularly when visitors were expected, making home management easier.³⁷ The first floor of dwellings above business premises was generally used as a living room, combining dining room and parlour with bedrooms on the upper floors. In comfortable but relatively modest homes of the period, such as Mary's, it was usual to dine at a table which was afterward, especially when entertaining, put against a wall to free space for dancing or musical evenings.³⁸ Mary commemorated in verse a friend's musical skill:

> A harp his energies drew forth,
> Upraised his soul and prov'd his talent's worth,
> Gaine'd him applause, esteme and well earn'd fame.³⁹

In 1831 she published her writings as *Serious Poems*. They celebrated the simple pleasure and contentment to be found in the beauty of nature, and in singing and music-making in the company of friends. Her writing also expressed the right of all, regardless of race, to freedom from oppression. Other poems reflected Mary's deeply held Christian faith.

Mary visited Southampton in April 1831 and accompanied her father to his lawyer, Mr Clements, to make his will.[40] After Mary's marriage, and sometime before June 1821, George Harris Snr had moved to Hill[41], where his second wife, Elizabeth, died in 1822.[42] Hill was a picturesque village on the outskirts of Southampton with thatched cottages and well-tended gardens. The village had expanded during Southampton's building boom to include larger dwellings[43] and George Snr had acquired two sizeable villas, with a garden and a small amount of land attached to each. Three months after making his will, Mary's father died at the age of 83.[44] His home in one of the villas, with its contents and his personal effects, he bequeathed to Benjamin Self, Ann's husband, and Robert Thomas inherited the other.[45]

Mary's father had also procured the lease of the Anchor Inn at Redbridge, near Millbrook on the outskirts of Southampton, and had then sublet it. Included as part of the inn were stables, a granary, outhouses, vaults, cellars, yards, watercourses and gardens. The right to operate it and its profits went to Ann, but from them she was required to pay her brother, George, an annuity of £25 per year. Mary's father had also retained the mortgage of £1000 on the business premises in High Street, Southampton, which he bequeathed to Mary along with the balance of its yearly interest after a further £5 annuity had been paid to George. Mary's inheritance amounted to about £50 a year, which at the time was a considerable sum. Ann was also left the residue of the estate after debts had been settled; it may have been that Ann was her father's favourite, or perhaps Mary had received the more generous marriage settlement. George's share was minimal and he was constrained, on pain of disinheritance, from contesting their father's will, indicative of some family tensions.

Despite the strictures he placed upon George, the action of Mary's father in making specific provision for his daughters demonstrates, what was for the time, a liberal-minded concern to provide them with a measure of independence. Mary would come to rely upon his bequest during the testing years ahead. George Harris was buried beside his first wife in St Mary's churchyard, Southampton. Mary arranged and paid for the headstone on her mother's grave to be replaced by a double stone dedicated to the memory of both her parents.[46]

About 18 months after her father's death, two of Mary's friends died within a few weeks of each other. They were elderly brothers – Mary was very fond of both and she memorialised them in her unpublished manuscript book of poems.[47] In the same book during 1833 she also commemorated the loss of a close female friend[48] and earlier, in *Serious Poems*, she had recorded her grief at the deaths of two other female friends.[49] Between about 1830 and September 1833, in little more than three bleak years, Mary had endured the deaths of six people to whom she was deeply attached. Mary's grief may have made the notion of emigration more acceptable to her and the parting from England easier to contemplate and less daunting. It may also have seemed to her that one phase of her life had reached a conclusion and that her life should now expand in a new direction and take on new interests and new challenges.

Chapter 2
The decision to emigrate

The first information about the proposed colony of South Australia reached Mary and Robert in mid 1835, through their friend Dr Inman of Portsmouth, who was in London to purchase land in South Australia for one of his sons.[1] At the time, their second son, William, was at home on summer holidays from his boarding school at Rickmansworth[2], and although he was only 13-and-a-half, Mary was already worried about his future prospects. He was, she believed, 'not likely to be placed in any business'.[3] The economy was experiencing one of its periodic downturns and without influential connections, the sons of the lower middle classes were hard-pressed to obtain positions with any likelihood of future prosperity or advancement – nepotism was rife. This worry, together with Robert George's wish to go overseas[4], and Dr Inman's enthusiasm about the opportunities for young men in the proposed colony, prompted Robert and Mary to make further enquiries.

It was only a short walk from the Thomas home in Fleet Street to the offices of the South Australian Commission and the meeting rooms of the South Australian Association at the Adelphi in the Strand, where Robert and Mary would have met the colonial secretary designate, Robert Gouger. He no doubt referred them – as he referred all enquirers[5] – to Edward Gibbon Wakefield's *The New British Province of South Australia*. This pocket-sized handbook, published in 1835, contained five chapters and was designed to give potential settlers an overview of the development plan for the new colony.[6] It provided general information, such as what was known of the geography and topography of Australia's southern coast, its climate and its suitability for agriculture, its relative position with regard to foreign trade (including a table of sailing distances from English ports), and the price and availability of livestock from New South Wales and Van Diemen's Land. A full chapter was devoted to Wakefield's concept of 'scientific colonisation' and its key principle – the systematic sale of land to fund the emigration of a workforce. It also discussed some of the problems facing other already established colonies, including the shortage of reliable, skilled labour and the dispersing of populations due to indiscriminate land grants. In his conclusion Wakefield emphasised the importance of establishing a newspaper – which would have been of particular interest to Robert who was contemplating setting up a printing business in the new colony.

At the Adelphi Mary and Robert met other intending colonists who gathered to exchange practical information, including the most suitable types of clothing, temporary accommodation, furniture and household items to be taken out. These groups also monitored the progress of the commissioners in their development of plans for the new colony, such as the appointment of its officers, and the progress of the land sales. Later, Mary and Robert almost certainly joined other would-be settlers at the Conversazione Club's fortnightly lectures and discussions, also held at the Adelphi. Among the topics relating to South Australia they reviewed were: geology, irrigation, artesian wells, internal water carriage and contact with the Aborigines. The club also organised sub-committees to examine matters like wages and industrial relations in the colony, the development of religious instruction, the building of churches, and the establishment of schools.[7]

From these sources, and from meeting and talking with long-standing supporters of Wakefield's concepts for the new colony (members of the South Australian Association, such as

Edward Wright, George Kingston and Osmond Gilles)[8], Mary and Robert became aware that the idea to found a new colony had been circulating in London since about 1829. It had been promoted by several successive groups, but finally came to fruition under the auspices of the South Australian Association, formed in December 1833. The proposed location of the new colony was influenced by Captain Matthew Flinders' charts of 1802, and by Captain Charles Sturt's exploration of the River Murray in 1830.

By August 1834 the British Parliament had passed legislation (*South Australia Act* 1834) to establish the new colony based on Wakefield's scheme for the systematic sale of land rather than the granting of land to colonists. This could be achieved, Wakefield argued, through investment in preliminary land orders in London and then the orderly surveying and allocation of land upon arrival in the colony. South Australia was to be founded without forced labour and to achieve this, funds raised from land sales would be used to provide for the emigration, from the ranks of the poor and the unemployed, an equal number of men and women with a range of trades and skills. Mary's distaste for slavery and any form of enforced labour meant that she would have welcomed this, and also the expectation that many from the labouring classes would prosper in the colony and acquire land themselves.

Robert and Mary noted that the act to establish South Australia provided for: the colony to be free of transported convicts; colonisation commissioners to oversee the sale of land set at a minimum 12 shillings per acre (0.4 ha); emigration to be delayed until land worth £35,000 had been sold; and for the establishment of a constitution when the population had reached 50,000. The colony was to be self-sufficient in meeting the costs of its foundation and governance; a loan of £80,000 – using the unsold land in the colony as collateral – was to be raised to defray these costs.[9]

The 12-member Commission – appointed under the chairmanship of Colonel Robert Torrens (a member of parliament and a political economist with an interest in emigration) – included George Fife Angas, a wealthy Dissenter, who was to emigrate later.[10] The commissioners had taken office only in May 1835, and with the Commission so recently established, it was obvious to Mary and Robert that there was still a great deal of work to be done before the first emigrant vessels could embark.

Mary and Robert were fortunate that they lived so near to the Adelphi – the sources of information there and the opportunities for contact with others intending to emigrate were readily available and easily made. They assessed and weighed up the material they had garnered and, according to Mary, were influenced by the view held by many that 'the plan on which this colony is founded is . . . [thought] superior to all others'. This, plus the belief that it was 'an excellent opportunity for young men' and the hope that Frances's health 'might be improved by a sea voyage and a change of climate', encouraged Mary to support Robert's 'inclination to become a landholder in this new Province'.[11]

By the end of September Mary and Robert had bought 134 acres (54 ha), at 12 shillings an acre for a total of £80, which also entitled them to an acre in the principal town.[12] The decision to emigrate had been made – Robert had definite plans not only to open a printing office but also to start a business as a general storekeeper. William did not return to school and was placed with a friend and printer in Fleet Street to learn as much as he could about the trade during the time left in London.[13] Robert George had already been working and developing his knowledge of draftsmanship, and his exhibition of drawings and maps at the Adelphi had brought him to the attention of the deputy surveyor-general designate for the colony, George Kingston.[14]

It is clear that Mary and Robert believed that their ambition for their sons 'to become possessed of considerable property' could not be fulfilled in England. Mary's hope was that emigration would provide the boys with a head start on their way to becoming men of wealth and substance. Her wish for herself was, ultimately, to return to England with the girls and Robert to enjoy a financially comfortable retirement, perhaps in the countryside near Southampton.[15]

By establishing the first store and first printing business, Mary and Robert anticipated having the whole of the local trade, at least for some time. Also, they reasoned, investment in substantial amounts of land at a fixed price before emigration provided the opportunity to profit later from real estate transactions in the colony. The purchase of a preliminary land order gave them a preferential first choice of land and the right to the 'free' passage of their tradesmen or labourers, which was to be to be funded through land sales.

As well, there is little doubt that Mary and Robert shared many of the social and philosophical values of those who promoted the new form of colonisation as a utopian experiment. Mary may not have considered herself an active reformer, but she would have felt comfortable in the company of social reformers such as Lord Shaftesbury and William Wilberforce, the anti-slavery campaigner. She shared the belief in the freedom of religious worship, which was so sought after by the non-conformist sects or Dissenters.

Many from the 'middling' class considered the *Reform Act 1832* to reform the parliament had not gone far enough to create a society that was both more just and more liberal. They saw the solution in a new beginning elsewhere – in a land where civil and religious liberty would prevail, where class structure no longer limited opportunities for the majority of young men, and where Dissenters could escape the tithes and strictures of the Established (Anglican) Church.

By the end of September 1835 the funds raised from the sale of preliminary land orders had not reached £35,000, the amount required for the colony to proceed. The bid to found the new colony was rescued through a major investment by George Fife Angas, one of the commissioners. He resigned from the Commission and was able to negotiate very favourable conditions for his joint stock firm that became the South Australian Company. Such a major investment in a very large parcel of land, predominantly in the control of one man, did not please many of the would-be settlers. They believed Angas's purchase breached the principles upon which South Australia was to be founded by introducing privilege and the potential for undue influence. If the colony was to proceed without long delays, however, there was little alternative but to accept Angas's offer.[16]

Further complications arose toward the end of December 1835, this time during negotiations between the commissioners and the Colonial Office. The Colonial Office had advised that 'the Government expected the Commissioners in fixing the boundaries of the Province to occupy ground only as it is unoccupied by the Natives'.[17] John Brown, the designated colonial emigration agent, pondered this new development.

> *What is to be the interpretation of the word 'occupy' is the question. The Act [to establish the colony of South Australia] itself declares the ground to be waste and unoccupied and the question, if raised at all, ought to have been raised before it was past [sic]. But it is not occupied according to any law regulating possession which is recognized by civilized people.*

Brown interpreted the government's edict as simply its attempt to avoid censure 'by Quakers or others upon the ground of supposed Humanity or Abstract Rights'. For Brown, however, it raised the question of the value of the land. He considered 'buying land by a few hatchets or old clothes may be a purchase in one sense', but it was dishonourable 'because the native is ignorant of a false price'. He posited that the Indigenous inhabitants should have what the settlers were paying for it, the price of the preliminary land order – 12 shillings per acre (per 0.4 ha).[18]

The matter continued to be debated during January 1836. A committee of settlers was appointed to draw up a memorial to the Colonial Office, requesting permission to start at once. Inspired by this committee, or perhaps as a part of it, and with Mary's support, Robert Thomas wrote to the parliamentary under secretary, Sir George Grey, on the 16th January. Robert's letter is significant because of the insight it provides into the attitudes Robert and

Mary held toward the Aborigines – a people they had not yet met – probably in common with most of their fellow emigrants.

> *I cannot but express my feelings of regret and disappointment [by the delay imposed upon us]. It is well known that the natives [of Australia] consist of wandering tribes, wholly independent of each other, who continually traverse from place to place without any fixed habitation, and, with all deference to superior judgement, I conceive these wandering propensities of the aborigines of Australia be sufficient reason why the millions of fertile acres over which they tread, like the beasts of the earth, unconscious of their value and ignorant of their use, may be taken possession of by a colony of civilized people, without doing them the smallest injury ... what wrong can it do them if others till that which is now a waste, but which is capable of maintaining many thousands of the over abundant population of Great Britain in comfort and affluence, and may soon become a valuable acquisition to the mother country? [The Aborigines] will be considered as brethren, not enemies; their ignorance pitied, not despised. They will be treated with kindness and compassion, and their wants, as far as may be practicable, relieved ...*

It is clear Mary shared Robert's views. The draft manuscript of the letter shows editing in her handwriting; she introduced a more conciliatory tone by softening some of Robert's phrasing although not his underlying meaning.[19]

The British Government's response to the ongoing debate and representations from prospective colonists was to insist upon a protector of Aborigines being appointed before allowing the colony to proceed. It was eventually, several months later, added onto the list of offices of the governor's private secretary, George Stevenson, as no other candidate was available. Much to the dismay of most of the intending colonists and the many Dissenters among them – whose ideals of religious freedom resented any suggestion of an established church – the Colonial Office also insisted upon a colonial chaplain on a government stipend, and appointed the

Reverend Charles Beaumont Howard. In order to avoid any further delay the commissioners eventually acquiesced to this last demand.[20]

After months of deferment the new colony of South Australia and its first governor, Captain John Hindmarsh RN, were gazetted on 2 February 1836.[21] The commissioners were now in a position to conclude the appointment of the colony's officials and to begin final preparations for the departure of the first settlers. Colonel William Light was appointed surveyor-general in early March 1836 and was given the huge task of surveying the acres that were to be taken up by the purchasers of preliminary land orders. It was intended that the surveyors should reach the colony in advance of the colonists and would have the survey well underway upon their arrival. Due to his ill health, Light's departure was delayed until May[22], but his deputy George Kingston, with his survey party, set sail on the *Cygnet* at the end of March. Sixteen-year-old Robert George Thomas joined Kingston as his apprentice.[23]

The final approval for the founding of South Australia[24] was the signal for Mary and Robert and others intending to sail on the first emigrant vessel to begin to put their affairs in order. All of the materials Robert required for his printing office and goods for the store had to be bought or assembled, packed and made ready for departure. February and March were months of hectic, exhausting, but nonetheless exhilarating activity – they were on the verge of an adventure and a new life. By the end of March, Mary and Robert had, as Mary put it, 'disposed' of their Fleet Street business, arranged temporary accommodation at Fish Street, sold the house near Southampton, and packed their personal possessions.[25] Hard decisions had been made in choosing what would be of practical use in the new colony, and what could be left behind. Tears were shed and sadness coped with; not all of their clothes or household goods could be taken, nor all of the treasures of individual family members – space on board emigrant vessels was at a premium.

For Mary, the task of organising and undertaking washing, ironing, repairing, making or purchasing the quantity of clothing required for the entire Thomas clan was onerous; and she had recently 'let go' her servant, who did not wish to emigrate.[26] This is to say nothing of the packing up of family furniture, furnishings, kitchen equipment and cooking utensils, and other personal possessions, including Mary's treasured clock made by 'William Poulton and Sons, Watchmaker to His Majesty the King of Spain'.[27] Supplies and dry stores were bought, boxed, crated and labelled for the voyage – there would be no readily available replacement for anything forgotten, lost or left behind. Mary also packed prints, muslins, gingham and scotch cambric for Robert's planned general store.[28] Packing cases were everywhere and the household was in uproar.

On 14 May, John Brown, the designated emigration agent, was informed that the passenger vessel, the *Africaine* 'has been conditionally engaged', and a few days later he advised intending passengers to confirm their arrangements. Under the supervision of her commander, Captain John Duff, the ship was being provisioned at the London Docks, ready for departure in a matter of weeks.[29]

On hearing this news, Mary and Robert set out from London to make their last visit to Hampshire, spending about a week 'taking leave' of old friends at Havant, Gosport and Chalton, where they engaged two agricultural labourers, Jacobs and Windebank, who were willing to emigrate, and a young woman, Mary Lillywhite, employed as a servant. Mary then left Robert to continue on by himself to Southampton. She 'absolutely refused to go . . . lest it should shake [her] resolution altogether'.[30] Mary's brother George Harris – from whom she was estranged at the time due to an upset over her sale of the house inherited from their father – and his family were still in Southampton, and her parents' graves were in St Mary's churchyard. It seems Mary could not quite face the reality that, in all likelihood, these ties to her childhood home were to be broken forever.

Her decision not to go to Southampton was also partly influenced by her concern at having left 17-year-old Frances to manage the care of the children: William (14), Mary Jnr (12) and Helen (10).

On her return to London, much to her distress, Mary found Helen in the throes of a serious illness, 'which soon proved to be scarlet fever of a very malignant kind'. This presented her with unforeseen difficulties just weeks before they were to set sail; particularly as, soon after, it became apparent that Mary Jnr also had the fever. Scarlet fever, although a commonplace childhood illness in the 19th century, was nevertheless a very serious disease and potentially life-threatening; sufferers frequently developed complications and could sustain long-term damage to the heart or kidneys. Frances 'had had the fever [previously] at Southampton when she was laid up with so severe a sore throat that her life was in danger'.[31] For Mary, the illness was an old adversary and she knew its dangers, but there was virtually no treatment, no antibiotics and little in the way of general medication. The only remedy available to try to combat the girls' fever was the almost continuous sponge-bathing of them with tepid water. Extreme swelling of the girls' throats could restrict their breathing and they needed Mary's constant attention – regular poulticing of their throats and frequent salt water gargles provided the only possibility of reducing the inflammation. Mary was desperate to get the girls well enough for their impending voyage as she was very apprehensive about how, in a weakened condition, they would cope with the rigours of ship-board life. The pressure upon Mary was unremitting, with the situation sufficiently grave for Robert to have 'applied to the captain of the vessel to delay the sailing for a few days, but it could not be allowed'.[32] Despite her assiduous nursing care, which provided some comfort and eased the girls' distress, Mary knew the illness had to run its course and that their recovery and the length of time it took was largely out of her hands.

Her energy was drained, not only from lack of sleep in attending to her sick children, but also due to her anxiety that the future of the entire family would be jeopardised if the girls did not recover sufficiently to allow the family to make the voyage. It was also possible that William would become infected, and if he had the illness at the time of their anticipated departure, they would not be allowed to sail. 'As all our luggage was shipped, as well as many tons of goods, such as paper, press, type etc and our money paid it would have been an awkward situation and a great loss to us as we must have waited for another vessel.'[33] Having sold their London business they had no means of income until they reached South Australia and re-established a business in the new colony. The cost of supporting themselves, possibly for many months, while awaiting berths on another ship would significantly erode capital intended for investment in the new colony. Mary's last weeks in England were fraught indeed.

Meanwhile, negotiations between Robert and George Stevenson to form the partnership of R. Thomas and Co., general printers, were at an advanced stage.[34] Before being appointed the governor's private secretary, Stevenson was employed as the joint editor of the *Globe and Traveller*, a London Whig newspaper.[35] He was born in 1799, the son of a gentleman farmer of Berwick-on-Tweed, and as a 12-year-old he went to sea with his uncle, the captain of an East Indiaman. Some years later Stevenson travelled through Central America and the West Indies and became a correspondent for the *Globe and Examiner* (later the *Globe and Traveller*). He was a tall man, six foot three (211 cm), of imposing physique, intellect and presence.[36]

Within weeks of his appointment by Governor Hindmarsh, he had married Margaret, the daughter of the former editor of the *Globe and Traveller*, John Gorton. Margaret was born in 1807 and, according to her granddaughter, Violet de Mole, was a very cultivated woman – an excellent German, Italian and French scholar. Both musically talented and possessing a good singing voice, Margaret had been a London art and music critic. Violet de Mole described her as:

> *small rather frail and dainty with fair hair and clear grey eyes of great animation. Her keen satirical pen and turn of wit would have perhaps made her many enemies but she was deeply religious and of a generous disposition.*[37]

Together, George and Margaret Stevenson made a formidable team.

It is not known when Stevenson met Robert and Mary38, but it is clear that it was at his suggestion that he and Robert join forces. Together they planned to publish the colony's first newspaper, the *South Australian Gazette and Colonial Register*; with Stevenson as editor and R. Thomas and Co. as printers and publishers. The business was awarded the government printing contract by the Colonial Office for the life of the partnership and Robert was designated government printer.[39] With this appointment and his new status as a newspaper proprietor, Robert and Mary were assured positions of substance within colonial society.

The formal partnership agreement between Robert and Stevenson, which gave Stevenson full editorial control over the paper, was signed on the 16th June, and just two days later, the first and only London edition of the *South Australian Gazette and Colonial Register* was issued.[40] It notified interested observers, and all those intending to emigrate, of the imminent departure of the first South Australian colonists. In his editorial, Stevenson rebutted the recent criticisms of the colony which had appeared in some London papers. He described the scheme for the foundation of the new colony:

> as possessing none of the characteristics of the rash projector, but is the result of the patient investigation of men qualified by years and experience to form a sound judgement, and who in all other relations of life, have acted on opinions cautiously adopted, deliberately confirmed, and fully capable of practical development ... the plan for the colonization of South Australia is one of the nature we have described [and its planners] His Majesty's Commissioners [are] gentlemen whose intelligence and honour are undisputed and indisputable.

A naval vessel, the HMS *Buffalo*, was provided by the government to take out Governor Hindmarsh and his family, George and Margaret Stevenson, the colony's resident commissioner, and other colonial officials, as well as a full complement of emigrants.

It required an extensive refit at the naval docks and was to sail three weeks after the *Africaine*. The Thomas family was now within two weeks of their departure on the *Africaine* and Mary's time and attention was still fully engaged in her desperate effort to get Mary Jnr and Helen well enough to cope with the voyage.

Chapter 3
To the Antipodes

On Tuesday 28 June 1836, despite the children still being ill, the Thomases left their accommodation in Fish Street and boarded the *Africaine* at the London docks. Mary had to carry Mary Jnr downstairs to put her in the coach as she was 'still unable to walk', and Helen was also 'very weak'.[1] Mary was too preoccupied with the plight of her children to remark in her diary upon the sad farewells among family and friends taking place all around her. Nor did she comment upon the hubbub and confusion on deck as the ship was readied for a voyage of many months.

During the early afternoon, the *Africaine* was towed by steamer to Gravesend, where she was berthed to await the boarding of the new colony's colonial secretary, Robert Gouger, and his wife, Harriet. Gouger recorded in his journal his observation of the distress his wife faced in leaving her family and friends.

> To those who know my wife's ardent attachment to her family and their unsurpassed love for her, a description of her anguish at parting and state on embarkation would be superfluous – they can imagine it all ... Fortunately the weather was delightful; the light winds that blew gave hardly any perceptible motion to the ship ... Sleep aided to restore her, and by Saturday afternoon when the Africaine anchored off Deal for the reception of the Captain and some of the party, she was in good health and spirits.[2]

Harriet's recovery was also helped by her husband's infectious optimism. The Gougers were young and newlywed and Robert was on the verge of bringing his long-held dream of founding the new colony to fruition – a cause for which he had worked tirelessly over a number of years. As one of the colony's leading officials, he anticipated a continuing and significant role in its development.

Confined to her cabin with the children, it is unlikely that Mary witnessed Harriet Gouger's anguish. The full reality and implication of their leaving Gravesend and London's precincts did not immediately impinge upon Mary as it had on Harriet – she 'did not feel the least alarm or repent having undertaken the voyage'; her 'greatest anxiety was to get the children well'.[3] However, two years later she recalled, 'I had not been long on board before I wept bitterly at the reflection as I often do now'.[4] Mary's distraction and subsequent failure to grieve as she left her homeland would have later consequences for her – almost uncharacteristically for one so resolute and committed, she was for many years dogged by severe bouts of homesickness.

By the time the *Africaine* had made its way to Deal, William was also in the throes of scarlet fever and was extremely ill. Meanwhile, the girls had suffered a relapse. 'Helen was so swollen as to be scarcely able to breathe' and neither she nor Mary Jnr were able to leave their berths for several days. Mary was particularly worried that William's infection would spread throughout the ship,

> as there were many children on board [particularly in steerage], but I kept him in my own cabin the whole time . . . he recovered and without the disorder spreading to steerage [where] the passengers were more crowded . . . You may suppose what a situation I was in, never at sea before and unable to procure many comforts which we might have had on land, [and] a very inattentive doctor . . .[5]

Mary continued her nursing of the children, albeit with minimal help from the ship's surgeon. She poulticed William's throat and administered the gargles prescribed for the girls that she had brought on board with her.[6] She did not become aware until after she and the family had boarded that provisions from the ship's stores would not be made available until the *Africaine* had left the precincts of London. The ship's mate was particularly unhelpful and made no effort to assist her. 'So if it had not been for some cakes that I had made for the children and a few other things . . . we would have been starved for the first week[7] having nothing but our own either to eat or drink.'[8] Even when the ship's provisions did become available, they were provided with 'little more than hard biscuits and salt junk, not very digestible food for children recovering from a dangerous illness'.[9] Fortunately Mary had included some honey in her cabin stores and was able to buy lemons when they docked at Deal[10], so by these slender means she managed as they awaited the boarding of the captain.

Captain Duff, accompanied by his bride of a few days, boarded the *Africaine* on 1 July and the next day they set sail – bound for South Australia[11], with 99 souls on board.[12] Mary, 'having been up all night in attendance on the children went on deck at daylight and saw the Isle of Wight hills', and reflected that in all probability it was the last view she would ever have of her native country.[13] Shortly after setting out from Deal, the *Africaine* encountered squalls and rough seas and Mary, anxious about the children, found them particularly frightening and unsettling. 'The expectation that the children would be tossed out of their berths generally kept me awake, and sometimes I was up the greater part of the night.'[14] The children were all continuously seasick, yet Mary, whether by dint of willpower or having a more robust constitution, was less affected, and Robert barely at all.

For the first three weeks on board, during the worst of William's illness, Mary did not get anything like a proper night's rest. It would be six weeks from the time Helen had first become ill in London until William was out of danger and the demands upon Mary eased. Mary's resilience and stamina got her children through this difficult time. She had faced misfortune squarely; transcending it by a mixture of optimism and acceptance, based in a deep religious faith and unadorned common sense. Clearly, Mary was not easily daunted.

As William's health improved, and with the girls' recovery assured, Mary and Robert considered what steps they might take to improve their onboard living conditions. They were upset by the general lack of consideration shown by the officials of the new colony, Robert Gouger and John Brown, who had arranged the contracting and provisioning of the vessel. Mary and Robert believed they had been misled about the standard of food and amenity that was to be available to them.

The *Africaine* was a barque – a three-masted ship weighing 320 tonnes and measuring just 30.5 metres in length and nine metres wide.[15] Conditions were inevitably cramped. Much of the deck space was taken up by the pens and coops of livestock, intended for use on board and as stock for the new colony. The cacophony from this sea-faring farmyard must have been intriguing and amusing, but the smells taxed the endurance, particularly of the squeamish, throughout the voyage. Robert's business partner George Stevenson described similar scenes on board the *Buffalo*.

> *The bulwarks of the Buffalo are six feet high. On both sides of the main deck are rows of filthy hogs kept in pens, generally in a horrid state of dirt and uncleanliness. The emigrants can only walk alongside these animals and inhale the stench from them. They are forbidden either side of the quarter deck, although the officers and passengers have the poop, or what remains of it unoccupied by hay trusses and hen coops, to themselves.*[16]

The *Africaine*'s four relatively spacious stern cabins, located under the quarter-deck, provided the ship's most comfortable accommodation. One of these was occupied by Captain Duff and his wife; another by John Hallett and his family (Hallett was the ship's part owner and Duff's business partner). The remaining two were reserved for the officials – Robert Gouger and the emigration agent,

John Brown, and their wives. These privileged passengers ate at the captain's table.[17] As all the stern cabins had been taken, Mary and Robert were allocated quarters in the intermediate section, which was below deck and on the same level as the steerage passengers. There were at least eight intermediate cabins, measuring 1.8 by 1.8 metres: Mary and Robert occupied one; and Frances, Mary Jnr and Helen, with Mary Lillywhite (their 21-year-old servant whom Mary refused to allow to travel steerage) were in the other. Two more couples, a Mr and Mrs Lewis, and the ship's surgeon, Dr Charles Everard, and his wife were also allotted intermediate cabins.

The rest were taken by young men: E. Osborne, Robert's apprentice printer; John Slater, a surgeon; Arthur Gliddon, a land agent's clerk; Charles Nantes, clerk to the colonial secretary; and John Michael Skipper, articled to the colony's advocate-general and crown solicitor[18], and who apparently 'fell in love with Frances at first sight when she went on board the vessel', as Mary explained later in a letter to her brother.[19]

The intermediate cabins opened onto a common room, measuring about 4.5 metres by 7, and William Thomas made do there with a hammock slung near Mary and Robert's cabin as his sleeping quarters. The total area occupied by intermediate was only about 9 by 8 metres overall. Nevertheless, Mary felt somewhat compensated that her family's cabins were located 'in the most airy part of the vessel'.[20] They were situated near the hatch that gave access to the deck, and which provided some natural light and ventilation; but the downside was the close proximity of the hatch to the ship's hold, with its store of dry provisions. Mary was continually cleaning up after the crew, as the trapdoor was opened every few days and clouds of dust were disturbed, while straw and other packing from the provisions being brought out for use were dumped at her door.[21]

In the lowest class (steerage), the *Africaine* carried 49 passengers, including six families who, between them, had 10 children ranging in age from four months to 15 years. The remaining steerage passengers were young, single adults, both male and female.[22] Although steerage passengers had to provide themselves with a month's clothing, plus linen, towels and soap, they were supplied with bedding, blankets and eating utensils.[23] Most adults in steerage were the employees of those settlers who, like the Thomases, had paid for their own passages and had invested in land in the new colony prior to leaving England. This entitled them to a 'free' passage for their emigrating workers and their families. Under this scheme, Robert's printer and two of his agricultural labourers travelled in steerage.

Although Mary noted in her diary that she 'did not expect to meet with many luxuries on board ship'[24], she was annoyed, as were other intermediate passengers, because she had been led to believe they would receive similar amenities – a cook and reasonably palatable food – to those provided for the stern passengers. 'This however was not the case, for not only ourselves but everyone in the intermediate, chiefly gentlemen, made loud complaints as to the quality of our provisions, the want of attendance and even necessary comforts.'[25] The £65 per passage paid for the stern cabins[26], it seems, related to the quality of meals provided for them at the captain's table. The £30 paid for the intermediate berths made very little allowance for food other than dry rations and mainly salt meat.[27] Mary believed those who were travelling intermediate received virtually the same provisions as the steerage passengers, and 'they [also] ought to have had better provisions than were often served us'.[28] What troubled Mary was not so much the type of food, but its quality. By contrast, stern cabin passengers dined 'sumptuously' as Robert Gouger recorded in his journal with lip-smacking satisfaction.

> Hot rolls for breakfast manufactured by our excellent black steward, eggs, rice, two sorts of cold meat, coffee, and very tolerable tea. At twelve luncheon: bread and cheese, the last of two kinds, both good, with admirable bottled porter, Hodgson's pale ale wine

and spirits. We dine at four, soup of an excellent quality, two joints, and poultry. As a sample: today we had pea soup, salt fish and eggs, haunch of mutton, fowls and pork – occasionally plum pudding. Then beer, porter, wine and spirits . . . Tea at eight and the grog bottles from nine to ten.[29]

Gouger had negotiated the charter of the *Africaine* and it was his responsibility to address the concerns of the intermediate passengers, as he noted in his journal on 23 July.

Some of the passengers in the intermediate cabin last week manifested discontent, and put up on their hatchway an impertinent notice. Excited by Mr Thomas the agitator of the ship, one complained of bread, another of beef, another of wine; indeed each had some one complaint to make, but rather a subject for marvel, no two agreed on the same complaint.[30]

Gouger dismissed each grievance, attributing the discontent to 'ennui', and there the matter rested. Even so he noted, 'Mr and Mrs Thomas, however, still preserve dignified silence, though all the rest appear to have forgotten their fancied wrongs'. Little changed with regard to food, and if intermediate passengers required special cooking, this had to be negotiated with the cook and a reward offered.[31] Mary's diary recorded, 'I afterwards saw other reasons for not in the least regretting our not being among the number of the cabin [stern] passengers'.[32] She felt Gouger's lack of empathy keenly, and was pleased to be without his company.

The monotony of the voyage and the stress of the ship's confined environment made the incidence of interpersonal difficulties and quarrels not uncommon. Although Mary was generally compassionate and tactful in her dealings with others, she found dissimulation distasteful, and could, when she believed circumstances demanded it, speak her mind. One irritation that would continue for almost the whole of the voyage was the difficulty the intermediate passengers had with the chief mate who seems to have targeted them, trying to oppress them with petty restrictions. Mary and Robert rejected officious authority; they were self-possessed and confident, and more than a match for him. Only a day or so after embarkation, he attempted to restrict the movement of the intermediate passengers around the ship, and as Mary noted in her diary:

> *This produced an altercation between Mr Thomas with some others and the mate . . . [who] said it was usual with all passengers who were not in state cabins, and he should insist on the order being obeyed, which they flatly told him they would not, and to show that it was disregarded we went to any part of the deck the same as before.*[33]

This would not be the only time the Thomases confronted the troublesome mate. Over the months Mary's patience became jaded and she took action just a week or two out from their journey's end. Throughout the voyage, Mary had continued to clean around her cabin and clear away debris left after stores had been taken from the hold. 'This we did for a long time without complaint but one day a larger quantity of rubbish than usual was deposited close to our cabin door.' She approached the mate for assistance from the crew. 'Not only did he peremptorily refuse to send anyone, but replied to my request with the most insulting language.' At the end of her tether with the mate's abrasive manner, Mary threatened to complain to the captain. 'He told me I was welcome to do that . . . "Tell him what you please" . . . Determined . . . to put a stop to, if possible, the mate's insolence I resolved to take his advice and appeal to the captain as the only way.'

As with many other early emigrants, Mary and Robert had been attracted to the new colony not only by its potential economic benefits, but also by the emphasis its promoters had given to individual rights and freedoms; they found the petty tyranny of the mate offensive. Although Robert had reacted to the problem by withdrawing the help of his labourers who regularly assisted the crew on deck, Mary took the mate's arrogant advice and made her complaint in writing to Captain Duff: 'I cannot suppose that you or any gentleman in the cabin would suffer his wife to be insulted.' The captain answered that she did him 'justice in assessing that he would not knowingly suffer anyone on board the vessel to be uncivilly treated while he had command of it and that he would take care that there would be no cause for complaint in the future'.[34] The refusal of the Thomases to accept injustice and bullying won them Captain Duff's respect, and ultimately, a grudging regard from the mate, whose manner and behaviour toward them changed. 'From that day [the mate's] churlishness seemed in great measure to have left him.'

There were, however, other diversions. Mary and all in intermediate had some cause for concern about the emotional stability of a fellow passenger, John Slater, whom Mary considered to be a kind-hearted man with gentlemanly manners. He was generally on good terms with his fellow passengers, but sometimes showed signs of a fiery temperament. 'I do not know what gave him great offence . . . [but on one occasion] after giving vent to furious passion he shut himself in his cabin with a loaded pistol in his hand, declaring that he would shoot the first man who dared to enter it.'[35] As his cabin was next to the one occupied by the girls Mary was rather anxious; otherwise she says she wouldn't have been troubled about his 'irritated humour'.

> *Osborne, however, went to him notwithstanding his threats, and not only induced him to lay aside the pistol but reasoned him into a calmer mood. This was not the only instance in which he succeeded, by his judicious arguments, in allaying the ruffled temper of Mr Slater.*[36]

And there was the occasional controversy that, no doubt, would not have escaped the attention of Mary. Gouger recalled the first Sunday prayers read by Dr Everard and attended by all passengers and crew, as being questionable, and requiring his intervention.

> *In consequence of the religious opinions of Mr Everard being unitarian he did not read the Litany nor some of the prayers in which the doctrine of the Trinity is prominently mentioned. This is to be altered against another Sunday.*[37]

About halfway through the voyage another event was to cause not so much a distraction but sorrow and anger for the Thomas family. Several of the young men in intermediate took Helen's kitten, Kate, from the hen coop on deck (where she was kept overnight) and threw her overboard, infuriating Mary. 'They had not only been guilty of a wanton act of cruelty to a harmless animal, but had committed a positive injustice, for the cat was our property and they had no right to destroy it.' The tragic fate of their pet caused the Thomas girls and Mary much distress and many tears, while Robert and his men were outraged, and 'vented their threats in no gentle tones if they could but fix upon the guilty party'. Mary found her own unique means of letting her indignation be known and circulated a verse throughout the ship in which, through a process of elimination, she identified but did not actually name the guilty men involved. She thought her method of dealing with them was more effective than Robert's as the guilty men 'began to be frightened at what they had done when they found their action was so deeply resented by almost everyone on the ship'.[38]

Once the children were convalescent, and despite the continuing irritations and distractions, Mary began to enjoy the novelty of life at sea; with her poet's eye, she closely observed its strangeness and beauty. She took a lively interest in the various fish and sea creatures that came around the boat – flying fish pursued by dolphins[39] and the delicate nautilus 'dancing on the waves with its transparent sails and little shell for a boat'.[40] An 80 pound (36.4 kilogram) albacore was caught which tasted something like veal.[41] On another occasion she peered at

> *a curious creature ... drawn up in a pail of water. It was called a glaucus ... and was of a dark purple. When the sun shone on it a*

variety of colours was reflected. It had four appendages about an inch long, with shorter ones again branching from each in different directions. Its length was about three inches, and its tail like a scorpion. The shape and general appearance were compared by some to the representations commonly given to His Satanic Majesty.[42]

As the *Africaine* approached the equator, Mary observed that 'the setting sun was remarkably brilliant, sometimes resembling a burning volcano, and then softening down to a variety of colours of the most delicate tints'.[43] She welcomed the evenings in the tropics.

> They were remarkably beautiful, the moon shining with a brightness that is not seen in England, so that I could sit on deck or at my cabin door and go on with [making] my fishing net with ease. The stars also presented a splendid appearance, and we could now see the Southern Cross.[44]

According to Mary, the *Africaine* crossed the equator at about 6 am on 22 August. She 'was up and intended being on deck, but was not aware we were so near to it'.[45] Mary's recording is at odds with Gouger's, who wrote in his journal that they made the crossing 'on the 21st at about nine o'clock', as, unknown to the passengers, 'the captain in consequence of the great number on board whose ire might be kindled by practical jokes, wisely forbade any procession of the sailors in honour of Neptune'.[46]

In the tropics the wind was very variable, and although both Mary and the girls – as with most other passengers – had a number of falls, Robert 'boasted that he could stand upon his feet as others could not'. However, on a day with 'a rough head wind which drove us every way but the right', Robert met his nemesis and, as Mary recorded, a little wryly, 'was thrown flat upon his back' like everyone else.[47]

On 20 September the passengers at last glimpsed land as the ship approached Simon's Bay at the Cape of Good Hope. As they drew nearer, Mary admired the 'grand spectacle' of a lofty mountain range – a magnificent vista after 12 weeks at sea.⁴⁸ They anchored in the bay on the following afternoon, and the Thomases went ashore with the Hallett family in a boat hired from some locals.

> *When we reached the shallow water, there being no jetty we were carried on shore in the arms of the men to our no small amusement, and my daughter Mary was the first of our party to set foot in Africa. There is a small town here as they call it which consisted entirely of one street, or rather, of one row of houses at the base of tremendous hills and facing the water. The whole much resembled a newly-founded watering-place in England. The inhabitants were chiefly English with some Dutch, but we saw a great many of the native Africans, quite black with woolly hair.*⁴⁹

The two families ate lunch at the inn where they were to stay overnight. The meal was simple fare – bread, butter and cheese with bottled ale – but it was fresh, and 'after being so long confined to ship diet', Mary had 'never relished anything so much'. She was equally impressed with their late afternoon dinner of 'boiled leg of mutton and rump steaks with potatoes and cabbage followed by a bread pudding and excellent pastry', accompanied by Cape wine. The landlord sat at the head of the table, 'assisting us and doing all in his power to make us comfortable, at the same time amusing us with many anecdotes respecting the Cape and its inhabitants'.⁵⁰

During their brief time on land, Robert ventured inland with Mr Hallett to buy milch goats. Two with young were obtained for 35 shillings. 'Livestock of every kind [as Mary recorded in her diary] was much cheaper than in England', but while 'the captain purchased a great many sheep and a cow and a calf', Mary and Robert limited themselves to some fowls.⁵¹ Mary also bought 200 small 'snatch' oranges for 1 shilling. Robert bought a 28 pound (12.7 kilogram) box of raisins, some seed potatoes, a roll of tent canvas, and a box of candles. All would be invaluable items for their home in the colony, and Mary's 'quart [2.27 litre] bottle of genuine cayenne pepper [bought for] 7 shillings and sixpence' – a considerable investment – was to last her for 40 years.

Within a few days of leaving the Cape, the *Africaine* confronted the ferocity of the Southern Ocean, with the sea 'running mountains high, but indescribably beautiful', as the wind 'increased to a complete gale'.

> *The sails had been all furled but two, and the ship rocked so much that everything which was not securely lashed was overturned and out of its place. The waves so incessantly broke over the vessel that it was almost impossible to stand on the deck. I ventured up for a few minutes to take a view of the raging seas, with its towering hills of water covered with foam, but grand beyond all description. I could have stood for hours to look at it, for I had become too accustomed to it to feel alarm. Although it inspired me with awe, it filled me with wonder and admiration.*[52]

About a week later, they encountered another huge storm. The oldest sailor on board had not seen such an intense storm for many years. According to Mary's diary it was one in which they could have foundered and gone down.

> *The vessel plunged and rolled from side to side, and the waves dashed over the ship with fearful violence. The captain, mates and crew were on deck the whole night ... I neither undressed nor lay down, but continued sitting at my cabin door, listening to and watching the progress of the storm, which from 9 to 12 o'clock was truly awful ... I have often said that I would like to witness a storm at sea, but I meant myself to be on dry land and only a spectator of the warring elements, for little did I conceive the terrors of such an awful scene.*[53]

The tedium of shipboard life was relieved not only by the storms but on 29 October, by the sighting of whales in the Great Australian Bight, and the excitement of seeing one come alongside and pass 'under the bow of the ship, spouting up water'.[54] It was exactly four months since the Thomases had boarded the *Africaine* at the London Docks and their journey's end was almost in sight. During the next few days they were tantalised by glimpses of land.

Then, on the last day of October, 'the point of Spencer Gulf was clearly visible' but, much to the frustration of all on board, the wind was contrary to their route; 'we could not make towards it, but steered away from it, and in a few hours it was again lost to sight'.[55] The anxiety of the new colonists to catch more than a fleeting glimpse of their new homeland was to be thwarted for another 24 hours. Nevertheless there was cause for celebration in having successfully survived their epic voyage across the vast and frequently storm-tossed oceans of two hemispheres.

Chapter 4
A tent village

On 1 November, much to the colonists relief, Kangaroo Island came into view as the *Africaine* tacked along its western coast. The weather was fine, and a number of young men sought permission to disembark and walk across the island to meet the *Africaine* at Angas's South Australian Company camp, recently established at Nepean Bay. The *Africaine* was en route there to seek news of Colonel Light and his decision regarding the site of the mainland settlement.

The six young trekkers included Robert Thomas's journeyman printer, Robert Fisher, John Slater and E. Osborne, who, as Robert's apprentice, had been 'consigned' to Mary and Robert's care by his father.[1] They were put ashore 'at Morrel's [Murrel's] boat harbour, between Cape Borda and Cape Forbin'[2], with a compass and a copy of Wakefield's handbook, *The New British Province of South Australia*. The volume included: Captain George Sutherland's descriptions of the island; a chart of his supposed 90-kilometre trek across it to Nepean Bay in 1819; an extract from his report of his eight months there; and additional information from Gouger's interviews with him in 1831.

Sutherland's report influenced Angas in taking up land on Kangaroo Island and in locating a whaling enterprise at Nepean Bay. Sutherland's descriptions of the terrain indicated that once the dense coastal brushwood had been penetrated, the interior plain of open woodland had a deep loam soil and ample freshwater ponds, while 'a plentiful supply of spring water [was] always attainable by digging for it'.³

Relying on this advice, the six *Africaine* adventurers carried no water and few provisions, believing they could find game and live off the land in what they anticipated would be a two to three day trek. Osborne asked Mary to exchange his heavy double-barrelled firearm for the Thomas's single-barrelled gun. When Osborne's friend, Slater, was in possession of it, Mary 'half in jest' admonished him not to lose it. He responded, '"I will lose my life first"'. Laughing, Mary explained, '"I did not mean that. I only . . . intended to caution you against laying it down under bushes, where you might not find it again"'.⁴ Despite this light-hearted exchange, Mary 'could not help feeling somewhat uneasy at their setting out on such a romantic expedition'.⁵

At dawn on the following day, the Althorpes, at the tip of Yorke Peninsula, were visible from the deck of the *Africaine*, and five hours later she entered Nepean Bay. 'The flag was hoisted and the guns were fired to announce our approach . . . Soon after, a boat with the mate and four sailors went ashore, and immediately returned with another boat'⁶, which carried Samuel Stephens, the South Australian Company's colonial manager, who came on board. Mary observed one of the crew members on Stephens's boat:

> *Nathaniel Thomas, had been a resident on the island many years but his appearance, I thought was more like that of a savage than an Englishman . . . [He] fell overboard, and . . . was watched . . . with considerable anxiety on account of the sharks . . . An oar, however, was thrown to him which he got astride till the boat reached him, and when he came again on the deck he shook himself as a dog does . . . and took no more notice of the matter.*⁷

Once ashore, Mary's attention was captured by the small population of eight or so ex-sealers, including Nathaniel Thomas, who had remained on the island after the sealing industry's decline and existed by the subsistence farming of small plots. Their Aboriginal wives had been abducted from their tribes years earlier, many from Tasmania and some from the mainland around the Murray mouth. The men wore skin-suits and shoes made by the women from the pelts of seals and kangaroos. It was these long-term residents who alerted the new arrivals to the dangers facing the young trekkers. Mary and the other *Africaine* passengers were told that Captain Sutherland had never crossed Kangaroo Island; his chart was a fabrication.[8] According to the sealers, the proposed journey was 'utterly impossible as the brushwood would so completely entangle the trekkers that they would lose their way and might never be found again, either alive or dead'. It was agreed that a search party should be sent out immediately.[9] An Aboriginal woman, Princess Con, was to be the main tracker and Mary was intrigued by her appearance:

> *Her clothing consisted of a red woollen cap, such as sailors often wear, and a shirt of the same material under a coat of thick leather, such as in England is used for harness and to cover trunks. Her hair was pleasing . . . perfectly black . . . long and straight on the forehead. Her legs and feet were bare, and around her neck hung several rows of glass beads. Her chin was also ornamented with a kind of beard, and whiskers grew at the sides of her face. But what most surprised us were her musical voice, and the pleasing intonation with which she spoke the English language . . . almost with fluency. Her height was about five feet six (165 cm) and her age apparently about twenty-five years . . . she talked with great confidence of being able to trace the young men, as she knew every part of the island.*[10]

Mary's original misgivings about the trekkers and the islanders' warnings were well placed as the men failed to arrive at Nepean Bay. Her fears for them were heightened by a walk on the island in which she and Robert were almost lost in the dense undergrowth.[11] When the search party had not found the trekkers by the time the *Africaine* left for the mainland, all at the depot and everyone on board were deeply concerned for their safety.

Mary's unhappy impression of Kangaroo Island would not have been mitigated by her experience of Angas's South Australian Company settlement; it was in disarray. The company's first vessel, the *Duke of York*, had arrived in July 1836, followed closely by the *Lady Mary Pelham* and the *John Pirie*, then a little later by the store ship *Emma*; by the time of the *Africaine*'s visit the settlement's population had ballooned to 379. Apart from the ex-sealers it comprised working men and their families[12] whom Angas expected to employ in his whaling industry and as tenant farmers. Although Samuel Stephens was Angas's distant relative and had been appointed by him, he proved a disastrous choice. The historian, Donald Pike, described him as 'excitable, irresponsible and too conceited to take advice' and 'too foolish when drunk to keep the respect of his subordinates'.[13] Stephens's mismanagement was compounded by the poor location of the settlement, which had been based upon Sutherland's faulty report; it proved to be without ready access to fresh water and the nearby soil was infertile. Additionally, Nepean Bay was not a suitable harbour for whaling activities, a venture for which both the *Duke of York* and the *Lady Mary Pelham* had been equipped. But even before this had become apparent, the whole settlement, under Stephens's ineffectual supervision, had descended into anarchy.

The *Africaine* left behind the troubled settlement, crossed to the mainland, and following Stephens's advice found Colonel Light at Rapid Bay – the inlet he had named for his survey ship – not far from the entrance to St Vincent's Gulf. In Mary's historic diary entry for that day, 6 November 1836, she described her first impressions of mainland South Australia.

> We anchored in Rapid Bay, in front of the most beautiful prospect imaginable. We could see some tents on shore belonging to the surveying party ... A party from the vessel went on shore and on their return gave the most enchanting account of the country, which everywhere resembled a gentleman's park – grass growing in the greatest luxuriance, the most beautiful flowers in abundance,

and birds of splendid plumage. They saw several of the natives, who the surveyors said, were of great service to them.[14]

Light informed them that he had not yet decided upon the site for the principal town as his exploration of the coast to find a suitable port was still underway. Without a designated port he had been unable to begin the surveys that would identify the land to be allocated to those settlers who had bought preliminary land orders in London. This delay was a severe blow and was a considerable source of additional anxiety to Mary and Robert, who, with their fellow colonists, had not anticipated facing an indeterminate wait before they could begin the work of building their homes and establishing themselves.[15]

Light piloted the *Africaine* for 40 miles (64 kilometres) up the gulf to the safe anchorage of Holdfast Bay, and the series of fresh water lagoons that lay just beyond its fringe of sand hills.[16] Kingston and his survey party, including Robert George Thomas, were already camped there looking for a site for the principal town. Once at anchor, Light ordered the immediate unloading of all the stores and goods on board the *Africaine* onto the beach – even household furniture, including Mary's precious 18th-century clock.

On 11 November Robert and his two agricultural labourers went ashore with the Thomas's tents and luggage, transferring them by hand, which was 'no trifling labour, especially through un-trodden paths often full of holes, and with grass three or four feet high'.[17] Mary and the girls remained on board with the other women and children while their temporary homes were set up. They disembarked on the 13th and were landed on the beach by way of the *Africaine*'s long boats; then on foot they followed the curve of the Patawalonga's estuary before striking due east away from the coast. After toiling through the sand dunes, and before reaching the plain on which they were to camp, they encountered a series of reed beds and then the lagoons, overflowing with freshwater. They waded through the lagoons 'up to [their] necks and no trace of human footsteps could be seen'.[18] Despite the strangeness of her new environment, Mary, in recording her first sightings of the colony's wildlife, recognised its unique splendour. 'The birds here were of beautiful plumage. White and black cockatoos were in abundance ... with large yellow or orange coloured crests ... Also there were wild ducks and flocks of geese with occasionally a black swan flying.'[19]

Light commandeered the *Africaine* to sail for Launceston to bring back stores, particularly sheep for fresh meat, and draught animals badly needed by his survey parties.[20] This was done so precipitately that most of Robert's type for his printing press – brought out as ballast – was left on board, and he was unable to retrieve it for many months.[21] The settlers established themselves about a mile from the beach, not far from the surveyors' camp and, for the first few days until their large marquee had been assembled, Mary, Robert and the girls made do in one of the smaller tents. Despite the park-like beauty of the plain upon which they made their first camp in South Australia and the pleasure of release from the *Africaine*'s cramped conditions, Mary's anxiety would not allow her to sleep. She was not only deeply troubled about the safety of the six young men on Kangaroo Island, but was very apprehensive about what lay ahead for her family in this unknown and exotic land.

Her anxiety may have been eased a little after the move into their marquee, their main accommodation, which provided them with some degree of comfort, greater protection from the weather, and more space to organise their stores and other possessions. Their makeshift home was within view of most of the 50 or so other settlers' campsites[22], 'near some gum trees ... about a hundred yards from the nearest lagoon'.[23] One of the trees was shaped like an arch and would later become known as the 'Old Gum Tree' and a South Australian icon.[24]

Robert, who, like many settlers, took advantage of the reed beds surrounding the lagoons to build rush huts, made one as a bedroom for the girls. Meanwhile, Robert Gouger took pride in using only six nails in the construction of his hut, which measured about 3.5 metres by 7. He cut the uprights, cross pieces, beams and joists from a 'copse about a mile distant', and tied them together with cordage.[25]

Some colonists, like Dr Everard, planted vegetables – peas, beans, potatoes and cabbages – which did very well until the sheep brought back from Launceston on the *Africaine* destroyed them as there were no fences to keep the stock out.[26] Some, like Mary and the girls, gathered local plants; Mary was delighted with a 'sort of samphire which grew in abundance and made an excellent pickle'.[27] Gouger discovered that game was very plentiful on the plains to the east of their tent village; he noted that it was almost impossible to walk for more than a few hundred yards without disturbing quails which, he said, 'provided for excellent eating'.[28]

Although they were making the best of their situation, the colonists, accustomed to the northern hemisphere's more benevolent summer climate, were no doubt challenged by the onerous conditions now confronting them. Before emigration, Mary, along with her fellow colonists, had been given the impression that the climate would be benign, but she very quickly recognised that this was far from her new reality. In her first letter to her brother from the colony she complained

> *[that the heat] is sometimes so intense as to be scarcely endurable . . . moreover, the atmosphere is subject to great and sudden changes from heat to cold, and cold to heat, so much more than the case with the climate of England, so long proverbial for it changeableness.*[29]

Mary and her family sweltered in their tents through temperatures reaching over 100 °F (38 °C), and endured summer storms and downpours that penetrated the canvas, and winds, which 'almost carried them away'. She coped with 'innumerable' flies and mosquitoes – 'one or another annoyed us incessantly' – and was literally faced by an infestation of rats in her primitive living quarters. '[They] would scarcely be driven away . . . they paid us nightly visits as well, for once I felt one run over my face.'[30]

A fortnight or so before Christmas, Robert's printer Fisher, and Nantes, two of the four survivors of the ill-fated trek across Kangaroo Island, arrived in Holdfast Bay on board the *Emma*, a South Australian Company vessel.[31] Mary noted in her diary that the two men made 'vague and contradictory' statements indicating that they had left Slater and Osborne near a lagoon, 'unable to proceed any further'.[32] The survivors told of their plight after leaving their two companions, describing how after eight days of severe hardship – they were without food or water for the last days – they reached Nepean Bay, having travelled about 70 miles (112.7 kilometres) over extreme terrain. According to Fisher's report, an extensive search from the settlement there failed to find Osborne and Slater, despite the assistance of local trackers, including the Aboriginal woman, Princess Con, who searched unsuccessfully for 16 days. It left little doubt that the unfortunate adventurers had perished. Mary was particularly distressed by the news; she was very fond of Osborne and her diary records that on hearing of their probable fate, she was given 'such a shock', that it was 'a long time' before she recovered.

Shortly after the survivors' safe arrival at Holdfast Bay, Fisher in particular was highly critical of Captain Duff's decision to leave Nepean Bay without news of the trekkers' fate. But the colonial secretary, Robert Gouger, rebuffed this attack, asserting that everything had been done to try to find the missing men before the *Africaine* had sailed for the mainland.[33] Mary never fully accepted Fisher's version of events and believed that some other misfortune must have befallen Osborne and Slater, concluding that 'whatever it may have been, a mystery hangs over it'.[34]

Although the loss of the young men cast a gloom over Mary's first Christmas in South Australia, the Thomas family celebrated it with a service held in George Kingston's rush hut, and afterward Mary 'kept up the old custom of Christmas as far as having a plum pudding for dinner, likewise a ham and parrot pie'.[35] William had constructed an 'ingenious camp oven' a few days earlier from the iron hoops of a barrel 'fixed in the ground in a half circle and covered with a thick coating of clay afterwards burnt'.³⁶ And so Mary had an oven to press into use as well as her campfire.³⁷

On the morning of 28 December 1836 the long-awaited *Buffalo* was sighted in the Bay, and Robert Gouger, as colonial secretary, was summoned on board to 'attend on' Governor Hindmarsh. Mary's diary for that day records that the governor's arrival 'made us all alive'; both Robert and Mary with their family were requested to attend the ensuing ceremonies. Robert Gouger read the proclamation of South Australia under a 'huge gum tree, a flag was hoisted, a party of marines from the *Buffalo* fired a *feu-de-joie*, and loud hurrahs succeeded'. After the formalities, the governor stood on a chair and gave the first toast – to the king, followed by the national anthem led by the colonial treasurer, Osmond Gilles. While the proclamation was being read, Robert Gouger's wife, Harriet, was in the early stages of labour – Henry Hindmarsh Gouger was the first white baby born at the settlement and the governor claimed him as a godson.³⁸ A day or so later, in order to print copies of the proclamation, the rush hut Robert had built for the girls' bedroom had to be vacated by them to accommodate the printing press.³⁹

What the Aborigines made of the new arrivals upon their shores is difficult to establish; the settlers ruminated as to what may have been their reaction. George Wilkinson, an early colonist, lived in daily contact with Aborigines on his property near Rapid Bay and was a close observer of their way of life. In his 1848 *South Australia*, Wilkinson claimed the Aborigines believed that after death 'their Great Spirit takes the soul and they are born again with a white body', and would be 'gifted with all the advantages and colour of the European'.⁴⁰ This view was also espoused by F.T. Whitington, the organising chaplain of the Anglican Bishop's home mission for Aborigines during the 1850s. In his 1888 biography of the first Anglican Bishop of Adelaide, Whitington claimed that Aborigines 'regard the white man as their former brethren whose spirits, purified after death, have passed into superior form'.⁴¹

It does seem that Aborigines may have, at first, considered white people as some kind of temporary visitation from the spirit world. However, these views no doubt changed when they began to recognise that the settlers were intent upon long-term residence, upon usurping their hunting grounds, and, as a consequence, desecrating their sacred sites.

The governor and his colonial officials, through the proclamation of December 1836, advised the first emigrants that the Aborigines were 'awarded' an equal entitlement with them to the full protection of British law, and that they were to be treated with kindness and respect. In general, the first settlers were mindful of these urgings.

Shortly after the proclamation ceremony, George Stevenson conscientiously took up the role thrust upon him as protector of Aborigines. He described in detail his first contact with one of the original inhabitants of what was to become known as the Adelaide Plains.

> *He was a young man of about twenty-five years of age, five feet ten inches in height, strong, and well built . . . Our Storekeeper supplied him with slop trousers and a military jacket, of which he was not a little proud. After an interchange of signs, I succeeded in making him understand that I wished to know the names of certain things in his own language, and at last obtained a few dozen words . . .*

Stevenson persuaded him to visit the *Buffalo*, still anchored in the Bay.

> *Ootinai . . . ate heartily . . . and after two or three attempts handled his knife and fork with as much dexterity as I could. He was greatly delighted with the pianoforte, which the Misses Hindmarsh played to him, also with Mr Hutchinson's flute . . . There is a degree of archness and quickness which places this race many degrees above the savage.*[42]

Clearly the early colonists believed that they could, by demonstration, introduce the Aborigines to a superior way of life. It was considered that, by patient example, they could be encouraged to come within the 'pale of civilisation'; which would be, the Europeans believed, ample 'compensation' for the loss of their land. The settlers had no doubt theirs was the superior civilization. It is evident that the vast majority of them had no knowledge or appreciation of the Aborigines' unique and intensely spiritual association with their land; nor of the custodial duties and responsibilities that each Aboriginal tribe fulfilled in those areas over which they travelled, and from which they won their food. The colonists' paternalistic views – encompassing notions of civilisation and superiority – were reflected by Robert and Mary while still in London, when they wrote to the Colonial Office expressing their frustration at the delays caused by the British Government's deliberations regarding the native population of South Australia.[43] The colonists believed that because of the Aborigines' nomadic ways, possession could be taken of their land 'without doing them the smallest injury'.[44]

The Thomases did not have their first contact with Aborigines until weeks after their arrival in Holdfast Bay. Robert Gouger expressed disquiet in his journal that no Aborigines had been seen around the area. He had felt 'somewhat uneasy at their lengthened absence ... two natives have been sent by land from Rapid Bay to inform the other tribes of our peaceful intentions'.[45] A day or so later one of the Thomas's fellow passengers, Williams, was out hunting when he came across an Aboriginal man and a boy, whom he persuaded to visit the settlers' camp. Mary's diary described her first meeting with them:

> *They peeped into tents and examined everything with perfect good humour, and were highly delighted. They shook hands with everyone, without at all being abashed. They were both stark naked, but we thought it most prudent not to appear shy.*

They were later given clothing and remained in the settlers' camp for three days. Before they left, the boy visited Mary again when she *endeavoured to excite his wonder. He was greatly astonished at the opening and shutting of an umbrella, the effect of a lucifer box, and seeing the water running out of a water filtering machine. But what most of all surprised him was a large telescope drawn out to its full length, which he at first took to be a gun . . . I persuaded him to look through it, when he expressed his astonishment by lifting up his hands and exclaiming 'Mawny! Mawny!' which is their word for anything wonderful.*[46] *. . . Afterwards we found that we were comparatively no strangers to them, though they were to us, for they had seen and observed our landing.*[47]

After this first encounter there were continuing visits from local Aborigines, and Mary became comfortable in their presence and grateful for their resourcefulness and their knowledge of a land, which to her was mysterious and incomprehensible. An Aboriginal woman visited Mary each morning for some weeks with a bunch of native watercress. 'Where she got it from I do not know. It was similar in flavour to the English cress. We were as glad to have it as she was to receive a biscuit in return.'[48] Mary was particularly grateful for these regular gifts of watercress — as she and her family had been living without fresh vegetables and fruit for many months.

Being unaccustomed to cooking out of doors, Mary was delighted to be shown a foolproof method of getting her campfire started. She had not understood how to place her wood to construct a good fire until two or three Aboriginal women, laughing at her 'lack of so basic a skill', reconstructed it to burn brightly.[49] Mary was especially glad of their local knowledge when fires, lit by the surveyors to clear high grass, got out of control. On more than one occasion she appreciated the quick action of her Aboriginal friends when they helped to 'extinguish fires, which at times came so near to us as to be extremely dangerous, beating them out with boughs from trees or treading them out with their naked feet'.[50]

By the beginning of 1837 the white population of the colony had reached almost 900[51], counting arrivals on the *Africaine*, the *Tam o' Shanter*, and the *Buffalo*, and including members of the surveying parties and those who came out with them on the *Rapid* and the *Cygnet*, as well, as the employees of the South Australian Company on Kangaroo Island. About half the population was living in the makeshift settlement at Holdfast Bay, providing excellent custom for the general store that Robert had established in a tent – his business was flourishing and his stock had been replenished by the arrival of the *Tam o' Shanter* in mid December.

Colonial matters were also progressing. Colonel Light and his assistants, including Robert George, were continuing their surveying work, although Light was still trying to gain agreement for his preferred site for the principal town. By the end of December, he had decided to locate it on the broad fertile plain that ran from the hills to the sea, along the central shore of the eastern side of St Vincent's Gulf; he believed this to be the most suitable coastal land in the colony for food crops. Following Kingston's discovery of permanent water – in the river to be named the Torrens – Light fixed the town's site on its banks, 5 miles (8 kilometres) from the settlers' camp at Holdfast Bay and about 6 miles (9.5 kilometres) from a safe harbour. After many attempts, much frustration and loss of time, Light had eventually found the elusive, southern arm of the Port River and thus a protected anchorage.[52] But, because of its lack of permanent fresh water, it was not feasible to locate the main settlement there; water would have to be carted a considerable distance even just to service the port.

Although, as surveyor-general, Light had been given sole responsibility by the South Australian commissioners to select the site for the principal town, his decision outraged Governor Hindmarsh who arrived in the colony just as Light had made it. Hindmarsh, a Royal Naval captain, found Light's decision intolerable, particularly his judgement in siting the principal town at such a distance from a safe harbour. He preferred Port Lincoln and others mooted Victor Harbor and Encounter Bay, both of which Light had seriously considered and dismissed as unsuitable.

As well as being the governor's private secretary, George Stevenson was appointed secretary to the Executive Council, which increased his influence significantly. He met daily with the governor and the already dissenting members of the council – the resident commissioner, J.H. Fisher, the colonial secretary, Robert Gouger, and the attorney-general, Charles Mann – to appoint officials and to pass laws. Meanwhile, Robert and his workmen, handicapped by the limited amount of type it had been possible to retrieve from the *Africaine*, were fully engaged in coping with the government printing. Mary, like the other women, was preoccupied in keeping her family healthy and fed and in maintaining her dusty, improvised home, while adjusting to new experiences, such as cooking outdoors.

On 6 January Stevenson, accompanied by his wife, Margaret, left for Kangaroo Island with another government official, Thomas Strangways, in the *Cygnet*, one of Light's survey vessels. Sent by the governor, the men were to investigate the lawlessness there and were away for most of the month.[53] Stevenson was rapidly becoming the governor's right-hand man. After an initial detestation of Hindmarsh's bluff quarterdeck manner, Stevenson's tolerance for the governor increased as his own position and power in the colony developed – a situation both he and Margaret relished. Later as editor of the colony's only newspaper, Stevenson's influence in colonial affairs continued to grow. Through the columns of the paper he mounted a vigorous defence of the governor and lashed his opponents, the colonial officials appointed by the London-based South Australian commissioners.

By May 1837, when Robert and William had moved the printing press to Adelaide leaving Mary and the girls to stay on, for the time, at their Glenelg camp, a group of Aborigines settled into Robert's abandoned reed hut.[54] Gradually, as neighbours, Mary and the girls had more contact with them.

> The women usually had mats fastened to their shoulders, in which they carry their young children and provisions. These they dexterously make from the bark of trees, but though I have often watched

them at this work I never could understand the method by which they made the meshes so perfectly even with their fingers only, without any of the implements we use for the purpose. [They] were generally covered with rugs made of opussum-skins, which they neatly sew together by means of twine made from the fibres of bark, and with a bone of the kangaroo for a needle.[55]

They became sufficiently trusted by their new friends to be invited to a corroboree.

The women took no part in it, but, like ourselves, were only spectators. We sat down on the grass beside them, while the men, decked with emu feathers and kangaroo bones, and their bodies ornamented with alternate stripes of chalk and red ochre, executed a sort of dance. They threw themselves into attitudes which we would have thought impossible, at the same time uttering the most fearful yells and screams that could be imagined . . . I believe these exhibitions never took place except when the moon was at the full.[56]

With continuing contact Mary and the girls learned to appreciate the Aboriginal sense of fun and their skill in mimicry.

[A] party of natives . . . performed some antics which caused us to laugh. These they immediately repeated with so much drollery that they made us laugh still more heartily. Then, as if determined not to be outdone, they all set up such a tremendous roar that we were actually obliged to hold our sides for breath.[57]

Helen and Mary Jnr explored the sand hills around their camp and, perhaps with Aboriginal help, became familiar with the native plants and bush tucker. They gathered 'cranberries', which were like small apples, making them into pies.[58] Mary and the girls continued to enjoy the companionship of their Aboriginal neighbours until they packed up their camp at Glenelg and left for Hindley Street, on the 1 June 1837.[59]

Part 2

Chapter 5
Makeshift dwellings in a forest city

The dispute over the siting of the capital which Governor Hindmarsh and his secretary George Stevenson had with colonial officials, particularly the surveyor-general, Colonel Light, and the resident commissioner, J.H. Fisher, unfortunately spread to include almost all decision making. However, despite these growing divisions, the establishment of the colony continued, and Light completed the survey of the principal town, which was named Adelaide in honour of the Queen consort. Under Light's instructions, his plan of Adelaide was drawn up by the young draftsman Robert George Thomas. The colonists, like Mary and Robert, who had bought preliminary land orders in London were allocated their town acres by means of a ballot toward the end of March, and the remaining acres were then offered for sale by auction.

Following his initial investment in land in September 1835, Robert had purchased a second preliminary land order. Thus he was allocated two town acres and in addition bought a further eight acres at auction, which included two in Hindley Street. Accompanied by William, he immediately set up the store and printing office in a tent on acre 56 Hindley Street, and began to build a pisé structure, which, because of its shape, became known as the long building. It was designed to accommodate both businesses and to provide temporary housing for the family. The store, although still in Robert's ownership, was now managed by James Coltman and traded as Messrs Coltman and Co.

When Mary and the girls joined Robert and William at the beginning of June, just before the first Adelaide edition of the *Gazette and Register* was published, the long building was still under construction. Robert borrowed a marquee to house them and they had to be content with spending their first winter under canvas.

Nevertheless, they were delighted to be in Adelaide at last, and to be camping on the acre where their permanent home was to be built. Mary longed to be settled and to have the months of making do behind her. She wanted a secure roof over her head and a permanent place for her things where they would be readily to hand, and so she was encouraged by the rapidly rising walls of the long building. While it was going up, Mary bore her discomfort under canvas with stoicism and good humour. Given her 49 years and the comforts and conveniences of her previous life in London, it is testimony to her even temper and optimism for the future.

> *Often I have got out of bed during a high wind and held the tent pole with all my strength, lest it should blow down upon our heads. Many times we have lain in bed with umbrellas spread over us and then stepped into a puddle of water, for no tent could be proof against the torrents which poured down upon us.*[1]

The production of the paper under these circumstances must have been daunting. Mary had assisted with the preparation of the first Adelaide issue just before her move to Hindley Street, having walked the 6 miles from her Holdfast Bay camp to do so, leaving the younger girls in Frances's care. Her work for the paper and 'her many meritorious contributions to the Press of the colony' in its early years were acknowledged by her contemporaries in her obituary.[2] She was also recognised by William Sowden, a later editor of the *Register*, in his unpublished history of the paper, for the 'active and useful part she played in the journalistic department'.[3] With the loss of his apprentice printer, Osborne, on

Kangaroo Island, and the increasing unreliability of his journeyman printer, Robert Fisher, Robert was chronically short-staffed. Mary lived alongside the paper during these early years and, being well educated and highly literate for her day, she was a very competent and readily available resource.

Conscious of the comparison that would be made with the London edition issued on 18 June 1836, just before the departure of the Thomas family on the *Africaine*, Stevenson commented in his first Adelaide editorial

> *[that the] difficulties attendant upon the novelty of our situation, the disadvantages under which the mechanical part of our labours takes place . . . will plead our apology should we not wear the same neat garb in which we made our debut in the great [?] emporium of our civilization.*[4]

The first Adelaide edition ran to six pages of single demy as against the eight of the only London edition. As a historian of the South Australian press noted: 'There was a considerable falling away in the quality of the paper used, and it was obvious that the printing machines employed by William Clowes and Sons for the first London issue were superior to Robert Thomas and Co.'s Stanhope Press.'[5]

For the colonists, the paper summarised very adequately the most significant events of the previous eight months. Of practical value was the listing of the names of all streets and squares, particulars of the sales of town acres, and details of the legislation proclaimed. For readers in Britain it gave a good account of the founding of the colony and, despite the divisions within it, the effective working of the transplanted British institutions – the operation of the Executive Council and the introduction of a legal system. Also, Stevenson's report of the installation of the governor and the proclamation of South Australia is an excellent account of this historic event. The *Gazette and Register* succeeded in demonstrating the systematic development of the colony and in creating, in a modest way, the impression of stability and order. All involved had good reason to feel pleased. Although the intention had been that the paper should come out weekly, at sixpence an issue, they could only manage two issues for July and fell back to one per month for the rest of 1837.

It is clear that Mary undertook a variety of important, if unspecified, tasks for the paper; given the circumstances of the paper and Mary's level of literacy, proofreading is the most likely regular activity. Such an intimate knowledge of the paper's contents – the colonial issues of the day and the details of the colony's growth and development – gave her a unique overview; her work alongside George Stevenson enhanced this perspective. Stevenson, as Governor Hindmarsh's private secretary and as secretary to the Executive Council, had access to information about almost every facet of colonial affairs. In general, along with Robert, Mary shared George Stevenson's stance on colonial issues and colonial development. She was a close and informed observer of the dissension and divisions within the colony during its early months. The *Gazette and Register*, in reports, in commentary and in publishing letters about them, brought these tensions to the notice of the public. The paper supported the governor and defended him fiercely.

Both July issues were controversial in their questioning of the role and powers of the South Australian commissioners in London, and by inference those of their delegate, the resident commissioner in the colony, J.H. Fisher. Stevenson, as editor, argued that Fisher's duties should be confined to two roles: directing the surveying and sale of land in the colony (with the prompt remittance of proceeds to London); and reporting to the commissioners regarding the colony's demand for labour.

Through his editorials, it soon became apparent that Stevenson believed Fisher was attempting to usurp the governor's powers. It seems that Fisher had attempted to diminish the validity of the Executive Council – the body through which Hindmarsh was required to govern – by refusing to attend its meetings. Two letters published in both July issues of the paper challenged Fisher, and by inference, Light's competence. 'A Purchaser of Several Sections' complained that after 12 months he still did not have his country sections. A second letter, written by 'A Colonist', alluded not so much to Fisher's inefficiency, but to his corruption. 'A Colonist' – widely believed to have been Margaret, George Stevenson's wife – asked Fisher to explain his official authorisation of the purchase of working bullocks, dairy cows and a large quantity of pork in Cape Town, and their later sale in Adelaide under circumstances which appeared to benefit a select few – including Fisher's sons.[6] Fisher refused to respond to the anonymous letter. Stevenson's editorial advised him that 'Nothing can be more unwise in the conduct of a public functionary ... than to hesitate for an instant in giving open and straightforward answers to questions touching upon official conduct'.[7]

Fisher's next move with colonial officials – Gouger, Light, Mann, Brown and several well-known private citizens – was to address a letter, published in the *Gazette and Register*, to 'Brother Colonists', advocating that an opposing journal should be established. And so the saga went on; attack and counter-attack, running through the paper during July and August 1837.

Mary supported 'A Colonist's' questioning of the resident commissioner. In correspondence with her brother some years later, she maintained that Fisher had committed many acts 'of glaring misconduct'.[8] Given the scarcity of draught animals and dairy cows, and the high price of meat during these early days, the allegation that Fisher – the most senior official in the colony apart from the governor – had failed to act in the public interest, to his own and his friends' private benefit, caused considerable disquiet among the colonists. More significantly, these claims and counter-claims were read in London.

The *Gazette and Register*'s detailed reporting in September of increasing tension between the governor and his officials, precipitated by the governor's suspension of two officers and the resident commissioner's attempts to reinstate them[9], further strengthened the hand of the Colonial Office in London in its ambition to combine the offices of resident commissioner and governor. The suspension of the colonial secretary, Robert Gouger[10], was the result of a fracas with the colonial treasurer, Osmond Gilles, in which Gouger was provoked into striking Gilles with a walking stick, while the emigration agent, John Brown, was suspended following his refusal – on the instructions of the resident commissioner, J.H. Fisher – to meet Governor Hindmarsh's request to arrange the burial of a pauper.

Despite the large number of columns occupied by the accounts of these disturbances, space had to be found for the more mundane and practical items of immediate benefit to the paper's readers. The September *Gazette and Register* made its first report of the markets in Adelaide.

> *[They indicated that] the recent arrivals of several vessels from the sister colonies have supplied our limited market with an abundance of every description of goods ... and it will be observed that our infant colony cannot be said to suffer under exorbitant prices.*[11]

Among the food items surveyed were preserved meats, fresh meats (beef and mutton), butter, tea, coffee, sugar, flour, dried fruit, vinegar, London soap, oil (for both cooking and lighting), ale and wines. Other items generally on sale were rice, potatoes, oatmeal, bran and pollard. With the exclusion of fresh fruit and vegetables, a reasonable variety of basic foods was available to the colonists.

By June 1837, little more than six months since the arrival of the *Africaine* and the first settlers, 34 vessels (including those belonging to Angas's South Australian Company) had reached the colony. About half of these ships were emigrant vessels originating from England – the majority from London – with the 600 ton (612 tonne) *Coramandel*, being the largest. Besides emigrants, almost all carried some cargo including food and other merchandise such as clothing, building materials and tools. The other half came from the 'sister' colonies and also brought in food and merchandise; but most of these coastal traders were quite small, less than 100 tons (102 tonnes).[12] These arrivals replenished the stock of Robert's general store as well as the official commissioners' store, which provided rations for those free passage emigrants who were without employment. Like Robert's during the early months of settlement, the commissioners' store had been based at Holdfast Bay before transferring to Adelaide.

Toward the end of 1837, South Australia's emigrant population was approaching 3000, including 600 who had come from other Australian colonies.[13] Vessels had continued to reach the colony at an ever-increasing rate, with six arriving in just two weeks during October 1837. Again, half were emigrant vessels from England, and half were coastal traders from Van Diemen's Land. All carried general cargo and one vessel, from Launceston, brought in stock – sheep, cattle and draught animals.[14]

During September, Robert, with the aid of tradesmen, had completed the long building. This was a considerable achievement, taking into account the rapidly growing demand for R. Thomas and Co.'s printing services, as particularly, with the loss of his journeyman printer, Robert Fisher (who had absconded), Robert was more short-staffed than ever. By October, Mary, Robert and the girls were well settled into their new home, sandwiched between the store and the printing office, occupying the short central wing that gave the long building its slight T-shape. Overall it measured 23 feet (7 metres) by 90 feet (27 metres), had walls of rammed mud and a roof of boards[15], with a calico 'ceiling' stretched across the rafters in an attempt to exclude insects and dust. Mary made no mention of a kitchen in a later letter to her brother, and it seems an outdoor fireplace 'of the most primitive description being no more than a square spot enclosed on three sides with stone to about 18 inches high and open in front'[16], continued as her stove with Mary taking cover under an umbrella when it rained.

Robert George didn't join his parents and sisters in their new dwelling – he was still away with Colonel Light's teams, engaged in the surveying of country sections; while William continued to share a room with an apprentice printer at one end of the warehouse. Despite an extreme shortage of skilled building tradesmen, within a matter of weeks of completing the long building, Robert had begun work on a stone house which he anticipated would be their permanent home.[17]

Mary and Robert's experience – from tent to pisé hut or something approaching a house – was the general pattern for most settlers. However, some prefabricated wooden houses (Manning houses), with the more luxurious providing four to six rooms, had been brought into the colony, mainly by officials – the colonial secretary, the treasurer and the chaplain, for example – and were successfully erected. Others, such as that brought out by the governor, were too flimsy to cope with colonial conditions.[18]

By November 1837 there were about 300 houses and huts in Adelaide[19], mainly clustered around the intersections of Morphett Street with Light Square and with Currie Street, and particularly around Hindley Street where – like the Thomas's – stores and other businesses were being established. Almost all dwellings were small and constructed from whatever materials were to hand: mud, native timber and native grasses for thatch. Even so, tents still provided the only shelter for many. Dotted around Colonel Light's survey camp on the banks of the Torrens, near the corner of North and West Terraces, were the makeshift homes of recent arrivals and those still waiting to obtain land. Government House, hardly more than a rush hut itself, was also on the river's bank.

An enclave of tradesmen associated with the building industry had settled in Waymouth Street adjacent to Gilles Arcade by 1838; and gradually more conventional building materials, both locally produced and imported – stone, bricks, timber and slate – were in greater supply.[20] A limestone quarry on the banks of the Torrens and a brick kiln at Hindmarsh, utilising the clays found there, were established, and eventually the stringy-bark trees in the Adelaide Hills were harvested for timber.

The homes and buildings concentrated in the north-west corner of Adelaide were generally becoming bigger and more substantial. And, although dwellings were scattered throughout the rest of the town's square mile, Adelaide was still a forest city. It was hardly more than a rudimentary settlement in a bush clearing and its streets and squares, although clearly marked on Light's plan, had barely begun to take form. Except for the area around Hindley Street, the streets were still largely covered with native trees and bush, and where clearing had been attempted, stumps and holes – some of them huge – were hazards for the unwary traveller. It was easy enough to lose one's bearings during the day, but at night, even with a good moon, most people became hopelessly lost.[21]

The ongoing clearing of trees and bush disturbed the natural drainage of the land, and without any man-made substitute to carry away the deluges after storms, the streets became seas of mud. Hindley Street was particularly badly affected, where carts and bullock wagons churned up and rutted the road. The business success of Robert and the other store owners was hampered by the state of the streets which presented a strong disincentive to shoppers, women especially, who often had a wretched walk in long skirts dragging through the mud and slush.[22] Mary, however, was more fortunate, with her easy access to Robert's store for basic food supplies and groceries.

In January 1838 Robert needed to find extra funds and, although the purpose was unspecified, Coltman's management of the store was causing difficulties. On the 11th an agreement was signed with the South Australian Company to raise £500 using eight of Robert's town acres as collateral, including acre 56 and the buildings on it.[23] Fortunately, 14 months later, due to the steep increase in land values, he was able to negotiate the exclusion of acre 56 and its buildings.[24]

Initially, the store had enjoyed 'all of the business of the place ... and it may have turned out a very profitable concern'[25], as Mary explained some months later in a letter to her brother George. Nevertheless, Robert dissolved the partnership in March 1838 due to Coltman's ineptitude, if not outright dishonesty. When Robert was in Hobart purchasing stock, Coltman 'contracted some heavy debts . . . entirely without his knowledge or consent', for which Robert was ultimately liable. Mary considered this happened 'through the villainy of . . . [Coltman] and [Robert's] own folly in not looking after him as he ought to have done'.[26] Even after he had ended the partnership, Robert continued to receive goods from London, ordered many months earlier, compelling him to maintain the store in order to clear this new stock, as well as that still on the shelves. A consignment arrived on the *Roxburgh* during early August 1838 and Robert advertised hats, linen drapery, jewellery, cutlery, perfumery, and ironmongery – 'all selected expressly for the colony'.[27]

Robert's chances of emptying the store easily and quickly were diminishing rapidly, due to the increasing competition from others setting up around him. V. and E. Solomon, merchants and auctioneers from Sydney, had established a branch store in Gilles Arcade during July, and only a few weeks earlier, Joseph Lazarus had opened on the corner of Morphett and Hindley streets. Two further stores had been operating in Gilles Arcade for about 12 months, plus others in Grenfell, Rundle and Franklin streets. There were nine in all, including Robert's, and as general stores they each carried much the same range of goods.[28] A year after Robert had ended the partnership with Coltman, he was still advertising dress materials and haberdashery 'at greatly reduced prices'.[29]

Entries in the directory of the *South Australian Almanack*, produced by R. Thomas and Co., reveal that at the end of 1838 there were at least 24 designated storekeepers, 24 merchants, 11 bakers, five butchers, and four auctioneers operating in Adelaide. As well, specialty stores had started to emerge in the retailing of clothing, with four tailors and drapers trading.[30] Although there was progress in the number and variety of stores and goods available, by October the price of food had started to rise as demand grew apace with the ever-increasing numbers of new arrivals. It was a constant worry.

Difficulties in quitting the stock of his defunct store and R. Thomas and Co.'s staff shortages were not Robert's only problems. Both he and Stevenson were in court for most of May 1838 answering libel charges brought against them by the resident commissioner, J.H. Fisher. Fisher claimed that the *Gazette and Register* had defamed him by accusing him of withholding land, for his own corrupt future private benefit, from the survey around Encounter Bay being undertaken to identify country sections intended for holders of preliminary land orders. After a number of delays and irregularities, the case was eventually decided in Fisher's favour, but with only minimal damages – 1 shilling – awarded. Because of the court case, Robert and Stevenson could manage only one edition of the paper for May.[31]

Only a fortnight later, on 2 June, the journal foreshadowed by Fisher and his faction 12 months earlier put out its first issue as the *Southern Australian*, with the former advocate-general, Charles Mann, as editor. It claimed to have been founded to combat the 'abuses' of the *Gazette and Register*, with 'its strong party bias', its 'disposition to make despotic use of its monopoly', 'insinuations', 'disgraceful personalities', and 'downright falsehoods'. Perhaps spurred on by the presence of its opposition, over the next two months the *Gazette and Register* became a true weekly. It continued to flourish, with both the journalistic and printing departments running smoothly.

Mann put out a second issue of the *Southern Australian* on 9 June in which he maintained that he and the resident commissioner's party opposed the governor in the cause of civil liberty, referring to Hindmarsh as 'that colonial autocrat'. The *Gazette and Register* defended Hindmarsh on the 16th: 'We have never yet found any of those most vociferous in abuse of His Excellency able to explain which of his public actions entitle him to the relief [recall] they contemplate.' In the following issue Stevenson published the Colonial Office dispatch recalling Governor Hindmarsh and, in support of him, attributed his recall to the commissioners' pressing for it in representations to the colonial secretary, Lord Glenelg. According to Stevenson, Lord Glenelg had only reluctantly complied with their demands for the withdrawal of

Hindmarsh's commission. In the last issue for June, having received information from a private source in London, Stevenson maintained that Glenelg could see nothing improper in the governor's conduct 'beyond troubling himself a little too much about matters which were better left alone'.[32] Stevenson concluded that the commissioners were 'grossly imposed upon by false information and that they have acted upon it'.[33]

Mary also abhorred J.H. Fisher's actions in which, as she reported later in a letter to her brother George, 'he contrived ... with other miscreants to get our late worthy Governor [Hindmarsh] recalled, deeply to the regret of all who wished well to the colony, especially as the misrepresentations sent home respecting him were the most base, false and cowardly imaginable'.[34] Hindmarsh did not wait for his replacement but, before leaving the colony in July, he appointed the attorney-general, G.M. Stephen, acting-governor.

The new governor, Colonel George Gawler, reached Holdfast Bay on board the *Pestonjee Bomanjee* in mid October, and wasted little time in implementing his instructions to suspend J.H. Fisher and to combine the role of resident commissioner with his vice-regal duties.

Gawler immediately directed his attention to the Survey Department, which had been in disarray since the resignations in June 1838 of Light and the majority of his surveyors and their assistants, including the young draftsman Robert George Thomas. As surveyor-general, Light had come under heavy and unfair criticism both from within the colony and from the commissioners in London; even though by May, 150,000 acres (60,000 hectares) – including 69,000 acres (27,000 hectares) around Adelaide[35] – had been surveyed and mapped by his team, and were available to the holders of preliminary land orders for the selection of their country sections. In this allocation of land Robert and Mary acquired two 134-acre (54-hectare) sections adjoining the River Torrens, a few miles east of Adelaide, near today's St Peters.[36]

But there had been delays with the survey, due largely to the nature of the terrain – virgin bush with neither roads nor tracks – and a shortage of skilled surveyors. Light had refused to be pressured into using a speedier but much less accurate method of conducting it. Although on Light's departure, his deputy, George Kingston, remained with the department, little more effective work was done until the newly arrived Governor Gawler expanded it dramatically and placed it under his direct supervision. Captain Charles Sturt[37] was appointed surveyor-general and Kingston resigned. Some of Light's former staff were reinstated – although not Robert George Thomas, who remained with the surveying firm which Light,[38] had established in partnership with his former chief surveyor, Boyle Travers Finniss. Gawler supplied his reinstated surveyors 'bountifully with labourers, equipment and stores', and within three months 'the survey was in full swing'.[39]

On 14 October, just two days after Governor Gawler's arrival at Holdfast Bay, Mary sat down to write her first letter to George from the colony. It was in response to his – the only letter she had received from her brother since leaving England. Mary and George had remained estranged after her emigration, and George's letter was seeking to restore their relationship. Mary received his letter 'with heartfelt satisfaction' and was taking 'the earliest opportunity to answer it'.[40]

She recounted the voyage out, describing the camp at Holdfast Bay and their present living arrangements in the long building, the progress in building the stone house, the failure of the store, but the prosperity of the newspaper and R. Thomas and Co. With some pride she told George of the rapid developments taking place: the expanding population, the forming of the streets, the increase in land values and the profits to be made through land transactions. A few days before Mary had begun her reply to George, Robert had sold a quarter of an acre (0.1 hectare) for 200 guineas. He had paid less than 10 guineas for the whole acre (0.4 hectare) at the end of March 1837. And during the course of her letter, which took Mary nearly a week to write as she had 'so little time to spare', Robert 'let a quarter of an acre on a building lease for 10 years for £40 a year'. It was part of another acre that Robert had bought for 10 guineas.[41] In spite of all of this, and Robert's infatuation with the country, she was homesick.

> *This is certainly a very fine country, and capable of the highest improvements . . . but to those who know what England is, and recollect the comfort there enjoyed, it never can bear a comparison, notwithstanding its luxuriant plains, its magnificent trees, its ranges of lofty hills, and scenery often sublime.*[42]

Perhaps in an attempt to assuage her longing for home, she asked George to send her some Hampshire produce.

> *It is only a childish whim, for I fancy I could relish a bit of Hampshire bacon more than anything to be got here . . . if you can prevail on Mr Kinggate [one of the executors of George Harris Snr's estate] to pay you for two flitches out of my money from the bank interest [her annuity]. But . . . do not send it unless you can have immediate payment.*[43]

Mary was troubled over her difficulties in arranging for her annuity to be collected. She had tried to negotiate for the mortgagee to pay the interest due on the Southampton property, which funded it, directly to her London agent, Mr Baugh. Her father's executors, including her brother-in-law Benjamin Self, objected, even though Mr Baugh's power of attorney had been drawn up by Mary's London solicitor. She suspected that her brother-in-law, and her sister, Ann, were behind the objection. Ann, she complained to George, 'was still possessed of such a selfish disposition . . . her jealousy must be a perpetual torment to her. She seems to grudge everything she cannot appropriate to herself'.[44] Mary told George that Robert planned to return a deed – sent to her some months earlier by her London solicitor for both her signature and Robert's – with the next government dispatches. She was hopeful that it might at last facilitate the collection of her annuity on her behalf and so provide the funds in England to allow goods to be sent out to her. In ending her letter Mary expressed her desire to end her days in peace and comfort in England, telling George that she had no ambition to be rich and that although she and her family may hope 'to obtain a competence here', they 'must go to England to enjoy it'.⁴⁵

It was only a few weeks before Mary wrote again. Believing that there should not be any difficulty now in George being reimbursed immediately, but urging him again to be sure of it before he purchased anything for her, Mary asked him to send with the bacon, six hams, a 12 to 14 pound pot of honey – to use as a substitute for butter which was very dear – and five or six dozen Isle of Wight cracknels [biscuits].

> *You will perhaps think me very childish to send 16,000 miles for a pot of honey and a few biscuits, but I am so attached to my native country, and especially my native county and its productions, that I fancy nothing like them.*⁴⁶

Mary considered that her garden would never produce what she thought of as the really useful and substantial fruits that were available in England, as she told George some months later. The South Australian climate, she maintained, was too hot and dry for apples, pears, gooseberries, currants and cherries to grow in abundance. To establish a kitchen garden and to acclimatise old-world plants to Australian conditions took time, but it was essential work for Mary if her family was eventually to have a consistent supply of fresh fruit and vegetables.

> *[In April 1839 she complained to George that] vegetables in our own garden ... arrive at maturity much sooner than in England, yet they get old and tough equally as quick. Though very nice if eaten young, if suffered to remain beyond a certain time they are good for nothing. This, I imagine will be the case with fruits if we grow them ...*

Then, more optimistically, she said:

> We had melons in our garden during January and February, but of course they were planted, and peaches, nectarines, and suchlike will doubtless be very plentiful in a few years' time.[47]

Twelve months later her garden had begun to produce an abundance of some vegetables as she gradually gained a better understanding of the seasons.

> [But she still considered the country strange, telling George that] the soil and climate seem to be as variable as the wind. The winter before last we had an abundance of carrots and onions in our garden, as well as peas and other vegetables, except cabbages, which ran to seed almost as soon as they were planted . . . Last winter our onions and carrots totally failed . . . [while the] cabbages continued to sprout all through summer in spite of the hot weather . . . I give a great deal away to those who have no gardens.[48]

Mary was fortunate to have a rivulet running through her garden, which flooded from time to time, providing irrigation for her vegetables and fruit trees.[49] For household use, she had a well dug and obtained an excellent supply of water at 60 feet (18 metres), free of the impregnated lime that caused most well-water in Adelaide to have a whitish, milky appearance. She was delighted with the clarity of her well, the convenience of having an unlimited supply of water readily to hand, and the savings it would mean, 'as water here is an expensive article, though the well has not cost much less than £40'.[50]

Before Mary's well was dug, all water for drinking and other household use was collected from the river or bought from one of the water carriers who supplied it from their carts, ladling it into water casks at each dwelling. It came from the Torrens, was not very pure, and was 'usually strained through muslin . . . before being used for drinking'.[51] Delivered water was expensive at 3 shillings a cask for customers in Hindley Street, and more in streets further away. The well also provided Mary with a cool place to store food.

Even when she had to pay for delivered water Mary was happy to share it, describing to George her encounter with two Aboriginal men who asked for bread and water.

> *[Mary gave them some bread and] took the jug to the water cask, not choosing that they should put their own dirty hands in it [when] one of them coolly told me to 'Wash the jug first,' though in truth there was much more occasion to wash it afterwards . . . I could not help laughing . . .*[52]

Much to her distress, Mary found it almost impossible, in her homemaking, to maintain standards of 'cleanliness and comfort according to English ideas'. It was 'out of the question and incompatible with the country altogether', particularly as 'clouds of dust . . . drove through every crevice' and covered the furniture three to four times a day. She was also troubled by the need to incessantly hunt fleas, bugs, flies and ants and to cope with 'spiders of enormous size'; and did not 'relish working so hard . . . at her time of life' but could see 'little prospect at present of its being otherwise'. Her servant, Mary Lillywhite, had left her, having married the absconding journeyman, Robert Fisher, and Mary was managing without a replacement, except for the German washerwomen who did her laundry. Servants were expensive and difficult to find.[53]

To add to her woes, between October 1838 and June 1839 the cost of bread rose by 33 per cent and fresh meat by 16 per cent; compared with Sydney, Adelaide's prices were dear. 'Housekeeping . . .' as Mary explained to George, 'is no joke and I fear it will be some time before things are cheaper'.[54] High prices continued throughout the winter of 1839 and into the following summer, due partly to a six-month drought when the country was 'so completely parched that nothing would grow'. The colony was without fruit and vegetables for several months, except for 'very dear' potatoes from Van Diemen's Land.[55]

Chapter 6
'A tree transplanted whole'

At the beginning of 1839, Mary's budget was boosted by additional income from the leasing of the defunct store to a Hugh McDonald and its conversion to the John o' Groats Inn. By March 1839, 45 public houses had taken out a full year's license under the recently passed *Licensing Act* 1839.[1] There were seven in Hindley Street, besides the John o' Groats, which, despite the competition around it, did well. It became 'a popular centre for dances, balls and small dinners'[2] and Mary occasionally provided suppers there for the apprentices of R. Thomas and Co.[3] Its location near the printing office and next to the Thomas's living quarters made it, in some ways, like an extension of the Thomas family home.

Hotels, however primitive in structure and design, played an important role during these boom years when migration was at its peak. They provided shelter and food for large numbers of the newly arrived, self-funded emigrants and their families until their country sections, and thus farms and dwellings could be established. Mary was impatient with the grumbles of some new arrivals

> because they could not meet with the accommodation to which they had been accustomed. Sometimes this induced me to retort . . . that if they had come out when we did exposed to all the weathers as we were, they would be glad to put up with what they could get, instead of complaining for what was not to be had.[4]

Accommodation and particularly meals were also required by colonists already settled in the outlying districts, when they visited Adelaide to transact business.

The early inns and hotels also provided stabling, and by c. 1839 a number of the larger establishments, the Southern Cross (Allen's) in Currie Street, for example, had hacks and spring carts for hire. Allen's was the depot for the mail carts that carried passengers between the hotel and Port Adelaide and to and from Holdfast Bay. Other establishments ran similar services to Willunga and to Gawler.[5] Adelaide's innkeepers were required to maintain lamps outside their doors from dusk to daylight and, as a result, Adelaide's main streets were reasonably well lit.[6]

At this early stage in the colony's evolution, inns and hotels were of prime importance in the development of Adelaide's social life and its social cohesion.

> *[They] entered prominently into the general domestic life of the people. For a number of years they were almost the only centres where suitable accommodation might be secured for meetings, dinners and general entertainments . . . For the ordinary individual, the 'sing songs' or 'free and easies' provided a form of relaxation . . . Probably at some of the popular diversions arranged in the better class inns, it would not be unusual to see the wives or women friends of the menfolk present.*[7]

Mary lived for almost 12 months with the bustle and activity of the John o' Groats to one side of her 'apartment' while the constant clatter of the printing presses resounded from the other. With the introduction of the *SA Almanack* early in 1839, R. Thomas and Co. was prospering and so was the *Gazette and Register*. The printing office, as Mary emphasised, in a letter to George, was extremely busy:

> *Mr Thomas, William and all have worked night and day for nearly a month past, seldom leaving off till 12 or one o'clock, and sometimes working all night . . . though seven hands are constantly*

> employed in the office we could readily employ three or four more, but printers and compositors are scarce.[8]

However, a month or two later, the smooth functioning of the paper was disrupted by 'agents of the opposition paper' [the *Southern Australian*] who, according to Mary's comments to George, 'have not scrupled to go on board vessels' and have taken all the copies of the *Gazette and Register* 'under the pretence of promising to forward them to their rightful owners, instead of which they were committed to the flames'. All of the papers that were addressed to the commissioners, to their agent in London, and particularly to London newspaper offices, were destroyed. As a result, R. Thomas and Co. had not been receiving reciprocal copies of London newspapers and the *Gazette and Register* had been deprived of this source of English news.

> *[Mary blamed this on a] villainous set here, who would overturn the government if they had it in their power, and convert everything into mismanagement and misrule by becoming tyrants themselves . . . inveterate against the Gazette because it has exposed transactions and laid bare truths which they did not wish the people of England to know.*[9]

Mary's accusations were consistent with a rumour circulating in London that the paper was defunct and was no longer available at the commissioners' offices. Stevenson commented in the *Gazette and Register* during March on what he believed to have been the commissioners' suppression of the paper to hide the divisions in the colony. '[If they] think it necessary in a political point of view to conceal the real occurrences that are happening around us, the good that can result is exceedingly questionable.'[10]

At about the same time, the *Gazette and Register* was caught up in further controversies in reporting the allegedly corrupt behaviour of another government official. The dubious dealings of the advocate-general, G.M. Stephen, in his attempt to inflate the value of his Milner Estate – selected from a special survey[11] on the

Gawler River – would eventually involve the two rival newspapers in charges of libel.

Late one evening, Stephen called at the printing office to leave a note for Stevenson just in time for its inclusion in the next day's *Gazette and Register*. In it he reported the sale of half of his estate [2000 acres (800 hectares)] for £20,000 – to two gentlemen recently arrived from India – which, on the face of it, gave Stephen a handsome profit on his outlay of £4000. Notice of the sale was included in the following day's paper, almost verbatim, as a news item. Within a matter of days it emerged that not only had Stephen, in his note, inflated the price by 100 per cent, but his sale had fallen through. He ignored Stevenson's instant request to correct this in the next issue of the paper.[12] Unfortunately, the story of the fabled sale had been immediately picked up and published by the *Southern Australian*, now under the proprietorship of Archibald Macdougall.

The *Southern Australian*, realising that in its earlier report it had been caught in a scam to inflate the estate's value, exposed Stephen's deceit. The paper also made reference to published statements from other colonies that were detrimental to Stephen's character:

> *We have carefully abstained from any allusions to the party who is said to be the proprietor of the estate since he arrived in our province . . . We cannot longer be silent. The colony has been sufficiently insulted by the appointment [as acting governor], further insulted by his impudent and insolent bearing, and we will take care that the colonists shall not have to suffer from his puffing propensities. It is a disgrace to the station he holds, so to employ himself as even to raise the shadow of suspicion of his honesty.*[13]

According to Mary's grandson, Evan Kyffin Thomas, in a later report of these events, Stephen started libel proceedings against the *Southern Australian*. On the day before the trial, he visited Stevenson and asked for the original note relating to the purported sale of half of the estate. Stevenson gave it to him reluctantly and only after making a copy certified by Stephen's signature. Stephen, who had not complained to Stevenson of any alteration to the note, immediately showed it to several witnesses to whom it appeared 'that there had been an attempt to convert the "2" [of the £20,000] into "1", in order to give the "2" the appearance of having been altered and changed from a supposed original figure "1"'. 'Stephen charged Stevenson with the alteration'[14], trying to make it appear that in his note to Stevenson he had reported a sale price of only £10,000 and that Stevenson himself had inflated the price in publishing it.

The *Gazette and Register* of 1 June covered the trial in which Macdougall, as a proprietor of the *Southern Australian*, was defended by Charles Mann, while Stephen prosecuted his own case. The note was not produced because Stephen cunningly limited his charges of libel against Macdougall to the imputations published about his character. This resulted in the judge disallowing any reference to the deceit over land sales as 'not material' and he instructed the jury to do the same.[15] Predictably, the verdict went Stephen's way. According to Mary in a letter to George, Stephen had obtained the guilty verdict against Macdougall by 'swearing he had never authorized the insertion of the article in the *Gazette [and Register]*'.[16] Stevenson was now forced to defend himself against Stephen's imputation that he had inflated the price of the land.

Stephen had denied on oath that he had ever intentionally deceived Stevenson about the sale and also claimed that Stevenson had dissuaded him from correcting the detail of the original news item – in fact the opposite was the case. In his defence, Stevenson published statements from Robert and William and other R. Thomas and Co. staff testifying that Stephen, himself, had told them of his extremely favourable land transaction the night he left the note at the printing office. Stevenson commented on the arcane byways of the law, which meant that Stephen's false statements under oath in a courtroom could not be considered perjury. He advised his readers that he had 'withdrawn from the

Magistracy and resigned the office of Coroner, declining to hold office while Mr G.M. Stephen continues connected with the Colonial Government'.[17]

This continuing debate – again involving the *Gazette and Register*'s questioning the probity of a public official – gave Governor Gawler the excuse he had been looking for to separate the government *Gazette* from the *Register*. Despite the fact that the paper was not originally involved in the scandal and the libel proceedings, Gawler strongly disapproved of Stevenson's – now characteristic – editorial attacks upon officials. The last *Gazette and Register*, published on 22 June 1839, advised readers of its separation into two papers. The *Register* would continue to be published on Saturdays with the *Gazette* coming out on Thursdays.[18] The cost of the division was to be born largely by R. Thomas and Co., and in its next issue Stevenson apologised for a steep increase in the price of the *Register* from sixpence to one shilling.[19]

The situation escalated a few weeks later when Stephen wrote to Robert threatening a libel action regarding the paper's accusations of his perjury in reporting the trial of Macdougall. Stevenson had not been named deliberately as Stephen wished to examine him as a witness.[20] Undeterred, Stevenson continued to pursue Stephen, commenting in the 27 July issue of the *Register* that he 'was egregiously imposed upon and scandalously hoaxed by Mr Stephen in common with the rest of the colonists'.[21] Presumably, Stevenson was aiming to precipitate the threatened action in order to have his day in court and to clear his name.

However, before the issue of Stephen's threatened action was realised, in August 1839, the disgraced ex-resident commissioner, Fisher, brought another libel charge against the *Register*, claiming to have been defamed by the paper's earlier printing of a letter from 'A Colonist' which implied his corruption regarding the pork and livestock saga. He had held over his original threat of legal action until after his appearance before the formal Board of Inquiry, established by Governor Gawler, into the same matter. Because of Fisher's refusal to answer questions, the inquiry returned an inconclusive finding, but Fisher was not exonerated and following his resignation from government service, he renewed the libel action against the *Register*. In a letter to George during the court proceedings, Mary's view of Fisher and his past activities was scathing.

> *This Fisher came out here as Resident Commissioner with a salary of £600 – a failed Attorney. His conduct was so atrocious in many instances that our Editor very properly called him to account, in the public papers as every public man is liable to be . . . These actions for libel were brought against Mr Stevenson nearly two years ago and everybody thought Mr Fisher would be wise enough to drop them but by bringing them to trial has once more brought to light what had nearly been forgotten . . .*[22]

Robert returned from the courthouse as Mary was finishing her letter. The verdict was decided against R. Thomas and Co., but on the lesser charge of printing and publishing improper language, with one shilling damages for the plaintiff – hardly a satisfying outcome for Fisher. He ultimately dropped two additional charges against the *Register* for publishing uncomplimentary remarks about his intelligence and honesty.

In early September, Stevenson and Robert were in court once more, this time responding to G.M. Stephen's libel action regarding the *Register*'s accusations of his perjury. A unanimous verdict was returned for Stevenson and, according to Mary, 'to the general satisfaction of the colony'. She wrote to George with obvious satisfaction that Stephen, a man possessing a character of 'one of the blackest dyes is now stigmatised as being guilty of both perjury and forgery by the plainest proofs'.[23] By this time, Stephen had been suspended from his official position as advocate-general, leaving the colony in disgrace.

Almost in spite of some of its public officials, South Australia continued to make progress, and by August 1839 the population was reported to be 8250, the result of an extraordinary growth of almost

40 per cent over the past year.[24] Ninety-nine vessels had reached the colony during the previous six months and virtually all ships from England had carried emigrants.[25] Under pressure from the increasing numbers of new arrivals, land prices continued to rise, with a town acre – which included a building valued at £500 – selling for £2000. Eighteen months earlier, in April 1837, the average price had been just £6 and 6 shillings.[26]

The surge in land values in and around Adelaide persisted and Governor Gawler's ongoing administration of the land department focused upon speeding up the survey, motivated by his recognition that the paucity of land available to new arrivals with ready money to invest was pushing up the price of land to untenable levels. An inflationary spiral was beginning to emerge, driven not only by the price of land, but also by the lack of land for food production and the increasing cost of imported food, particularly from New South Wales which was in the grip of a severe drought. Gawler wanted to continue to get the colonists away from the town and out onto the land producing food. By the end of the year, the marking of a further 200,000 acres (80,000 hectares) had been completed 'in spite of a wet winter and intricate, uninhabited territory'.[27] Gawler's dramatic expansion of the Survey Department to a staff of almost 200 men was accompanied by an astronomical increase in expenditure. Although his annual allowance from the commissioners totalled only £16,500 to cover all government outgoings, during the last quarter of 1839 Gawler had spent £10,000 on salaries and stores for the survey alone.[28] Given the circumstances he was facing, he believed that, despite its escalation, either the commissioners or the British Government would meet his expenditure in full.

The early settlers, like Robert and Mary, who had benefited financially from land transactions and whose businesses were booming, shared Gawler's optimism for the colony's continued prosperity. But the Aborigines of the Adelaide Plains were not prospering, and tensions between the white and Aboriginal populations were beginning to arise with the spearing of sheep as

Aborigines attempted to compensate for a loss of access to their former hunting grounds. As Mary explained to George, '[They] very logically exculpate their own misdemeanours by saying, "White man come kill black man kangaroo. Black man kill white man sheep"'.[29]

These tensions were heightened by the Aboriginal killing of two white shepherds. The three Aboriginal men implicated were tracked and charged and appeared in the Supreme Court before the recently arrived chief justice Charles Cooper. Two of the men were found guilty and convicted. Their public hangings were witnessed by a considerable number of colonists and a group of Aborigines, and as Stevenson passed the native huts immediately after the execution, he 'found women and children and many of the men lamenting in a most piteous manner'.[30]

The colonists, alarmed at the murders, had called a public meeting a few weeks earlier to discuss ways to improve their rapidly deteriorating relationships with the Aborigines. Sadly, little of value was achieved by the meeting and Governor Gawler rejected both its criticisms of the protector of Aborigines, Dr William Wyatt, for his alleged inefficiency, and the suggestion that the Aborigines should be disarmed.[31] To add to the Aborigines' already parlous plight, their population was declining rapidly with Aboriginal deaths exceeding Aboriginal births.[32]

Despite these difficulties and tensions, only a few months later, recreational and educational activities open to the general public were beginning to develop, as Mary Jnr noted in her journal. In August 1839, a week or two before her 16th birthday, she began the journal which she was to continue for the next seven years. While her first entry recorded a music lesson both she and her sister, Helen, took with a Miss Margaret Williams, the daughter of R. Thomas and Co.'s chief clerk; her next reported that on the following day, accompanied by Helen and Margaret Williams, she attended the first of a series of public lectures planned by the recently combined Literary and Scientific Association and

Mechanics' Institute.³³ The lectures were not only educational but provided an opportunity to meet up with friends and to make new ones.

The Literary and Scientific Association had been founded in London just prior to the departure of the first colonists.³⁴ It was formed to become a South Australian replacement for the Conversazione Club which, in the Adelphi rooms of the SA Association in London, had provided lectures and discussion groups on practical topics as well as cultural matters of relevance to the intending colonists.³⁵ E.G. Wakefield's metaphor for the society to be formed by South Australia's first emigrants was the transplanting of a fully grown tree 'removed whole and uninjured such that its several parts are established in the same relative situation as they occupied before'. The prospective colonists were aware of the importance Wakefield placed upon 'rendering the colony as like as possible to England from the very beginning of its career', and the establishment of the Literary and Scientific Association was the embodiment of Wakefield's principles in practice. Some intending settlers, before leaving England, were involved in planning for the development of secular and religious education, a newspaper, and artistic endeavours. 'Such a society', Wakefield considered, 'will remove with order and can hardly fail to be established in peace and prosperity'.³⁶ The Literary and Scientific Association, however, did not develop its activities in South Australia until Governor Gawler founded the Mechanics' Institute, and within a matter of months, in July 1839, the two bodies had amalgamated and became known as the Institute.³⁷

The Congregationalist, the Reverend T.Q. Stow, gave the first lecture in August on 'The Pleasures of Literature'. The next lecture reviewed 'Animal Production in the Colony'; and the third, also in September, was presented by George Stevenson on horticulture, with his topic continuing in November and December. As reported in the *Register*, his focus was on the plants most suited to the colony's Mediterranean climate.

South Australia must eventually become the peculiar country of the orange, the pomegranate, the fig, the olive and the vine, and every description of grain most prized as animal food . . . of first importance is the grape vine and next the orange and the olive.[38]

With considerable prescience, he vigorously promoted the establishment of a grape and wine industry, and as an adjunct, a brandy industry.

Mary Jnr, Frances, Helen and Margaret Williams attended both September lectures; and their friend Harriet Holbrooke, a teacher in the infants' school associated with Trinity Church, joined them for the second.[39] In October the Thomas girls and their friends heard Charles Platts give his lecture on music at Richardson's Auction Rooms assisted by George Bennett on the violin and William Ewens, an ex-chorister from Chichester Cathedral. Platts was organist at Trinity Church and the proprietor of a music store and circulating library. Mary Jnr thought the music 'very poor' apart from George Bennett's playing.[40]

A few months later, Charles Platts held another concert in Solomons' Auction Rooms, again with the assistance of Bennett and Ewens. Tickets were expensive at 7 shillings a single[41] but, despite their cost, Mary bought four – for Frances and John, Mary Jnr and Helen – an indication of the Thomas's affluence at that time. It was an occasion for dressing up and Mary Jnr wore her dress of India taffeta, 'a silk well suited to our climate'. But because of heavy rain and muddy streets, the concert had to be postponed from Wednesday to Thursday evening. Mary Jnr, who was now having two music lessons a week with Margaret Williams, judged the concert to be 'very good considering all things'.[42]

The *Register* reported the first Annual General Meeting of the Institute on 18 July 1840. It had maintained its early momentum: classes run by volunteer teachers 'for study among junior members' were promoted; a museum was proposed to aid the preservation of the colony's distinctive natural history; and a library of 417 books (many donated from England) had been established in the previous October. Charles Platts, as volunteer librarian, opened the library each weekday evening in the South Australian School Society schoolroom on North Terrace, only a short walk from acre 56 Hindley Street.[43] The series of lectures, the first initiative of the Institute, had continued and covered zoology (Dr M. Moorhouse), chemistry (M. Weston), botany (J. Bailey), minerals (J. Menge), geography and geology (Captain C. Sturt), as well as literature, music and horticulture. Captain Charles Sturt was appointed president with George Stevenson as one of several vice presidents, and Robert Thomas a committee member.[44]

Education for their children was of major concern to the colonists and after the first months of the all-absorbing struggle to establish themselves, they turned their attention to the founding of schools. The South Australian School Society's school was supported by the society's headquarters in London, and was sponsored by the merchant and philanthropist, G.F. Angas. It was one of the first schools to open in Adelaide, and by the end of May 1838, with Mr J.B. Shepherdson as teacher[45], it had been set up in the brick building on the western corner of Morphett Street and North Terrace, previously occupied by the Bank of South Australia. The society's charter was to provide schooling for children of the less affluent, who paid sixpence per week for an elementary education.[46]

One of the first private schools in the colony was run by a friend of Mary's, Mrs Jane Hillier, who had taught the Thomas girls in London. Initially her Adelaide school, which Helen Thomas attended, was located at the foot of Montefiore Hill by the ford over the Torrens, and by January 1838, she had transferred it to the Pavilion Cottage near Gilles Arcade.[47]

Two years later, in the *Register* of 22 February, Margaret Williams announced the opening of her school. She offered tuition to young ladies at premises on North Terrace (near King William Street), and Mary enrolled Mary Jnr for the 1840 school year. Tuition covered 'all the essential branches of instruction', including French. Boarders were accommodated at £60 per annum and day pupils at 12 guineas, while fees for music lessons were 2 guineas per quarter plus 1 guinea for the use of an instrument.[48]

Almost simultaneously Charles Platts announced that, as well as providing pianos for hire, he was offering piano lessons in conjunction with George Bennett, who taught the violin. And the *Register* also advised the opening of another school in Rundle Street for boys under nine, as either boarders or day pupils. A year or so later, there were six more schools in Adelaide – three for boys and three for girls – as well as an infants' school. Schools had also opened in the newly established villages of Hindmarsh, Thebarton and Walkerville.[49]

Developing and sustaining their religious environment was of prime importance to the colonists. Most gave high priority to the building of churches and chapels, thus ensuring the freedom of religious worship for each denomination. But church services in the early months were held in very flimsy structures, some purpose built and others borrowed for Sunday use.

Adelaide's first Anglican services, attended by the Thomas family, were held in the courthouse, which Mary described as a wooden building with only 'a few loose boards for a roof, which could afford but little protection in rough weather'. As Mary had witnessed, its seating was very insecure and liable to give way, laying the occupants 'flat on their backs'.[50] The Anglicans were the first to put up a permanent building, and both Mary and Robert made individual donations to its establishment fund. Trinity Church was a very modest stone structure with a tower, which housed a town clock provided by the SA commissioners. Its single face looked out over North Terrace and its bell struck the hours. Trinity was dedicated and opened in mid 1838, but to cope with a rapidly expanding congregation, it was considerably enlarged during 1839.[51] Then, within a matter of months, three further substantial church buildings had either been completed or were in progress. The Wesleyan Chapel in Gawler Place – for which Robert had contributed £1 – was finished at about the same time as Trinity's extensions. A few months later tenders were called for the

Congregational Chapel in Freeman Street (southern end of Gawler Place), and in October the foundation stone of the Anglicans' second church, St John's in Halifax Street, was laid at a service attended by Robert, Mary Jnr and Helen.[52]

The last weeks of December 1839 were particularly hectic for Mary, Frances and the younger girls. As well as preparing festive season fare, they were getting ready for Frances's marriage to John Skipper in Trinity Church a few days after Christmas.[53] The wedding celebrations were to be held in the almost finished cottage being built on acre 56, which was to become the Thomas's new home.

Chapter 7
A wedding celebration in a new home

In planning the wedding finery, Mary's only regret had been – as she later wrote to George – that bonnets she had ordered from England for the bride and bridesmaids had not arrived in time, and did not reach Adelaide until July. Mary Jnr's journal recorded that 'Frances's bonnet . . . was . . . trimmed with orange blossom and is made of white silk. Helen's and mine are pink silk and they are all stylish'.[1] Mary didn't comment to George about how the problem of the missing bonnets was solved, but bonnets were listed in the large variety of goods advertised by a number of Adelaide's general stores – although they were perhaps not as fashionable as Mary would have wished.

She gave no indication that any difficulty had arisen about gowns for the occasion. By 1839 specialty clothing stores were beginning to advertise their wares. In the *Gazette and Register* of 9 March, Flaxman and Rowlands of Rundle Street, as well as Murray, Grieg and Co. and Pearce, tailor and draper – both of Hindley Street – were all offering a variety of dresses and materials: printed cottons, silks, crepes, muslins and linens. Straw bonnets, shawls, parasols, silk gloves, 'fashionable jewellery', and ladies' shoes were also available. And according to the *Gazette and Register* of 17 February 1838, there was at least one 'Dress and Cloak Maker' in Adelaide, a Miss Rogers. She was to be found, presumably under canvas, on the bank of the river opposite the commissioners' store.

Men, too, were well catered for. As early as 1838 I.J. Barclay, tailor of Alpha Cottage, Rundle Street, announced his opening in the *Gazette and Register* on 15 September, advertising stock for fashionably inclined gentlemen including, 'Superfine west of England cloths' in blacks, blues, olive greens and browns, cassimeres (a twilled woollen cloth) in blacks, drabs and fancy colours, and a variety of waistcoats in silks – figured, plain and check – were available. There was no shortage of formal attire suitable for weddings and there is little doubt that the Thomas family, both men and women, including John Skipper, would have been elegantly turned out for the occasion.

Just before 8 am on 28 December, in the cool of a summer morning, the Thomas family procession – with Mary Jnr and Helen as Frances's bridesmaids – left acre 56 Hindley Street. It took them only a few minutes to walk to Trinity Church by way of Morphett Street and North Terrace. The church, despite its squat stature, was one of the largest buildings in Adelaide and dominated the tiny cottages nearby. The wedding procession was escorted by the Thomas's large hound, Rio, who refused to be sent home. During the ceremony, she lay quietly at the feet of the Reverend Charles Howard as he married Frances Amelia Thomas to John Michael Skipper.[2]

Mary and Robert were pleased to welcome John into their family. His romance with Frances on the *Africaine* during the voyage out had continued in the colony. Within a few months he was to be admitted to the Supreme Court to practise in association with Charles Mann. John Skipper came from a well-connected Norfolk legal family.[3] He was proficient in the classics and modern languages and an accomplished painter of watercolours. His maternal uncle, James Stark, with whom John had studied, was a well-known English landscape artist.[4]

Among the wedding guests were Mrs Wright, the wife of the Thomas family's physician, Edward Wright, and their son, Robert. Charles Wright, another son, was John Skipper's best man. Also included were George and Margaret Stevenson with Margaret's mother, Mrs Gorton; William Williams, R. Thomas and Co.'s chief clerk, and his daughter, Margaret, the Thomas girls' teacher; as well as a number of other young friends.[5] The Thomas's new seven-roomed cottage provided a gracious venue for the wedding celebrations, although there had been a rush to complete it, and the parlour was still being papered the night before.[6] Mary's management of the cooking for the celebration held during the evening must have been a triumph of ingenuity if work on the cottage was not sufficiently advanced for her to have had access to the kitchen in her new home, leaving her to make do with her old outdoor fire at the long building. Alternatively the use of some bakers' ovens and ovens in smallgoods shops could be had for a fee and this may have helped Mary out.

Rather than a cottage, Robert's intention had been to build a substantial two-storey stone house on the Hindley Street frontage of acre 56 as the Thomas's permanent home. A start was made on it but, although there was a stone quarry on the banks of the Torrens, a shortage of other materials and skilled workmen delayed its progress. As Mary explained to George in March 1840, she was anxious to be settled.

> [Robert] had in the meanwhile commenced building two small cottages nearly at the top of the acre, with the view of letting them. I persuaded him to unite them in one and to occupy it ourselves, and when the other house was finished to let that. He expects to get at least £300 a year for it either as a hotel or for some other public use.[7]

Just four days after Frances's wedding, Mary and Robert, with Mary Jnr and Helen, moved the few yards from the home they had shared with the printing presses since October 1837 to their new home, which they named Rhantregwnwyn after Robert's birthplace in Wales.[8] Mary and Robert were to occupy Rhantregwnwyn for the rest of their lives. Although Mary makes no mention of the two boys in the move, it seems that William kept his room in the warehouse and Robert George remained living in his apartment at the offices of Colonel Light's surveying firm in which he was now a junior partner. Frances and John's new home was in Waymouth Street, only a short walk from acre 56.

Overall, Rhantregwnwyn measured 38 feet by 34 feet (11.6 metres by 10.4 metres). On the east-west dimension it was in the centre of acre 56 and set back from Hindley Street by only about 30 feet (9.2 metres). Thus, as Mary indicated in her letter to George several months after the move, the cottage was almost at the top of the acre. It faced east toward the hills and Helen described it in later life as being 'on the exact spot where Register Street now is'.[9] In Mary's day, as shown on Kingston's 1842 map of Adelaide buildings, a private roadway (not Register Street) ran along the eastern boundary with acre 55, from Hindley Street to the back of the acre – to the John o' Groats Inn and the *Register* printing offices. Mary's garden was slightly to the rear, but mainly on the north-western side of the cottage, and took up well over a quarter of the acre. It was fenced off from the private road, the *Register* offices and the inn.

> *[Mary's letter to George depicted Rhantregwnwyn as having] two sitting rooms, three bed rooms and a kitchen on the ground floor with two attics above, and is altogether very neatly fitted up, quite in the English style. Indeed it is the envy of almost everyone who has seen it.*[10]

According to Kingston's map, the cottage was timber framed, with boarded outer walls and built on a brick foundation. It is clearly apparent in the middle ground of an 1840 drawing, *Clarendon House* (the two-storey stone building), by John Skipper.[11] Its origin as two cottages 'united' is obvious in its symmetrical façade of a verandah with four bays, and four windows between front doors at either end.

Altogether the cottage suggests a very pleasant, modest formality. The two front doors and large windows indicate that, in their original state, each of the cottages had a door opening to the verandah from a double-fronted living room which included a fireplace. Two additional rooms to the rear also opened from the living room. This was a common design in Adelaide during this period.[12] It is apparent from Rhantregwnwyn's footprint in Kingston's map that there were additions at the back; these included a masonry fireplace and chimney – the kitchen to which Mary referred. She gave no detail of how the ground floor rooms were disposed, but the cottage's timber structure provided for a considerable degree of flexibility. In the basic (single cottage) design, the dimensions of the front room or living room would have been in the vicinity of 17 feet by 12 feet (5.2 metres by 3.7 metres). Mary told George that she had 'two sitting rooms', but it is not clear whether both were front rooms. It was common practice in colonial Adelaide to have both a front and a back sitting room or parlour. The front parlour was used like today's sitting room, while the back, usually adjacent to the kitchen, was similar to today's family room and frequently provided additional sleeping space.

Mary made no mention of the contents of her rooms in her brief description for George, but from the details of the furniture she bequeathed in the March 1870 codicil to her will, it is evident that she retained two parlours over the years. Mary referred to furniture in the parlour adjoining the spare bedroom (arguably the back parlour) as well as to furniture in the parlour next to her own bedroom (front parlour).[13] The codicil also gave some indication of Rhantregwnwyns's contents, itemising silver candlesticks, silver table settings, china and glassware. The only two identifiable pieces of furniture, known to have been brought out on the *Africaine* and used in Rhantregwynwyn, are a small mahogany occasional table and an early 18th-century clock. The clock, which Mary left to William, is said to have had a 'place of honour at Rhantregwnwyn Cottage', and is an indication of the quality of Mary's furnishings.[14] It stood three feet high and was 'of elegant design, the material the very best Spanish mahogany, sound, and of beautiful grain, mellowed by age and taking a fine polish'. It was decorated with brass fretwork and had been made by watchmakers to the King of Spain.[15]

Despite her pleasure in her new home, Mary confided to George, 'I must endeavour to be contented, or at all events, not to repine . . . But there is nothing will induce me to give up hope of returning to England and ending my days where they began'. And even though she was very relieved to be settled at long last, she declared:

> *For my part I would exchange it [Rhantregwnwyn cottage] for a cow pen in England, even if I could have those comforts which are incompatible with this country or at least be free from the annoyances to which this climate subjects us . . . if I were now in England with the experiences I have had and recollecting the dangers and difficulties I have undergone nothing would induce me to return to South Australia. Yet on the other hand if I were a young man of enterprising disposition nothing is more likely than I would try my fortune.*[16]

When Mary sat down to begin her long letter to George, she was frustrated over inefficiencies at the Port, which had caused a month's delay before she could gain access to her parcel from him. On 3 March, Robert was finally able to collect Mary's Hampshire produce, but in spite of her impatience, he got home so late that the parcel remained unopened until the next morning. Continuing with her letter, Mary told George that Robert had grumbled about her order, believing the bacon would be spoiled by the time it reached Adelaide, but when she fried some for his breakfast, he had praised 'the Hampshire bacon as much as he would a tub of Welsh butter'. Although the pot of honey had broken and leaked, Mary managed to save a pound, which she clarified. She refused an offer of 7 shillings for it – English honey was considered 'quite a treasure'. As for the cracknels, 'everyone was astonished at their being so fresh after being packed up [for] . . . upwards of eight months'. She had 'given the greater part away to those who had young children' for a treat.[17]

Mary celebrated the arrival of her delicacies by arranging for a swing to be put up in the stables for Mary Jnr and Helen. She enjoyed herself with the girls in, as Mary Jnr's journal put it, 'that childish amusement called swinging'. And she baked one of the hams for a family dinner party, which included Frances and John as well as Robert George and William.[18] During the same week Mary had three other guests. Firstly a Mr King, an out of town visitor, came to breakfast and was probably served rashers of Mary's prized bacon – Mr King was the brother-in-law of Mary's *Africaine* fellow passenger, John Hallett. Then Margaret Stevenson and her mother, Mrs Gorton, also called and stayed to afternoon tea, when they were no doubt offered some of the Isle of Wight cracknels.[19]

In returning to her letter to George, Mary expressed concern that he had not received payment for the things he had sent. She was still having difficulty in receiving her annuity and, although the deed she and Robert signed had arrived in England some nine months earlier, the trustees had once more refused to pay her London agent, Mr Baugh. Mary's London lawyer had responded by enforcing payment, but it could only be paid up to the date of her most recent letter to Mr Baugh:

> *This is strange yet I was not greatly surprised at it, for I have always suspected there would be difficulties in obtaining that money when I came abroad, especially when I consider what jealous beings I have to deal with...*[20]

Her unpaid annuity had accrued to £157 and 10 shillings, a considerable sum. But, as she told George, with payment of what she owed him and also Mr Baugh, 'I do not expect there will be much left as about £50 will go to pay for [the cost of returning] Mr Osborne's effects' (Robert's apprentice who perished on Kangaroo Island).[21] There were other items 'ordered for myself and the girls', expected before Frances's marriage, and Mary believed that accounts for the piano for the girls and surveying instruments for Robert George would 'amount to £70 or £80'. Mary was very put out, not only because George and Mr Baugh had both been financially inconvenienced, but also by the legal fees she was incurring.

What there will be to pay to lawyers I know not, but I cannot help thinking that Mr Clements' conduct in advising the trustees not to pay Mr Baugh, as he informs me, after I had signed the deed . . . was most scandalous and I wish I had an opportunity to tell him so, which if I had I should not hesitate to do so in plain terms . . .[22]

She intended to write immediately to Mr Baugh and, as she explained to George, by the time Mr Baugh had her letter, a further payment of her annuity should be due. On this basis, in the expectation that George would be able to reimburse himself, Mary asked him to double the order for cracknels and to repeat the rest of her previous order, including the honey.

Only a day or two after Frances's wedding, Mary Jnr had developed a throat infection, which, despite Dr Wright's best efforts, nothing seemed to cure. By March it had become persistently ulcerated and Dr Wright had needed to separate 'one part of her throat from growing to another'. He used the handle of a tablespoon for this procedure, but no anaesthetic. Mary Jnr's discomfort must have been extreme and Mary not only had to witness the procedure, but to assist Dr Wright in performing it. By the end of March Mary Jnr appeared well enough to attend Margaret Williams's first-term break-up party with 11 of her classmates. But it was a very short-lived recovery and a few days later Dr Wright called in a surgeon, Dr John Woodforde. Of course, there were no antibiotics, and surgery without an anaesthetic was a horrendous option, so very little could be done.[23] It took until May for her throat to heal.[24]

Despite her preoccupation with Mary Jnr's health, Mary followed up her very detailed letter to George, which had taken most of March to complete, with a short one on 6 April, explaining that she was only now sending him the parcel in which she had enclosed her March letter and the poems that she had mentioned in several earlier letters. She had been waiting weeks for a vessel to sail directly to England, rather than via the other colonies, as it was the most reliable means of getting her manuscripts to him. Months earlier, anticipating that she would be able to forward her poems more quickly, she had remarked to George

> [that if he thought it] proper to publish any other pieces that I may send now or at any other time, either in newspapers or magazines, you are at full liberty to do so, and if they may chance to turn a pecuniary advantage . . . apply it to your own benefit, but do not affix my name, only my initials.[25]

Ten of the poems Mary sent were from her manuscript book of poems and were composed before her emigration. Although the 11th, 'Finding an English Poppy in my Garden', had been written in South Australia, no copy appears to have survived. The whereabouts of any other poetry she may have written in South Australia is unknown.

Mary also enclosed three drawings in the parcel. One by John Skipper showed Rhantregwnwyn, with the stone house in the foreground, and Robert, Mary Jnr and Helen, with Mary at the front door of the cottage as she farewelled the Skippers. The other drawings were of Trinity Church by Frances, and the Wesleyan Chapel by Robert George.[26] Mary apologised for the brevity of her letter – not for want of news, but because she did not have time to write more – telling George, 'even now I have the materials for another long letter, for I am never tired of writing when I once begin'.[27]

Chapter 8
Prosperity

Mary had concluded her April 1840 letter to George on a very optimistic note, telling him of the success of R. Thomas and Co.; wages paid in the previous week totalled £50 and they had undertaken printing business 'amounting to £194 besides stationery [sales]'. 'This is no trifle for one week in a new colony established but little more than three years.' With pride and a sense of her place in South Australian history, she explained that 'we were the first who ever sold anything in the colony ... the printing and our store were for several months the only businesses carried on in Adelaide'.[1]

A few weeks earlier, their problem of perennial staff shortages had been solved when Robert acquired another newspaper, the *Adelaide Chronicle*. For £800 they were able to buy the 'whole concern – press, types and all ... and [had] engaged most of the hands lately employed on it'.[2] The former proprietor, William Caddy Cox, joined R. Thomas and Co. as manager of the printing works and James Bennett became subeditor and editor of the *Almanack*.[3] Mary was elated by their progress and their achievement;

> our establishment now has a formidable appearance – 10 compositors 3 pressmen, 2 binders and 1 boy, 1 errand boy, 1 collector, 1 clerk, Mr Stevenson (Proprietor and Editor), and Mr Thomas (Proprietor and Manager), besides an old man who is constantly

> *employed in sticking bills and delivering newspapers, making, in the whole 22 persons. One of the compositors is also Sub-editor, and my son William is Overseer.*[4]

The circulation of the *Register* had reached 900 and was expected to pass 1000 in a matter of months. This demonstrable success gave Mary a new view of the colony and its potential, but even so she was still homesick for England's mild summer weather.

> *So you may suppose there is something to this 'Humbug Colony', . . . I trust it will not turn out such a humbug after all and if it had but a more agreeable climate I might perhaps be tempted to make up my mind to stop here . . . But as it is, nothing will induce me to give up the hope of returning to England.*[5]

R. Thomas and Co. was expanding and flourishing. The *Adelaide Chronicle* was to be issued on Tuesdays and the *Register*, running to six pages with an average of three pages of editorial copy and three of advertisements, would continue on Saturdays; while the *Gazette*, the government's official paper, was to keep to Thursdays.

Another new venture for the firm was a dictionary, *The Native Language*, compiled by the German missionaries G.C. Teichelmann and C.W. Schürmann, which included the grammar, phraseology and vocabulary of the tribes to the north and south of Adelaide. The *Register* of 30 May called for 200 subscriptions – 80 copies had already been ordered by the governor, Judge Cooper, the colonial secretary and the manager of the South Australian Company. Publication would proceed as soon as it was fully subscribed. It was considered to have potential value for settlers in frequent and close contact with Aborigines by aiding communication and understanding and so assist in reducing tensions.[6]

In early August, Robert and Mary, with Frances and John Skipper, dined at the Stevensons' and, as Mary Jnr reported, she and Helen joined the others for tea when she 'played the piano from memory'.[7] The dinner was held during the afternoon – the usual practice of the time – and may have celebrated the arrival of the imported Columbian press and the anticipated change in status of the *Register* to a broadsheet with the edition of 29 August 1840. As Mary told George in her letter written a few days after the party, counting the new press, they now had 'five presses at work, including a small one for cards and such-like which came out with the Columbian'.[8]

But the main topic of conversation during the dinner party must have been the tragic news of the massacre of survivors from a vessel wrecked on the Coorong coast. In its first August issue, the *Register*, under the headline 'Suspected Shipwreck, and Murder by the Natives', published a report from the Encounter Bay police station. It advised that, about a week earlier, local Aborigines had seen members of a neighbouring tribe, the Milmenrura (Big Murray tribe), wearing bloodstained European clothing and were told that 10 white men, five white women and some children had been killed at a site about two days sail down the Coorong. Their ship was thought to have been wrecked near Rivoli Bay. The *Register* also advised that the marine surveyor, Captain W. Pullen, had already been sent to investigate. Based on information from two Adelaide merchants, the paper established that a brig, the *Maria* from Port Adelaide, was overdue at Hobart Town and that the number of passengers on her, as far as it was possible to ascertain, agreed with the Encounter Bay report of the massacre victims.[9] Mary, in writing to George, outlined these awful events:

> *Adelaide has for some time past been greatly agitated owing to some atrocious murders which have been committed on the crew and passengers of the brig Maria (which was wrecked in a violent hurricane a few weeks since) by a party of natives called the 'Big-Murray Tribe' . . . Those called the Murray tribe are not generally on very friendly terms with other blacks . . . and are said to be cannibals, an imputation which all the other natives disdain.*[10]

The identification by relatives of rings taken from the bodies of two of the murdered women confirmed that they were survivors from the *Maria* and it was established that, as well as the crew, 16 passengers had been on board, including women and children. The women's rings had been brought back to Adelaide by Captain Pullen who had searched the Coorong coast and hinterland exhaustively over 16 days. He found eight bodies in shallow graves and Aborigines in the vicinity with bloodstained clothing, but no sign of other survivors or of the wrecked vessel. The commissioner of police, Major Thomas O'Halloran, was dispatched with a mounted party to find and punish those guilty, and to search for survivors.

On 4 September, news reached Adelaide that the wreck of the *Maria* had been found near Cape Jaffa, many days' walk from the massacre site discovered earlier. Major O'Halloran had executed an Aboriginal man, pointed out by others of his tribe as one of those involved in the killing, and another who was known to have killed a sailor from an earlier shipwreck. Both were hanged in front of members of their tribe and two other Aboriginal men, also implicated, were shot and wounded as they escaped capture.

> *[The official announcement concluded that] there is great reason to believe that the prompt execution of the guilty parties, on the spot where their crime was perpetrated . . . will have a very beneficial effect in deterring the natives of that district, for the future, from making wanton unprovoked attacks on the persons or property of the Europeans who are about to settle in that neighbourhood.*[11]

Stevenson's comments, in publishing the announcement, were restrained. 'Before our next the official documents connected with this sad transaction will be published . . . we feel bound to pause until the fullest possible information be obtained.'

The *Register* published O'Halloran's detailed report on 12 September and, after reading it,

> *[Stevenson had no difficulty in] entertaining the moral conviction of the guilty participation of the Big Murray Tribe generally, or of the particular guilt of the individuals executed, and it is in the*

> hope that such moral conviction will be confirmed by the evidence itself which satisfied Major O'Halloran of the actual criminality of these individuals; we urge its publication without delay.[12]

Mary agreed with him, telling George, 'For my part I said from the first he [Governor Gawler] had done wrong in executing such summary vengeance on them, and yet under such aggravated circumstances I can hardly blame him'.[13] But Stevenson had difficulty in reconciling the executions with his belief that the Aborigines were given the full protection of the law and had been declared British subjects by Governor Hindmarsh in the proclamation of the colony. Stevenson claimed, and was widely believed, to have composed the proclamation document as private secretary to Hindmarsh. He reminded readers that this declaration was officially approved by the British Government in Lord Glenelg's dispatch of August 1837.

> [T]he government is at least bound by its own act. In its eyes the Aboriginal inhabitants of South Australia can only be regarded as British subjects... Our present object is... to record... a distinct and earnest protest against the right of the Colonial Government of South Australia to authorize the summary putting to death of any human being save under circumstances recognized and specially defined by the law of England, and the constitution of the British Empire.[14]

Stevenson returned to the topic in the next *Register*. Notes of the evidence that led to the executions were presented to the Executive Council. The attorney-general considered 'though conclusive in a moral point of view, [the evidence] was not of a nature which was capable of trial by jury, or which could have led to a conviction'.[15] Stevenson refuted the argument that the governor had proceeded on the principle of martial law, which gave him extended powers to order an execution. Stevenson noted that martial law had not been declared because the colony was not in a state of general disturbance, and therefore the extended power claimed and exercised by the governor had no legal basis. He maintained that, contrary to the belief of some, his protest was not 'to claim impunity for atrocities, but to protect the key-stone of British liberty, and to save those who have not been proved legally guilty of crime from being put to death'.[16]

Public opinion was divided and heated. In the last issue for September, the *Register* published three columns of letters, one supporting its stance and two objecting to it. Mary, commenting to George, considered that the summary executions

> *had caused some severe censures to be passed on our Governor for having exceeded his power . . . [in executing] British subjects . . . without regular trial and conviction according to the law. Others contend that the necessity of making an immediate example, especially in the case of such brutal savages, justified him in what he has done. No doubt the matter will be taken up in England.*[17]

Many who opposed the *Register* maintained only a specific mention in legislation could give the Aborigines British citizenship, and that, as both South Australian acts were silent on the matter, Gawler's summary executions were lawful.

On 17 September, Gawler advised R. Thomas and Co. that he was acting upon a previous threat to remove the government printing, apart from the publication of the *Gazette* and the printing of the acts of council, from the firm on 1 January 1841. Handbills, special notices, forms of bills, etc. and bookbinding were to be placed with other presses.[18] Since June 1839, when the governor had insisted upon separating the government *Gazette* from the *Register*, there had been, whenever the *Register* opposed aspects of Gawler's administration, veiled threats that he intended to 'divide the government printing as far as practicable among the several presses in Adelaide'.[19] Robert made strong representations to Gawler regarding R. Thomas and Co.'s agreement with the South Australian commissioners and the Colonial Office that, because of the capital investment made and the risk taken in establishing a printing business from the very first months of the colony, the firm was to have the government printing for the life of the partnership of Robert Thomas and George Stevenson.

While initially conceding the fairness of this arrangement, Gawler later maintained that the partners' lack of documentation negated its validity. He asserted that he could not leave the printing with a firm who opposed him so vehemently – not only regarding his actions following the *Maria* massacre, but also regarding his recent bill for the Prohibition of Internal Distillation 1840. Gawler wanted support from the press and believed he could buy it from the rival *Southern Australian*. He declared himself 'free to give encouragement to other journals'.[20] It was Stevenson's strong belief in the significant economic benefits for the colony in the establishment of grape and wine industry, and as an adjunct a brandy industry, that set him at odds with the governor's Prohibition of Internal Distillation legislation.

Despite Gawler's reduction of R. Thomas and Co.'s printing contract, Stevenson, in the first *Register* for October, again declared that the Aborigines were British subjects, maintaining that 'a Governor has no power under any circumstance, to supersede the established civil tribunals and to order an execution of any human beings within a British Territory'.[21] And a further letter in the same *Register* highlighted the continuing disquiet and controversy in the general community; it reminded readers that earlier survivors of a shipwreck had, for over a month, been well cared for by the Big Murray Tribe (Milmenrura), who had then guided them, unharmed, to the edge of their tribal lands. 'A Colonist of 1836' attributed the 'conversion of the once friendly natives' to ruthless killers to the brutality they had experienced at the hands of the 'degraded [white] ruffians employed by droving stock'.[22]

As something of a diversion from these distressing events, on 14 October 1840, the opening of the new Port Adelaide was celebrated by some 5000 colonists – the largest gathering ever assembled – and was reported in the *Register*. Port Misery, as the old Port was known, was to be a thing of the past. The Port River, which provided the only safe natural harbour in the vicinity of Adelaide, was for most of its 10-mile (16 kilometre) length, surrounded by mangrove swamps, and Adelaide's original port had been sited to avoid them. But the river there was so shallow that only small vessels could reach it, and passengers and goods had to be offloaded into 'jolly' boats and then wade, or in the case of goods, be floated to a crude landing.

Port Misery posed significant problems, not only for passengers but also for merchants in the safe landing of their goods. Although Governor Gawler's preferred option was a port at the North Arm (near Torrens Island), the deepest part of the river, he was eventually persuaded to accept a port 4 miles (6.4 kilometres) further along it. The manager of the South Australian Company, David McLaren, offered to build a road through the swamp to a point halfway along the river. McLaren's choice was driven by the commercial interests of his company, which had acquired a 134-acre (54-hectare) country section in the vicinity at Albert Town (today's Alberton), as well as six other sections along the main channel. Gawler negotiated an interest rate of 12 per cent per annum on the £14,000 put up by the company to build the road.[23]

Construction of the permanent causeway through the swamp from McLaren's preferred port to Albert Town had begun in May 1839, and at its termination he built a wharf, a two-storey warehouse, stores and a six-ton crane for an additional £13,000. The government's wharf was established nearby, but it was markedly inferior to the South Australian Company's because of inadequate supervision during its construction. McLaren, on completion of his development, was able to sell nine of the Albert Town acres, for which he had paid about £1 per acre, for a total of £14,000. He was in the mood to give the inhabitants of Adelaide and nearby centres a grand party.[24]

On the morning of the opening day, the weather was very hot and dusty. Frances's first baby was almost due, and Mary remained at home with her while Helen and Mary Jnr went with Robert to the South Australian Bank, the assembly point for the procession to the Port.

> *[As Mary Jnr described in her journal, she and Helen] were put into a yellow wagon filled with people and proceeded with a long line of carriages and horsemen in the direction of the Port, until our traces broke and we broke from the cavalcade. After some time spent in repairs we arrived safely at our destination ... The ceremony of opening the Port was performed by Mrs Gawler ... After that was over a very large number of ladies and gentlemen adjourned to the Company's rooms to partake of a handsome cold collation. The place was built as a warehouse and in a style which I think highly creditable for these early times. Our dining room was prettily decorated with flowers.*[25]

A day or two later, a feature article in the *Register* of 17 October, 'Opening the new Port', added to Mary Jnr's description:

> *[The governor was escorted from Adelaide] by the officers and brigade of the Adelaide Corps, assisted by a strong party of Mounted Police... The river was ... studded with boats, sailing and pulling, and a very large concourse of people had already assembled on the wharf and along the line of the road.*[26]

Speeches by McLaren and the governor, as the *Register* noted, were mutually congratulatory and foretold great future prosperity for Adelaide, as 'a box of tea and a small box of spices were ... brought up from the hold of the *Guiana* and landed on the wharf amidst a thundering round of applause'. It was less than four years since the first colonists had stood in the sand hills at Holdfast Bay for the proclamation of the new colony and they were now celebrating their remarkable progress and their prosperity.

While most of the spectators were entertained by a regatta on the river, the governor and 600 invited guests 'retired to the Company's warehouse and partook of refreshments'. The catering was undertaken by Fordham of Fordham's Hotel, who, amidst further speeches and toasts, provided 'his usual excellence and abundance'. Mary Jnr's journal recorded that:

> *The scene in the evening after the feasting was all over ... was indescribable. Such a confusion of men, women, bullock carts, noise and novelty ... Helen and I were comfortably stowed along with Mr Skipper in a stage coach, when we returned to Adelaide; but most of the others must have been exposed to a storm of dust and rain with which we were visited.*[27]

Notwithstanding the celebrations surrounding the new Port, life's ongoing pressures still had to be dealt with. The *Register* kept alive the issues of principle involved in the summary execution of the two Aborigines by reporting the recent court martial of a British officer in India. He was found guilty of having 'caused five persons who had been taken prisoner ... to be summarily put to death', and was struck off the army lists despite representations as to his past good service and character. Stevenson categorically denied that, in reporting these events, he was making a 'cowardly charge of murder against His Excellency and Captain O'Halloran'.[28]

On 24 October, Stevenson acknowledged that, in support of the governor's actions against the Milmenrura, 'sentiments at variance with our own have been expressed by very many colonists'; and Gawler's response thanking the colonists for their support was reported in the same issue. In it the governor maintained that his policy of an 'energetic system' was the 'best calculated to promote the ends of justice and humanity towards the Aborigines, and of due peace and protection towards settlers in contact with them'. This, Gawler believed, could be achieved by leaving the 'administration of justice towards both parties in the hands of the government', rather than within the independent legal system and the courts. Stevenson was highly critical of the governor's approach considering that it cut across the basic tenet of British justice – the right of access to a judicial system that was independent of government.[29]

On 27 October, only a few days after the publication of Stevenson's most recent criticism of his pronouncements, the governor divided the printing even less in favour of R. Thomas and Co. The *Gazette* was to remain, but the acts were to be printed by the *Southern Australian*, and the miscellaneous printing split between them. An attempt was made to reason with the governor that the government printer, himself, exercised no control over the editorial or political columns of the *Register*.

> *[As a separate and independent paper] the Register has given the Colonial Government, except on two recent occasions, the best support in its power but it has done this in no degree because it was bound to do so, or because the existence of our engagement as Government Printers depended on it, but because the measures and general proceedings of the Government were such as could in the estimation of the Editor be conscientiously advocated.*[30]

The letter went on to argue that as the *Register*'s editor had written the proclamation document which, he believed, extended the full protection of the British law to the Aborigines, he could not in conscience support the governor's proceedings regarding their summary execution. Stevenson also maintained that before publishing his opposition to the Prohibition of Distillation bill he had made his views known privately to the governor. These appeals to the governor were to no avail; the new regime was to begin on 1 January. In her December letter to George, Mary's commentary on these events is scathing.

> *The first intimation was given in a kind of half-civil way as if His Excellency considered it unfair that one office should monopolize the whole, although the right of printing for the Government he knew to be as much our property as the types with which it was done. Notice was then given that another portion would be taken away . . . and finally it was notified that the whole would be removed to another office, though without any reason being alleged than the opposition of 'the Register' to the conduct of the Governor, as if it was bound to uphold him in every action, good or bad, and obliged to commend him in all he did, right or wrong.*[31]

In continuing her letter, Mary was firmly behind Stevenson and his editorial stance.

> *His Excellency assumed to himself power which even the Sovereign does not possess, that of taking the lives of British subjects without a formal conviction. For this he has been most justly called to account not only by 'the Register', but by almost all the papers of the neighbouring colonies ... Mr Stevenson has, however incurred the heavy displeasure of His Excellency, though he could not suppose that any independent journalist would approve of measures diametrically opposite to the laws and constitution of England ... According to his proceedings, these poor natives are at the mercy of any Governor, who, out of caprice or spite, may think fit to issue orders either to destroy their property or affect their existence, for not only were they made amenable to laws which they did not understand, but the huts and property of themselves and their tribe were burned down because the former were found to contain some articles which had belonged to persons of the Maria, though it is not known whether these articles had been given to them, or whether they had been stolen. For these ... and some other arbitrary acts of the Governor ... he has been very properly rebuked by The Register.*[32]

In a last stand, none the less valiant for its defiance, R. Thomas and Co. advised the governor that

> *His Excellency erroneously assumes that our political opinions were to be subject to those of the Colonial Government ... Neither as a firm nor individually have we ever acknowledged the alternative of being ... obliged to give venal support to His Excellency ... If His Excellency has not already discovered, he soon will discover, that no support of a hack newspaper writer – that no political advocacy which can be purchased – no subversion of the Press – is worth a straw.*[33]

The governor's response was the immediate removal of all printing from R. Thomas and Co., and the denial of verbal contracts to supply government stationery, for which orders had already been placed in London. Incensed, Mary broke the disastrous news to George in one of her last letters to him:

> [T]his act of injustice has caused a greater sensation here than the colony has ever experienced since its commencement. The Governor's unjust conduct towards us will now, I believe, oblige Mr Thomas to go to England for redress, for which purpose Mr Stevenson is now preparing a memorial to lay before Lord Russell [colonial secretary] ... an income of from fifteen hundred to eighteen hundred a year is not to be given up so easily.[34]

This blow to the wellbeing of R. Thomas and Co. severely dampened what had been Mary's growing confidence in the future of the colony and her family's place in it. During the early months of 1840, with the business success of R. Thomas and Co., the move to her new home and the amenity of having a well in her garden, Mary had been optimistic that much of the hardship and privation – which had tested both physical endurance and nerve – was behind them. In March 1840, with pride in what had been achieved, Mary had told George:

> Our population is increasing and is I believe now upwards of 12,000. Houses and warehouses are springing up in all directions, and trades of all kinds flourish. We have some shops as handsome as may be seen in any country town in England and generally as well supplied with goods.[35]

The colony's prosperity over the previous two years had resulted in the erection of more substantial buildings, and the streets were at last cleared of scrub and stumps; Adelaide was beginning to take on the character of a provincial town. Government House, the government offices on the north-eastern corner of Victoria Square, the Wesleyan Chapel in Gawler Place, the Congregational Chapel in Freeman Street (now part of Gawler Place)[36], and hotels such as the Adelaide in Franklin Street and the Exchange Hotel near the corner of Hindley and King William Streets[37], were all public buildings which gave the town an air of permanence and urbanity. This developing character was supported by a substantial number of sizeable private buildings, including the stone house of two main floors and 13 rooms that Mary and Robert had built on their acre in Hindley Street, and the guesthouse of Miss Jane Bathgate, the principal guesthouse in the colony, on the south-eastern corner of Pulteney and Rundle Streets.

Mary and Robert had continued to benefit from the boom in land prices, having sold a further quarter of an acre in Hindley Street for £900 in July.[38]

But given the events in which R. Thomas and Co. and the *Register* were embroiled in the latter half of the year and the difficulties and losses experienced as a result, Mary's mood was once again one of pessimism and distress in coping with the onerous nature of her life. In her last letter to George for the year, she once again expressed her desire to return to her 'native country, if only to die there'.[39]

Mary was also deeply troubled by Frances's health and her failure to recover from the birth of her first child, Jane Georgiana Kyffin Skipper. According to Mary Jnr's journal, Mary's first grandchild was born on 16 October at 7 am, after a seemingly uncomplicated delivery – Dr Wright and the nurse, Mrs Moss, were not sent for until 2 am.[40] Frances's difficulties were not the after-effects of having given birth but were due to tuberculosis, from which she had suffered since before her arrival in South Australia. In her letter in late December, Mary explained to George:

> *Frances was obliged to wean [the baby] at two months and has never been well since her confinement. She has been with me the last six weeks but is now better and went yesterday on a visit to a friend, who lives a considerable distance from the town, for a change of air and I hope will soon recover. The child is out at nurse.*[41]

Unfortunately the improvement in Frances's health did not last. As Mary Jnr recorded in her journal, just over a week later Frances was very ill again and returned to Mary's care. A few days earlier, Mary had brought baby Georgiana, also extremely ill, home from the nurse at North Adelaide. She hired a wet nurse to live-in and by the week's end, Georgiana was much improved.[42]

Frances's health and that of her baby daughter were not the only causes of Mary's anxiety. She was also troubled about the future of R. Thomas and Co. The loss of the government printing was a severe blow. During the last quarter of 1840, Robert, concerned by the inevitable decline in the firm's income, began to advertise the now completed stone house on acre 56 as a first-class venue for a hotel or banking chamber[43], and by the close of the year, plans were well under way for him to seek redress in London for the loss of the government contracts.

By the end of 1840, the first signs of the colony's future economic difficulties had begun to manifest themselves in London. Inevitably, the commissioners were unable to keep up with the huge demands on their resources being made by Governor Gawler's large expenditures on the survey and on public works. News items, derived from English papers and published in the *Register* toward the end of November, advised that the commissioners had made their first attempt to borrow £120,000 in July 1840: 'with the £80,000 already borrowed, [this] completes the sum of £200,000 which they are allowed to raise under the South Australian Act.' In reporting these developments, Stevenson maintained that there was a great deal of dissatisfaction in London regarding Gawler's actions, and that the need for a loan had been forced upon the commissioners to provide for Gawler's 'unexpected and unauthorized drafts which ... were pouring in ... to an alarming extent'. It was anticipated that new orders would be sent to prevent the governor from exceeding his instructions under any circumstances, and that 'any bills drawn for unauthorized purposes would not be paid'.[44] As reported in the *Register* of 21 November 1840, the commissioners' initial loan-raising attempt failed due to the negative rumours circulating in London that questioned the colony's future. Subsequently, all sales of land and all emigration under the land fund were suspended. But the colonists, as yet blissfully unaware of the significance of these events and what was to befall them, continued to enjoy Adelaide's apparent prosperity.

For Mary, however, 1840 did not end well, nor did the New Year bode well for her. In addition to her other worries, it is apparent from her December letter to George that access to her annuity was still problematic. Much to her irritation, she was required to forward a declaration, as proof that she was still alive, each six months to enable it to be collected on her behalf.[45] Mary was also alarmed by the lack of letters from George – she had not heard from him for 'more than fourteen months'.[46]

Part 3

Chapter 9
An ongoing crisis

As Mary had foreshadowed in her letter to George, Robert was due to sail for London toward the end of January to seek reinstatement of the government contract. But Mary and Mary Jnr were able to put aside the stress associated with his impending departure, at least for a few hours, when they were given an unexpected tour of the newly built Queen's Theatre. It was the third to open in Adelaide – the first had had its origins in the Adelaide Tavern, at the western end of Franklin Street. Considered, c. 1838, one of Adelaide's principal hotels, it operated the small Theatre Royal from its first-floor dining room.[1] And at the end of the following year, Samson Cameron announced the opening of his Royal Victoria Theatre on North Terrace near Morphett Street.[2] As an historian of Adelaide's theatres noted, 'pioneer theatres were tiny, crude, makeshift affairs, where the scenery might be ruined by the rain coming in, or the seats collapse'.[3]

In January 1841, however, the pristine Queen's was preparing for its premier performance and, a few days before its opening, Mary and Mary Jnr called at the home of their family friends, Mary and Emanuel Solomon, who were major investors in the Queen's Theatre. Emanuel, originally from Sydney, was an Adelaide merchant and auctioneer. Mary and Mary Jnr were introduced to two members of a visiting Sydney theatrical company, John Lazar and his daughter, Rachel, and then Emanuel offered to show them over his new theatre. On approaching the main entrance off Gilles Arcade, they faced an imposing façade of three floors. An engraving made in 1842 and a later photograph of the theatre suggest 'a pleasing brickwork architecture – Georgian perhaps – with a white trim . . . The inscribed stone set in the apex of the façade carried the Solomons' initials and the date 1840'.[4]

It was an elaborate and very expensive venture for such a young colonial town – initially its cost was estimated at £3000, but the final outlay was probably almost £10,000. The dress circle and private boxes opened onto a saloon, with a promenade and a retiring room for ladies, and it was anticipated that patrons occupying these seats would maintain theatrical tradition by wearing evening dress. There was additional accommodation in the upper circle and room for a further 700 in the pit – altogether the Queen's could hold about 1000. Lighting was initially supplied by candles, with lamps introduced later, and ultimately Emanuel imported a chandelier from Sydney.

Other theatrical refinements included overhead equipment for 'magical appearances and disappearances', plus trapdoors in the stage which allowed 'ghosts or wizards to rise or sink', and backstage there were at least two dressing rooms.[5] Delighted with their chance preview, the two Marys walked the few hundred yards home to acre 56.

The Queen's held its premiere performance on 11 January and, apart from Mary, who remained at home with a seriously ill Frances, the rest of the Thomas family attended, including Robert whose departure for London was still a fortnight away. Adelaide welcomed the theatre – it was so popular that the Thomases were too late to reserve a box and had to be content with the dress circle, except for William who could only get a seat in the gallery. The company from Sydney performed *Othello*, with Mr Arabin as Iago and John Lazar playing Othello, to a house 'crowded with respectable people'. Mary Jnr considered John Lazar's acting very clever and she approved an entertainment by his 15-year-old daughter – 'she dances very well'. The programme ended with the farce, *Our Mary Anne*, but because of a delay between the acts, this final offering did not conclude until 1 am.[6]

Seemingly, not even Shakespeare was immune from what was a tradition in colonial theatre for an evening's performance to include several plays (with the last a farce) frequently interspersed with other items such as dances and songs. The Queen's *Othello* may have been an abridged version, possibly with songs and other changes included. Similar variations were made 'by minor theatres in England to escape infringing the rights of Covent Garden and Drury Lane', and it is probable that these precautions were taken by the Queen's.[7]

Robert left the colony on 24 January 1841 on board the *Lalla Rhook*, armed with a memorial addressed to the colonial secretary, setting out the claims of the firm for redress. A day earlier, Stevenson's editorial had advised that Robert was seeking compensation for the 'tyrannical conduct of Governor Gawler in depriving Messrs R. Thomas and Co. of the colonial printing . . . and of his illegally pirating the *SA Gazette*', which was the property of the firm. 'That Mr Thomas will be successful in the object of his visit no doubt is entertained.'[8]

None of the letters between Mary and Robert during his absence have survived and what management arrangements were made for the firm are not clear, but given Mary's day-to-day involvement with the paper, her participation in decision-making is probable. Between Mary's letters, and reports of the colony in the English press, Robert must have been well informed of the difficulties at home. With these anxieties, he would have had little pleasure in his return to England.

The printing office, while completing the last of the government printing and adjusting to the loss of Robert's input, was extremely busy. The 1841 *Almanack* had gone on sale in January priced at 5 shillings, and maintained its earlier format as a veritable South Australian yearbook, but with increased information on the progress of the colony, colonial laws, statistics, climate and geography. The usual diaries, calendars and directories of previous years were continued. Also during January, R. Thomas and Co. were preparing for the publication of *A Guide to the Preservation of Health in South Australia* by Dr A.V. Fitzpatrick, ex-physician to the Polish and Belgian Armies, and the *Register* of 23 January called for subscribers. Mary may have assisted in its production, given Stevenson's preoccupation with the *Register* and James Bennett's responsibility for both the *Almanack* and the *Chronicle*.

In the last *Register* for the month, the firm gave advance notice of the establishment of a reading room on the ground floor of the Thomas's stone building and subscriptions were invited at two guineas per annum, payable in advance. Papers from all the Australian colonies were to be available, as well as those from India, New Zealand and the British Isles, plus the leading French journals, and 'the last and most authentic shipping news [would be kept] . . . on the table'. It was to open daily (except Sundays) between 9 am and 8 pm from 22 March.[9] The front room of the stone building, which faced Hindley Street, had already been fitted out with cedar shelves as a 'bookseller's and stationer's shop'.[10] During January, R. Thomas and Co. advertised stationery with their latest *Almanack*, and in March published an extensive list of books for sale in their new bookstore.[11]

It is clear that the firm was developing new initiatives in an attempt to cover the loss of the government contracts. Although stationery had always been a component of the business, it was now being given greater emphasis as part of the stock of the new shop, and was being advertised in more detail and more frequently. On sale were account and memorandum books, foolscap, wrapping and cartridge papers, quills, pens, ink and ink powders, sealing wax and so on. The cedar bookshelves were well filled with some 200 volumes on religious themes (a recognition of the significance of religion in the colony). Other diverse titles included: *Every Man his own Gardener*; *Book of Table Talk*; *Johnson's Dictionary*; *Buchan's Domestic Medicine*; *Diamond Edition of Shakespeare*; *Beauty's Mirror*; *Henderson's Scottish Proverbs*; *Comic*

Annuals; and *A Pictorial History of England*. The last no doubt helped to assuage the homesickness of many, including Mary[12], who would have recognised the potential appeal of this volume. But despite these efforts, as she told George in her March letter, 'business of every kind has been dull for some time past' and 'there is very little money showing'.[13]

Only a few weeks after Robert's departure, sensational news reached Adelaide regarding South Australia's debts. As reported in the *Register* of 13 February, the London creditors of a number of Adelaide merchants had dishonoured bills forwarded by the merchants to cover their debts. The bills had been drawn on the commissioners by Governor Gawler as payment for goods and services provided by the merchants to the Colonial Government. These unfortunate merchants had then remitted the bills to London, in good faith, in the belief that, when their London creditors presented them to the commissioners for payment, the commissioners would meet them. The bills related to government outgoings for the first quarter of 1840 and included those that had been drawn to meet expenditures not authorised by the commissioners. Stevenson's editorial maintained that all of the bills drawn by the governor over the preceding 12 months would meet the same fate, involving an estimated £165,000.

Although there had been no communication from the commissioners to explain their refusal to honour the expenditures, the troubling news had been reported by several London journals in September 1839. It was from these – just arrived in the colony at the beginning of February – that Stevenson gleaned his information. As Stevenson noted, the bills drawn by the government were used as legal tender in the colony; they were 'freely purchased by merchants and private individuals and remitted home to meet their various engagements, as cash'.[14] He argued that the British Treasury must eventually provide the loan to meet these commitments because the colonists were in no way at fault in the difficulties they now faced. They had had no say in government expenditure and, although the colonists knew it exceeded official authorisation, various similar drafts had been accepted before. Besides, the colonists had no means of knowing the extent of government overspending without the regular publication of its accounts.

On the 20th, the *Register* published Governor Gawler's explanation to the Executive Council regarding the commissioners' refusal of two particularly large bills – totalling £10,582 – involving two Adelaide merchants in a potentially disastrous situation. Gawler dismissed the suggestion that the bills were rejected because they had exceeded the expenditure authorised by the commissioners. He claimed to understand from private sources – there was still no official word from London – that the bills were dishonoured only because of 'the want of funds on the part of the Commissioners'. He also claimed he had reason to believe that sufficient funds would be provided by the British Government.[15]

In the last *Register* for March, Stevenson was highly critical of Gawler's excessive and unauthorised expenditure and recommended that, if the Governor was to remain, constraints must be placed upon him; but he believed that Gawler was very likely to be recalled.[16] Although there was no official word from the Colonial Office, London papers issued toward the end of 1840 and just received in the colony, confirmed the governor's recall. Details appeared in the *Register* of 3 April, alongside a report that suggested that the British Parliament had now approved guarantees to support a second attempt by the commissioners to raise a £120,000 loan. According to the English *Spectator*, it was the 'intention of the commissioners to pay the debts already incurred, and to honour Governor Gawler's bills'.[17]

With these economic uncertainties, conditions were hardly optimal for the establishment of a new theatrical venture; nevertheless, the Queen's went ahead with its second programme on 16 January. A few days later, with complimentary dress circle tickets from Mary Solomon, Mary Jnr and John Skipper saw *His First Champagne* and *Ask No Questions*.

Frances's illness, according to Mary Jnr's journal, had come to a crisis in early February. By the end of February she was well enough to make her first visit to the Queen's, accompanied by John. They also had complimentary tickets and enjoyed *The Brigand* and *Advice Grates*.[18] A slowing of the economy was beginning to be felt, however, and in its last advertisement for February, the Queen's offered half price seats, even for Saturday evening. Mary Solomon again provided complimentary tickets for Mary Jnr and Helen who were escorted by William.[19]

Despite the increasing amenity in the practical day-to-day life of the colony and the development of recreational pursuits such as the theatre, bouts of homesickness still bedevilled Mary, even after almost five years in South Australia. In her letter of March/April 1841, her last to George – he had been dead for some months, although she did not know it – she wrote with great poignancy:

> *I feel as much interested now as ever I did in the prosperity and happiness of my own dear native land, and shall never think of myself at home until I get back to it . . . I really long so much to hear from you that when an English ship comes in it makes me quite nervous till the mail arrives, and when I find myself disappointed of a letter I am almost ready to cry.*

But there were some things in which Mary could take pleasure:

> *Mr Stevenson has the finest garden in the colony, and the best cultivated containing yam, bananas, pomegranates, and almost every tropical fruit, besides those of English culture . . . For us, we have little to boast of at present besides vegetables and melons, both of which we have in abundance for our own use . . . [and] our meat is as fine as any in England.*[20]

This approval of South Australian meat, given Mary's love of England and her loyalty to the mother country, was high praise indeed.

The baked ham dinner party of March 1840 – celebrating the arrival of the Southampton delicacies sent by George – was only one of a number that Mary put on, mainly for family birthdays and for Christmas and Easter. At Easter 1841, she lamented that she 'tried to get some [apples] for an apple pie with which to treat my boys and girls . . . but I could get none under six pence each, and that would not do. So I substituted plum pudding with roast beef'.[21] For William's 18th birthday, she had held a supper party for nine of his printing office work mates and, despite the tightening of finances beginning to be felt generally, during February, Mary hosted a dinner for Robert George's 21st birthday in the long room of the stone house with six invited guests besides the family. She also ensured that Helen did not miss out, acknowledging her 16th birthday with a tea and supper party for six of her school friends and the three young daughters of the Reverend Charles Howard. A few weeks later, the long room was back in use to celebrate the joint birthdays of Mary and Mary Jnr, with both Margaret Stevenson and her mother, Mrs Gorton, and William Williams (R. Thomas and Co.'s chief clerk) and his daughter, Margaret (the girls' teacher), as dinner guests.[22] It seems Mary was determined that Robert's absence and the problems facing R. Thomas and Co. should have as little impact as possible upon their family life.

Her cottage was frequented by the friends of her adolescent sons and daughters – not only Harriet Holbrooke and her husband, Thomas Taylor, but also Elizabeth and Agnes Reid and Elizabeth's future husband, John Primrose, a Kent Town brewer. She was particularly welcoming to Charles – the son of Dr Wright – and his four brothers. The Wrights were very hospitable to Mary Jnr and Helen, who were regular visitors at their East Terrace home; and the party the Wrights held each January, after the traditional New Year's race meeting in the parklands opposite, became a highlight for the girls. But for the first race meeting held there, in January 1841, near the site of the future Victoria Park racecourse, they had to be content to view the races from the East Terrace home of their friend, Mary Hillier. They saw the races 'very plainly from the verandah, but they were not very good'.[23]

Although food costs had remained high for almost two years,

early in 1841 meat, bread and butter dropped to below their October 1838 prices as a very relieved Mary told George.[24] This was due in part to more land becoming available for agricultural and pastoral production. The first flocks of sheep and herds of cattle were brought overland from New South Wales during 1838. Two years later the routes were well established and the number of sheep in the colony was reported as 150,000 with 25,000 head of cattle, and an anticipated wheat harvest of 60,000 bushels for the year.[25] The first bread made from South Australian wheat, grown at 'Mackgill' (Magill), and ground at Dr Kent's steam flour mill, was advertised by James Sanders in the *Register* of 6 March 1841. The colony was, at last, beginning to cater for its own needs.

Toward the end of April, Frances and Mary Jnr called on Mary Solomon with a present of a 'helmet hat' for her new baby boy, and she invited them to the theatre on the 20th. The Thomas's party on this occasion included Mary as well as John and Frances and the two younger girls. It was Mary's first visit to a performance at the Queen's, and she enjoyed *All for Love* and *The Illustrious Stranger* as well as a dance by Rachel Lazar. But it was not a good house; apart from the Thomases, there were very few people in the boxes.[26] Despite the improvements in the availability and price of food, the economy, overall, was declining, and the citizens of Adelaide, preoccupied with forebodings for the future, were not in the mood for theatre going.

The long expected and overdue dispatch from the commissioners, with revised instructions for the governor in his management of the economy, finally arrived on board the *Siam* on 25 April and details were published in the *Register* of 1 May. As anticipated, the governor was prohibited from drawing further bills, leaving him only the minimal funds raised within the colony (mainly from tariffs) with which to govern. Several more dishonoured bills were also returned to the colony in the same mail.

Gawler attempted to justify his excessive spending by claiming that he had no alternative but to exceed the funds allowed by the commissioners. He had been forced to greatly enlarge the Survey Department to meet the demand for surveyed land made by the large numbers of self-funded emigrants entering the colony. He maintained that, until land was in production and required the labour of agricultural workers, he had little choice but to embark upon a programme of public works to ensure jobs, food and shelter for the newly arrived and unemployed assisted emigrants. Stevenson, unmoved, was scathing.

> Colonel Gawler knew that the whole of the means at the disposal of the Commissioners did not exceed £120,000 and he draws upon them, notwithstanding, for twice that sum . . . [w]ith the certainty that his bills, sooner or later, would be dishonoured . . . [27]

Later assessments judged Gawler's management of public works to be poor, observing that each had run substantially over budget. They included the road to the Port, a hospital, a jail and sizeable administrative buildings in Victoria Square, as well as Government House. Government House, which cost a massive £10,000, was considered to be self-indulgent and extravagant, as were the jail and the administrative buildings.[28]

On 15 May, the *Register* reported the arrival of the new governor, Captain George Grey, who brought with him the dispatch advising Colonel Gawler of his recall. It was Gawler's first official intimation of the withdrawal of his commission.[29] In his editorial farewelling Gawler, Stevenson set out three major regrets: Gawler's improvident spending of excessive sums (contrary to his official instructions); his failure to inform members of the Executive Council that they had the right to exercise control over his expenditure (so denying them any check or veto); and finally, the legislation that, due to the change in administration, would now be delayed – the Marriage, Bankruptcy and Registry Bills were all urgently needed.[30]

Through his government's expenditure, Gawler had bought his way into popularity, creating catastrophic problems for the colony. In his dual role of governor and resident commissioner,

Gawler had seen himself as having unprecedented emergency powers to call upon the funds of the commissioners, and he assumed that the British Government would meet any outlays over and above their reserves. His government's expenditure during his two-and-a-half years in office totalled £320,000, which exceeded the colony's revenue raising capacity by £250,000, and was £120,000 in excess of the commissioners' reserves.[31] By the time the commissioners in London had realised the degree of Gawler's spending, it was almost too late for them to act effectively.

In June 1841, almost 12 months after the commissioners' second unsuccessful attempt to raise a loan, general uncertainty about the financial future of the colony and retrenchments due to the scaling back of government expenditure were affecting business confidence. At the end of July, further details of the proceedings of the British Parliament were received and were published in the *Register* of the 31st. Given the commissioners' lack of success in loan raising despite government guarantees, the British Parliament had granted financial assistance to South Australia – but only just enough to stave off absolute disaster. Although some of the immediate worries of Adelaide merchants were to be relieved by the payment, at least in part, of Gawler's dishonoured bills, businesses generally were still in trouble. The economy was in serious decline and the government's Treasury loan was too little too late to stimulate even a limited recovery.

The economic crisis, however, was not Mary's only preoccupation. She had had only a few months' respite from her anxieties about the health of Frances and baby Georgiana when, on 12 May, a Southampton paper arrived for her. She anticipated news of the passing of an elderly aunt, but instead found the death notice of her brother, George. Although Mary had been troubled by his long silence, she was taken by surprise and was shaken by the sudden and unexpected news.[32] She wrote immediately to her sister-in-law reassuring her that Robert would arrange to meet any monies that might be outstanding for the goods George had sent out. Despite her own potentially difficult circumstances, Mary offered financial assistance should her sister-in-law need it, and asked that she accept the £5 annuity previously paid to George which, according to her father's will, should now revert to Mary. She then told her sister-in-law how much she had hoped to have met George again in this world:

> *[I] often dwelt in my own mind on the joy I should experience if ever I returned to my native country and went to Southampton, which would have been my first aim, but Heaven has denied it, and we must submit to its decrees. Indeed this melancholy event has greatly lessened my desire to return to England . . .*[33]

To honour her brother and observe custom, Mary decided that she and the girls would change into mourning clothes as soon as possible. They visited Murray and Grieg's store to buy black bombazine and crepe for their dresses and bonnets. Their dressmaker, Mrs Boswarva, was to make their bombazine walking out dresses, but their cotton ones and their silk bonnets were to be sewn by the girls and Mary at home. Mrs Boswarva took only a few days to complete their order, and within four days they were 'in mourning'.[34]

Despite this gloom, there had been some consoling news at the end of the month. Frances's baby was to be brought home to be weaned by Mrs Quin, who was to live-in at Rhantregwnwyn for a week with her own child, to allow Georgiana to be 'weaned by degrees'. By the middle of June, baby Georgiana had returned to Frances's care and, growing well, she looked forward to a healthy childhood. A few weeks later the baby was robust enough to be vaccinated by Dr Woodforde, probably against smallpox.[35] Frances's health seemed stable and she was maintaining her strength for the time being.[36] She and John were now living on acre 56; Mary had offered them the empty rooms on the upper floors of the stone building rather than encourage their return to Waymouth Street. Mary and the girls would be closer to hand should Frances need help.

The Thomas family continued to support their friends' theatrical venture, thus gaining some occasional, short-term respite from the general despondency which was beginning to envelope the colony. At Emanuel Solomon's request, Mary, accompanied by her family and a guest, attended the performance of *The Naval Engagement* and *The Young Queen*. They were entertained before the theatre at the Solomons' home. Unfortunately, although the show was very enjoyable, it did not attract a full house. Within two nights they were at the theatre again – Mary had bought eight tickets in support of John Lazar's benefit. And the next month, in spite of another packed programme for the benefit of one of the other players and the attendance of some of the Thomas family, there was again only a poor house.[37]

Chapter 10
A battle for survival

During June, the contraction in the economy was beginning to be felt by businesses generally, and R. Thomas and Co., seemingly in an attempt to stimulate some activity, took out an unprecedented column and a half of advertisements for their bookshop in each issue of the *Register* for June and for the first three issues for July.[1] The advertisements bulked up the declining classifieds columns, giving them some semblance of normality. There were also individual advertisements for copies of the 1840 and 1841 *Almanacks*, which were still on the shelves, as well as the *Sheet Almanack* for 1841. The classified columns, now reduced to only about half of their August 1840 peak (when they ran to the equivalent of two full pages of broadsheet), had been falling away for months, and so too had the *Register*'s revenue. During the previous month the paper had reduced the cost of classifieds by 25 per cent, as well as reducing its annual subscription of two guineas to £1 and 15 shillings. R. Thomas and Co., like all other businesses, was being hit by the severity of the economic downturn.[2]

The number and size of the advertisements for the Queen's Theatre was similarly unprecedented, with three very large advertisements during June, perhaps at a reduced cost in return for the Solomons' generosity with theatre tickets.[3] Members of the Thomas family attended the theatre on five occasions during the month. Several were benefit performances for members of the company and Mary, to help her friends, bought tickets for three of them.[4] The last benefit evening for June was Mary Solomon's, with Mary taking six tickets. There was a good crowd in the dress circle and, with entry at half price, the pit was well attended. It does seem that the Thomases and the Solomons were providing mutual support to each other's enterprises in an effort to keep both the classified columns of the *Register* reasonably well filled and the seats in the theatre occupied in an attempt to produce an appearance of normality.

A few nights earlier, Mary had also been at the Queen's, not for a theatrical performance, but to hear Dr Richard Penny deliver his lecture on the Aborigines of Encounter Bay. His audience was sizeable and included, as well as Mary, the Skippers, Mary Jnr and Helen. Some months earlier, before Dr Penny had been invited to give his lecture, the *Register* published the report which the German missionary, Dr Teichelmann, had made to the Wesley Missionary meeting describing his early work with the Aborigines of the Adelaide plains. The missionary advised that, after spending 12 months acquiring some knowledge of their language, he had opened a school for Aboriginal children in Adelaide. Although they were taught in their own tongue, the overwhelming orientation was toward Christian teaching and Bible study. When Aboriginal adults objected to this emphasis by suggesting that, as not all white men believed in the Christian God, this religion should not be forced upon their children, it seems Dr Teichelmann told them that if they did not believe in or obey Jehovah, they would be thrown into hell.

The *Register* was highly critical of the missionary's approach, which was thought to have been supported by the protector of Aborigines, Dr Matthew Moorhouse. Stevenson maintained that

> *before attempting to teach them christianity he [the protector] ought to have taught them to till the ground, and to have shown them by what means they could have taken an evident and useful step towards civilization . . . [the Aborigines] crowd into Adelaide*

to beg or to steal or to become the prey of horrible disease ... the general neglect of the aborigines – in spite of fine speeches and big words – [is] alike scandalous and disgraceful.⁵

A few weeks later, in April, Dr Penny – in the aftermath of the continuing tensions generated by the *Maria* massacre, and in an attempt to diminish them – gave an account, also published in the *Register*, of his recent chance meeting with members of the Milmenrura tribe on 10 April. It gave him an opportunity to discuss with the Milmenrura the circumstances of the *Maria* massacre. He understood

> that they had brought the whole people [the survivors of the ship-wrecked Maria] up a long way [along the Coorong], showed them water, fished and carried their children for them. That when they came to this point [where the massacre took place], they could not take them any farther as their country ends there and the piccanniny Murray begins. Then they claimed some clothes and blankets for their trouble, but the white people refused to give them any, yet said that if they took them to Adelaide they should have plenty. This they could not do, so they began to help themselves, and, this being resisted, ended in the murder of the whole. The white men did fight for some time, but they broke their arms with waddies and speared them. They were also jealous of the next tribe into whose territory they [the survivors] would have passed, and who, being in the habit of visiting Adelaide, could have taken them up and obtained the reward promised to them [the Milmenrura].⁶

Penny believed the massacre of the *Maria* survivors had been provoked by misunderstanding, and in his report to the *Register* he was providing an explanation for that tragic event. He also considered that the Milmenrura had received 'on one or two occasions shameful treatment from overland [droving] parties'. 'There was not the slightest ground for apprehending any further trouble from these people ...' Penny was determined to continue to do whatever he could to ameliorate the circumstances of the Aborigines of the lower Murray.

Stevenson, in his editorial of 24 April accompanying Penny's report, maintained that Penny's revelations vindicated the stance of the *Register* regarding the summary execution of the Aborigines involved. 'The unfortunate passengers of the *Maria* were not murdered in cold blood, but in an affray evidently provoked by the resistance and ungrateful conduct of the white party.'[7]

In his June lecture, Dr Penny attempted to promote tolerance of Aboriginal ways. His aim, according to the *Register* of the 26th, was to refute general claims that Aborigines were incapable of responding to educating or civilising influences. He also used the lecture to stress the need for greater acceptance and understanding, particularly at a time when violence between settlers and Aborigines in frontier situations was becoming more frequent. Aborigines were responding to the occupation and stocking of their tribal lands by spearing stock, which then prompted retaliation from the settlers. Dr Penny told his audience that both the violence and the 'dreadful condition to which the natives [particularly of the lower Murray] were reduced by disease' had prompted his appointment to enquire into their circumstances.[8]

He described his perspective of the Aborigines' way of life and made comparisons with the North American Indians and the progress some Indian tribes had made as settled farmers and artisans. He believed that this was a cause for optimism, and pointed out that some Aborigines had already become good and useful labourers. Penny did not agree with the frequently expressed opinion that 'the child of nature must necessarily disappear before the advance of civilisation', and again he emphasised the need for forbearance, warning that change would be slow. But he was unable to offer concrete solutions and the thoughts and energies of his audience became easily diverted by the demands, difficulties and preoccupations of their own lives – Mary Jnr was one member of his Queen's theatre audience who remained unmoved. With the incisiveness of adolescence, her journal records that Dr Penny's sentiments 'were undoubtedly good but he expressed himself so badly that the lecture was rather more ridiculous than instructive'.[9]

About a month later, Mary and Frances were out walking and, in passing the Queen's Theatre, they met Emanuel Solomon. He escorted them to his home for tea to celebrate Elizabeth Solomon's second birthday and then presented Mary with a theatre ticket for the coming season.[10] In the context of the social prejudice of the time, Mary's support for the theatre and her willing acceptance of her family's friendship with the Solomons are noteworthy. Frances, particularly, was a close friend of Mary Solomon, who, in having been given a benefit evening, a privilege reserved mainly for actors and those closely associated with the theatre's day-to-day operation, was almost certainly at least a part-time actor.

Clare Tomalin, the biographer of the 19th-century actresses Dora Jordon and Nelly Tiernan, in describing 19th-century attitudes toward actresses commented:

> *To pretend to be what you were not and to make a good job of it made you morally suspect. Alongside the admiration was a steady stream of abuse directed against actresses on the grounds that their work was of its very nature damaging to character. The point was made by many writers throughout the century. In Fanny Burney's last novel,* The Wanderer, *which was published in 1814, her heroine Juliet has no hesitation in preferring the prospect of starvation to a perfectly good offer of work as an actress, because she considers its very nature corrupting. In the same year Jane Austen in* Mansfield Park, *although it addressed itself only to amateur players, held up the most skillful and enthusiastic participants to particular disapproval . . . [Elsewhere] the association between prostitution and the stage was made over and over again.*[11]

It is quite apparent that neither Mary nor any of her family held these views, although they were commonplace enough for the Thomases to have been fully aware of them. Their friendship with the Solomons suggests that Mary and her family disregarded such notions, even though they may have been held by other colonists, and that the Thomases would not be swayed by what they considered the unreasonable prejudices of others. It is a further testament to Mary's strong, self-assured character that she had no sympathy with anti-Semitic views – also widespread in the 19th century, though less endemic in South Australia with its emphasis upon religious freedoms – as both the Solomon family and their friends the Lazars were members of Adelaide's small Jewish community.

Mary, with the Skippers and Mary Jnr, attended the opening of the Queen's second season on 29 July. *The Dancing Barber* was, according to Mary Jnr, 'excellent, laughable and well acted'; but 'The house was not full'.[12] Despite her own financial worries, with the *Register*'s revenue from classified advertisements halved, Mary maintained her support for the theatre. She selected a box for her family for an evening performance under the patronage of the Freemasons' Lodge. Although the dress circle was well filled, there were fewer than expected in other parts of the house. The next morning Mary, Frances and Mary Jnr called on Mary Solomon who showed them through the backstage of the theatre – the scenery store, stage furniture and costume wardrobe – where she told them that the theatre was likely to close as its profits were so small.[13]

Mary Jnr completed her schooling mid-year in 1841, a month or so before her 18th birthday. This reduction in school fees perhaps eased Mary's budget a little – even though she immediately hired a piano from Platts's music store so that Mary Jnr could continue her music lessons with Margaret Williams.[14] Nevertheless, Mary must have been deeply troubled about her family's financial situation, as in three successive *Register*s – the first on the 31 July – an advertisement appeared offering Rhantregwnwyn for immediate lease at £60 per annum. Although this effort to increase her income came to nothing, Mary's circumstances must have been dire for her to even contemplate giving up her beloved cottage to strangers. It seems she was forced to explore every opportunity to find some financial relief and, in September, she brought an action in the Magistrates Court to recover the value of a plough that had been borrowed from Robert several years before and not returned. But the case was decided against her and she was ordered to pay her own costs – seemingly little was to go right for her.[15]

Many others were in a similar predicament – unemployment was widespread and the ranks of out-of-work labourers continued to swell. By September 1841, some 500 labourers (with their families about 1200 people, close to one 10th of South Australia's population) were reliant on the government for support and employment.[16] In his editorial of 25 September on the 'State of the Working Class', Stevenson was less than sympathetic to their plight. Earlier in the week, the labourers had called a public meeting to censure Governor Grey's denial of their constitutional right 'to publicly express grievance . . . with a view to its redress'. In seeking effective relief from their destitution, they had presented him with a petition, which he thought contained a veiled threat of violence. Their petition had argued that obedience to laws 'seldom or never obtain when want, destitution and misery prevail'. The governor objected to the perceived threat and refused to countenance their grievances.

Stevenson rebuked them for the 'strong feeling' shown at the public meeting they had called to censure Grey, referring to them as 'those classes'. He argued that they had no unequivocal right to relief payments; these had been paid during the first years of the colony only because the resident commissioner was given the authority to provide them, but with the new restrictions imposed by the commissioners, this authority had been withdrawn. And the governor had been able to find only enough funds to make very limited assistance available to them.

The current financial difficulties, Stevenson acknowledged, had 'operated with the greatest severity on the working classes', with the 'sudden transition from a steady demand for labour at high wages to a precarious employment at low rates'. But he was convinced there would be ample work during the coming harvest. Although it was at least two months away, he had no suggestions to offer about how the unemployed workers and their families would live in the interim. And he admonished them not to 'make any attempt at ... combination or any attempt to force labour to an undue price'.[17] The workers, however, prevailed to the extent that the governor received a working class deputation, as reported in the *Register* on 16 October, but he refused their pleas for greater financial relief.

Those of the unemployed who were experiencing near destitution were not the only section of the population whose plight demanded the government's immediate attention. During the previous month, news had reached Adelaide of a clash between Aborigines and an overland party droving stock from New South Wales, in which 15 Aborigines were shot. Robinson, the leader of the party of 26 drovers, was bringing in 6000 ewes and 500 head of cattle when a confrontation occurred with about 300 Aborigines massed at Rufus River. The protector of aborigines, Dr Moorhouse, accompanied by a squad of police, was sent to negotiate with the tribe, but, despite their presence, a second clash lasting 10 to 15 minutes killed 30 to 40 Aborigines and injured many more, including women and children.[18] News of this further affray reached Adelaide and answers were demanded.[19]

A bench of magistrates' inquiry investigated the incident and their findings were reported in the *Register* of 25 September. According to Moorhouse's evidence, approximately 150 Aboriginal men, with 400 or so spears, had confronted the overlanders in battle array. An Aboriginal interpreter, who had been present at the battle site, told the hearing that the Aborigines could not be allowed within spear-throwing range because an attack was imminent. It had been apparent to him that their intention was to steal the sheep and other goods, and Moorhouse, convinced of the accuracy of this advice, had then handed over command to the police. But Robinson fired the first shot before any spears were thrown, claiming that it was for the safety of all. Moorhouse apparently agreed with this assessment, as once Robinson had fired the police also opened fire.

This description was confirmed by an Aboriginal prisoner

who, speaking through an interpreter, acknowledged that his tribe had been planning to attack. The inquiry found that 'the conduct of Mr Moorhouse and his party was justifiable and indeed unavoidable in their circumstances'. The explorer and former overlander, Edward Eyre, a member of the inquiry, said he knew 'the spot where the blacks had posted themselves ... and that a collision was unavoidable'. He had little sympathy for the Aborigines and his concern was that 'the example made was not yet sufficient'. Nevertheless, the prisoner was released and returned to his own people.[20]

The findings of the inquiry did not satisfy the *Register*. Stevenson editorialised that it was 'very plain that Matthew Moorhouse cannot act as Protector for it was under his protection they were shot down by the dozens ... before they had thrown a spear'.[21] With the intention of preventing further clashes, Eyre was posted to the area as a resident magistrate. During the next 12 months, however, these confrontations ceased, as overland traffic dwindled to a trickle when sheep numbers in the colony began to equate with the available pasture.[22] In the settled areas, Aboriginal resistance to colonial incursions onto their land had been overwhelmed, and the dramatic decline of the Aboriginal population was continuing.

Meanwhile, there was still no respite in the difficult economic circumstances prevailing throughout the colony. Businesses were continuing to contract; there were no jobs; a large number of bankruptcies had begun to emerge among the colony's merchants; and a great deal of property changed hands at prices that ruined its former owners.[23] As part of this general stringency, the Queen's was forced to close for several weeks, reopening only at the end of September to bring some sorely needed diversion from the general dejection. Helen, Frances and John attended the new production and, despite continuing poor houses, the theatre valiantly foreshadowed a further season for the coming year.[24]

Notwithstanding these failures, a new paper made a brief appearance when R. Thomas and Co. printed the first two issues of

Nathaniel Hailes' *Free Press* in October. Mary Jnr reported that another paper, the recently established *Independent*, was 'not quite dead', though she thought it would not last long, as 'there are too many papers already'. R. Thomas and Co. went ahead with preparations for the 1842 *Almanack*, and an advertisement on the 16th called for information to update its directory.[25]

In spite of the difficulties confronting the government, new legislation continued to be drawn up and, during October, the *Register* reported on a new Marriage Bill drafted to replace the one that Governor Gawler had set aside. In summary the bill ensured: the due public notice of all marriages; the validity of marriages through the maintenance of a registry and authentic government records; and that – as marriage was legally a civil act – ceremonies associated with it should in no case either interfere with the religious scruples or offend the consciences of the contracting parties.[26] This last stipulation recognised the colony's principle of religious freedom of worship, rejecting an established church and the requirement in England of the enforced performance of marriages according to its rites. The editorial commented favourably that the bill covered all of the essential provisions effectively.

At the beginning of November, Mary received the first news of Robert since he had left the colony 10 months earlier. According to Mary Jnr's journal, a recently arrived vessel from England carried the confirmation that the *Lalla Rhook* had arrived safely in London.[27]

In mid December 1841, as some relief from the encompassing economic bleakness, Mary made arrangements to lease a cottage at the Bay for a seaside treat for her family away from the heat of Adelaide. Perhaps Robert, in person, had been able to sort out the problems with her annuity and, by this time, she had received the long overdue accumulated arrears, which boosted her finances. Mary accepted a two month lease, which included the services of Mrs Cousins 'to attend on them' and the use of Mr Cousins' cart. The cottage was 3 miles from Glenelg, probably in the Hove or

North Brighton area. While waiting the few days for their cottage to become available, Mary Jnr, Helen and the Skippers were invited to dine onboard the Solomons' brig, the coastal trader, *Dorset*. Driven to the Port in the Solomons' cart, they were entertained onboard by Emanuel and Mary Solomon, and Captain Walsh and his wife. To round off the day, on their return to Adelaide, the Solomons extended an invitation for tea and Mary Jnr noted in her journal that they had been 'highly gratified with the excursion'.[28]

A day or so later, Mr Cousins drove the girls and baby Georgiana with their friend, Elizabeth Reid, to the Bay. At dusk, after tea, Mary Jnr and Elizabeth crossed the sand hills and visited the beach. Next morning the two young women gave the baby her first sea-bathe, and they all bathed each day, both mornings and evenings, after walks along the beach.[29]

Robert George, and presumably John Skipper, joined the beach party for Christmas Day but neither Mary nor William was with them – an issue of the *Register*, published on the 25th, kept them in Adelaide. The seaside Christmas dinner 'consisted of fried fish and a huge plum pudding that could have served as an Australian curiosity for some museum'. In the evening, accompanied by Robert George, they took 'a delightful walk towards Periwinkle Point' but, by the time they returned to the cottage, the weather had become so cool that they lit the fire in the sitting room. Surprisingly, it had turned out to be like 'an English Christmas evening in some respects'.[30]

On Boxing Day, modesty did not allow the girls to bathe because of the numbers of people on the beach but, with Robert George, they made a 2-mile excursion, walking the full distance to Periwinkle Point – perhaps in the vicinity of Seacliff – and Mary Jnr thought it 'a very fine place'.[31]

The girls remained at the Bay throughout January, missing the opening of the Queen's 1842 season but enjoying visits from Mary and William for a few days between issues of the paper on the 15th and 22nd. Mary was there on the 16th but back at Hindley

Street again by the 19th. While at the Bay, she invited her friends, Mary Hillier, Henry Wigley and Henry Jickling, to ride over from Glenelg for tea and 'they all three rode back in the evening'.[32] While William was with them, and with his protection, the girls were able to bathe by moonlight, dancing 'a quadrille in the water' and enjoying it as 'excellent fun'. Mary Jnr returned to Adelaide for treatment for an eye infection, which responded quickly, and she rode back on a pony Mary hired for her, escorted by their 'man' Black. She joined the others for three more days before they all returned to Hindley Street.[33]

Early in the New Year, R. Thomas and Co. at last had reason to feel vindicated as, on 22 January, the right to the publication of the government's *South Australian Gazette* was returned to the firm by Governor Grey. Although this was the less lucrative aspect of the government printing, Mary, who had earlier expressed faith in Governor Grey's goodwill toward them, was delighted. It reinforced the hope that Robert's trip to London for the total reinstatement of the contract would be successful.[34] Within a few weeks, the Thomases had further cause for celebration as Mary had confirmation from Robert, in a letter dated October 1841, that he had taken a passage on the *Lady Fitzherbert*[35], due to leave London at the beginning of January.[36]

Chapter 11
Financial failure

There was little good news in Adelaide in March 1842, and Mary Jnr confided to her journal that the colony was

> *in a very desperate condition . . . merchants are failing and everybody is desponding under a general want of money. I hope that there will be a favourable turn in our affairs soon, or else I cannot tell what will become of us all . . . We want some good capitalists from England, though doubtless many who are inclined to emigrate will be deterred from coming by the present ill opinion of this place in the home country.*[1]

Nevertheless, some of the Thomases enjoyed the respite of a visit to the country section of Mr and Mrs Henry Mildred, with John driving Mary Solomon, Frances and Mary Jnr in the Solomons' carriage. 'The house [was] prettily situated near the river with garden etc. and shaded with a pleasant verandah', where eight of them, including the Mildred's son, Hiram, sat down to dinner. Henry Mildred, riding in his gig with his married daughter, Claripa Hay, had accompanied the visitors' carriage from town 'and rode home with them in the early evening . . . [as] they were afraid of being on the road after dark' – perhaps because of the state of the roads or for fear of losing their way. At the Solomons' they 'all took tea' before the Thomases walked the few hundred yards to Rhantregwnwyn and the Mildreds returned to their farm.[2]

Robert's return was anticipated almost daily from the middle of May, in the expectation that the *Lady Fitzherbert* would have left London in January. R. Thomas and Co. was facing increasing difficulties and a lack of advertisers led to the closure of the *Chronicle* on 25 May. Mary's unhappiness over the failure of the *Chronicle* was exacerbated, not only by the lack of news concerning Robert's wellbeing and the whereabouts of the *Lady Fitzherbert*, but also because Mary Jnr was experiencing a severe recurrence of her throat infection. It required almost daily cauterisation of the affected areas 'with caustic mixed up with ointment'[3] and although the administration itself was very painful, the pain immediately afterwards was much worse and truly 'dreadful'.[4] Mary Jnr's illness reached its peak early in May when, in the middle of the night, she was 'taken so very ill with violent shivering fits and fever' that Mary had to get Robert George up to fetch the doctor. Charles Wright diagnosed 'a kind of ague', and prescribed medicine which Robert George collected immediately from the Wrights' home. Mary Jnr remained weak for about 10 days; nevertheless, she was allowed no respite from the daily treatment except that the caustic was now administered dry, 'in its pure state', and seemed less painful.[5]

A week or so later, Mary Jnr thought she was sufficiently recovered to attend Helen's school break-up party and a performance at the Queen's Theatre, but the next day, she was so ill that Mary had to call Dr Wright again. Both Dr Wright and Charles visited and explained that her relapse 'arose from the attempts to cure [her] throat' – perhaps a toxic reaction to their treatment of it with caustic. Although she was still feeling very unwell, her throat was cauterised yet again within 24 hours of her latest attack. Charles reassured Mary Jnr that her throat would benefit from the treatment and then left a glass tube of caustic with instructions for Mary to continue to apply it.[6]

On 18 June, the *Register* reiterated the view regarding the economic plight of the colony, which Mary Jnr had so eloquently expressed earlier in her journal – there was no marked improvement in the commercial or financial position of South Australia. This stagnation was attributed to the uncertainty caused by the absence of any advice or communication from the British Government, 'The latest news from England direct is dated about the 20th November – nearly seven months since!'[7]

The long-awaited information reached the colony in the form of a report and was published in the *Register* of 9 July. The British Parliament was introducing new legislation for the regulation of emigration and the disposal of wasteland, which would remove South Australia's special arrangements and status regarding these aspects of its administration. Most of the recommendations of a committee of inquiry into South Australia had been incorporated into the Bill for the Better Government of Australian Colonies. The committee had been set up following the financial failure of the South Australian Commission, which, in line with the committee's recommendations, had now been reformed and given the extended responsibility to supervise land sales and emigration for all Australian colonies.[8] Included in the bill were the requirements that the minimum price of land was to be fixed by the British Government, with the power given to Colonial Governments to raise but not to lower it, and that land was to be classified into the sites of towns, suburban allotments and country lots. But the bill ignored Wakefield's plea, made during the committee's hearings, that land should be sold at a fixed price, and, instead, continued the practice of sale by auction. It did, however, include the committee's recommendation that only half of the land fund should be devoted to emigration, with the balance, after provision for the Aborigines, available to be used at the discretion of the Colonial Government. A further clause required that loans from the British Treasury would be designated the public debt of the colony and incur interest of 4 per cent per annum.

Stevenson hailed it as the beginning of 'a rational system, which in all its leading points, can scarcely fail to work fairly and beneficially'. He suggested that country land should be further divided into its likely use – tillage, pasture and timberland – with an appropriate price for each.⁹ The legislation, but without Stevenson's suggestions, was eventually enacted during the early months of 1843.

There was at last some certainty about the future for the colonists, but for Mary and her family, there was no certainty about Robert's whereabouts. Finally, after having anticipated Robert's arrival every day for almost two months, on the morning of 12 July, Mary learned that a ship from England had been sighted in the gulf. William and William Hillier, one of R. Thomas and Co.'s clerks, 'went down to the Bay to see if it was the long expected *Lady Fitzherbert*'. At last, late in the afternoon, from the roof of the stone house, Mary and Mary Jnr saw 'a cart coming up the road' with Robert and William in it.¹⁰

The unhappy task of telling his father of the predicament of R. Thomas and Co. had fallen to William. Their creditors were closing in; they owed the Bank of Australasia £1543 and the bank was about to foreclose – the firm was insolvent.

Just two days after he stepped ashore, Robert signed his interest in acre 56 and all of the assets on it into Mary's name. At the time, married women could only own land through a trust – not in their own right – and John Skipper and Henry Wigley (a family friend and lawyer) became Mary's trustees. This served to protect the Thomas home, the acre on which it stood, and the buildings that surrounded it from the creditors of R. Thomas and Co.¹¹

In less than a fortnight, Robert was back at sea on the Solomons' coastal vessel, the *Dorset*, bound for Sydney. He took with him 'some consignments of Mr Hannan's to dispose of them there to prevent them from being seized by the creditors of himself and Mr Stevenson'.¹²

On 4 August 1842, the *South Australian Gazette* reported that George Stevenson had been declared insolvent by Judge Cooper of the Supreme Court. Robert Thomas was ordered to appear before him in chambers on 19 August 'to make a full discovery and disclosure of your estate and effects'. A fiat had been obtained by the Bank of Australasia on 12 August against the partnership of R. Thomas and Co.[13]

The notification of a sheriff's sale was advertised in the *Southern Australian* on 5 and 9 August. The sale had been initiated by the directors of the South Australian Insurance Company for the disposal of 'all the Stock-in-Trade of a Printer and Bookseller . . . [and] in one or more lots as may be agreed on – the Types, Press and Copyright of the Newspaper called the *South Australian Register*'.

The last *Register* published under the imprint of R. Thomas and Co. came out on the 6th, and Stevenson advised their readers:

> *Circumstances the history and the bearing of which are sufficiently notorious have led to the dissolution of the copartnery between the original proprietors of the Register and, it may be, will lead to the immediate transfer of this journal to other hands.*[14]

It was a devastating blow for Robert and Mary when, only a few days later, the copyright of the *Register* plus its presses and all its working equipment and supplies were sold off for a mere £600 to the editor of the *Southern Australian*, James Allen.[15] Robert and Mary were deprived, not only of a livelihood, but also of any means of recouping lost capital. Their dream of colonial prosperity and a comfortable retirement had been shattered.

Robert – en route to Sydney on 19 August – is very likely to have been represented in court by John Skipper for the 'full discovery and disclosure' of his estate and effects before Judge Cooper. Robert's decision to take the cargo he had brought out on the *Lady Fitzherbert* to Sydney was to avoid its inclusion in these proceedings and its subsequent sequestration.[16] In London, he had chartered the *Lady Fitzherbert* (a 500-ton vessel) and had 'freighted the ship – about half of her tonnage'. Robert had entered 'into some mercantile transactions with a Mr Hannan, purchasing merchandise for shipment to Adelaide'.[17] How this transaction was funded and whether it was a wise business decision is not clear. It is possible that land that Robert had purchased in 1822 in London ('eight pieces or parcels of ground at South Richard St, Churchfield,

Limehouse') was sold to finance his time in England and his venture with Hannan.[18]

In London, 'after several attempts to interview the Secretary of State who, (the Parliament being in recess) was not to be easily found, [Robert] abandoned the object of his visit to England'.[19] Faced with defeat and frustration in his dealings with the Colonial Office, it seems Robert sought to gain at least some benefit from his potentially wasted 18 months by returning to the colony with a consignment of goods. His involvement in yet another awkward business arrangement, given the predicament he was then in, may not have been as totally ill-considered as it appears. Perhaps it was always his intention to take the goods on to Sydney if he found South Australia's economy still in difficulty.

It is sad to contemplate that, if the funds Robert used to meet the costs of his return to England had been used instead to support R. Thomas and Co., the firm might have been saved. The firm's debts were almost balanced by what it was owed. Book debts (£3,563) very nearly equalled the total the firm owed to creditors (£3,889).[20] Most of the amounts owed to R. Thomas and Co. were relatively small sums – with the majority less than £5 – and had been incurred during the 1841–1842 crisis[21] when there was a general expectation that creditors would be forbearing, particularly with regard to fairly small debts. Although it may not have been possible to continue to publish the *Register*, at least sufficient stock and equipment could have been salvaged to continue in business as a stationer and general printer, thus ensuring the retention of capital and the means of making a livelihood. It was, however, fortunate that Robert had little, if any, personal debt, as shortly before he left for England he had sold valuable land – several town acres and one of his country sections – to meet debts of £1,500.[22] A £500 mortgage appears to have been paid out earlier, following Robert's very profitable land transactions during the land boom.

With regard to the failure of R. Thomas and Co., both Robert and Stevenson were discharged from bankruptcy without formal court hearings.[23] The two major creditors of the firm, the Bank of Australasia and a J. Baker, it seems under directions from the court, were appointed as trustees for the liquidation and distribution of the assets of Robert and Stevenson for the benefit of the firm's creditors.

What Stevenson's assets were, apart from some shares in a cattle company and a parcel of land in the Barossa (Valley) survey is not clear. Unfortunately, Stevenson had used these as security to raise loans for his personal use; thus they were the subject of mortgages and not available to assist in meeting the firm's debts.[24] His home and large garden at North Adelaide, which he retained, was very likely to have been protected through an arrangement similar to Mary and Robert's protection of acre 56.

Robert's assets are also not easy to establish. His known purchases of land in the colony amounted to 10 town acres, including three at North Adelaide, and two country sections of 134 acres (53 hectares), each on either side of the River Torrens in the vicinity of today's St Peters.[25] But various records (General Registry, items in the *Register*, letters 'home' to England, a descendant's papers) indicate that Robert progressively sold land to meet debts – particularly those incurred by his failed partnership with James Coltman in the general store – and to finance the expansion of R. Thomas and Co.[26] It is by no means certain, however, that Robert made no other land transactions apart from those discovered; as, at the time, details of transactions did not have to be lodged with the General Registry, and not all were. This aside, if those discovered represent the large majority, then Robert would have paid into the trust for disbursement to the creditors of R. Thomas and Co. three town acres at North Adelaide and, excluding acre 56 Hindley Street, one in Hindley Street and one in Rundle Street. Given Stevenson's personal financial difficulties, there is little doubt that Robert paid the lion's share of the monies ultimately distributed to their creditors. There is no record of what proportion of debt was cleared through the trusteeship but it must have been considerable for the Insolvency (Supreme) Court to have, in anticipation of the liquidation of assets, provisionally discharged both partners.[27]

In effect, with the exception of acre 56 Hindley Street, nothing remained of the investments Mary and Robert had made with the substantial capital they had brought from England – proceeds from the sale of their Fleet Street business, from the sale of the house at Southampton inherited from Mary's father, and from the sale of the leases of two cottages at Clerkenwell. The financial rewards of their life's work had been swallowed up in the black hole of South Australia's economic crisis and their net income was halved.[28] Basically, they were reduced to relying upon rent from the John o' Groats Inn and Mary's annuity from her father's estate. It was barely enough for four adults – Mary and Robert and the two girls – Mary Jnr was now 19 and Helen 17.

To add to the Thomas family's distress, Mary Jnr was still battling her, by now, chronic infection and her throat was incised in two places on the inside, probably to relieve the swelling. The operation was performed by Charles Wright using a pair of scissors and Mary Jnr's discomfort must have been extreme. A month later, when another incision was contemplated, Dr John Woodforde was called in for a second opinion. He recommended raising 'blisters' on either side of Mary Jnr's neck, by using 'drawing plasters'[29] made up with a paste which included the skin irritant, powdered cantharides (Spanish fly).[30] The blisters were then opened up and, by applying an ointment, prevented from healing with the intention of withdrawing blood from surrounding areas to reduce inflammation. When the ointment was unavailable, Mary used cabbage leaves to keep the wounds open.

It seems this procedure was repeated throughout October with little effect – she remained unwell and Dr Wright prescribed a tonic to strengthen her. Mary paid Dr Wright £4 for his services[31], and decided upon a remedy of her own – arranging for Mary Jnr and Frances, with Helen, to go down to Glenelg in December to stay in one of Henry Wigley's seafront cottages. Frances was also in need of recuperation after the birth of her second daughter, Frances Mary, on 10 October 1842.[32]

Meanwhile, the whole Thomas family, particularly the girls, would have been saddened by the closure of the Queen's Theatre, although, given the state of the colony, it was inevitable.

> *[The] last Performance was held on Monday November 28, 1842. The opera 'Der Freishutz' went off with 'great éclat'* . . . *at the end of the performance [John] Lazar gave a farewell address* . . . *The closing of the theatre, of course, simply added to the general distress of the colony.*[33]

By inviting their friend Mary Solomon to spend Christmas with them at the Bay, the Thomas girls hoped to help assuage her unhappiness.[34]

Henry's 16-year-old son, Tom, drove Mary Jnr and Helen down to the Bay in his father's cart while the Wigleys' dray followed with their furniture. Until Frances and her two daughters, driven down by Henry, arrived the following day, the girls stayed with Mary Hillier at Henry's home. While there, before taking up residence in their cottage, Mary Jnr walked across the Patawalonga with Tom and gathered native fruit growing in the sand hills. Mary Jnr had not 'visited this place since our first landing in this country, when we spent seven months at the primitive settlement'.[35] On Christmas Eve, Frances, the two girls and Tom helped Miss Hillier with the Christmas dinner preparations – Tom and Mary Jnr picked plums 'with especial injunctions not to eat any'. Following the arrival of Mary Solomon and her children on Christmas Day, they all dined at the Wigleys' on 'roast beef, roast sucking pig, plum pudding and mince pies'.[36]

Not only a spring cart, but the bullock dray and Tom Wigley on horseback, were required on Boxing Day to get the whole party down the south coast to Marino where they drove through the sea to Periwinkle Point. The scenery was very beautiful, 'large rocks communicating with a range of mountains while innumerable smaller ones stretch[ed] away into the sea . . . when the rocks were reached [and] the carts could proceed no further', they made 'a general halt there and dined upon the beach in the most picturesque manner possible'. Mary Jnr's dining room was the dray that she shared with a couple of companions while others picnicked on the beach.[37] She loved the seaside[38], the pristine beaches were part of the charm; the beach after a storm was littered with a wealth of shells and other sea treasures, to the delight of the children.

To allow Mary to escape Adelaide's heat for a few days, Mary Jnr returned to Rhantregwnwyn on 28 January.[39] Helen, perhaps with Mary, walked on the beach in the vicinity of the village of St Leonards, near the Patawalonga Creek, and noticed that:

There had been a high tide, and the sea on receding washed away the sand from the beach laying bare for some distance great trunks of trees buried in broken shells and hard sand. The trees were lying flat very close together, and much worn and honeycombed. The next tide covered them, and I saw them no more. And it has often made me wonder how these trees came to be there, where they came from and at what period they got buried so close to the sea; I would very much like the opinion of a geologist on the subject.[40]

They were the remnants of an ancient mangrove forest in which Aboriginal artefacts lay hidden. Glenelg's natural oyster beds, which would soon be exhausted, were nearby.[41]

After her short respite, Mary and the girls packed up to return to Adelaide – for Mary, her return meant facing the last bleak phase in the winding up of R. Thomas and Co. Matters relating to the firm were officially concluded at the end of January 1843, when Robert Thomas and George Stevenson, 'both individually and jointly', signed agreements that conveyed to the Bank of Australasia and J. Baker, trustees for the creditors of R. Thomas and Co., all freehold property and all other assets including 'goods and chattels and personal estate' for their liquidation and payment of creditors.[42] The only possessions not included were personal and family clothing and household goods and utensils, with the Stevensons retaining their home and garden and the Thomases, through Mary's trustees, retaining acre 56 Hindley Street.

George Stevenson's inability to meet his considerable private debt resulted in his personal bankruptcy in August 1843. Besides the listing of his personal finances in the Schedule of Estates, which he was required to lodge with the court, Stevenson included a statement in which he detailed the failure of R. Thomas and Co. He claimed that the difficulties of the firm had contributed to his personal insolvency:

> *Failure of R. Thomas, Insolvent's partner, in February 1838 and expenditure of monies taken from the firm by him subsequently on buildings on his acre in Hindley Street believed to exceed £4500 in amount. Irregularity of the books kept by Robert Thomas and consequent losses in bad debts. Withdrawal of Government printing in October and November 1840. Great expense of workmen on the printing establishment – falling off of advertisements and circulation of the Register. Loss upon the Chronicle; payment of interest on loans, general decadence of the province since 1840 and depreciation of property.*[43]

This is a very harsh and unjust judgement of Robert, given that it was Stevenson's uncompromising editorial policy that had ultimately cost the firm the right to the government printing contracts. According to their partnership agreement, it was Stevenson's sole prerogative to determine the *Register*'s editorial policy.[44]

Robert met his debt in relation to the 1838 failure of his business venture with James Coltman (to which Stevenson refers) by the sale of land, owned by him personally, for £1500.[45] It is Robert's prudence and judgment which should be questioned, not his honesty. As Mary stated in her letter to George of October 1838, James Coltman had involved the firm in large debts, for which Robert was liable, without his 'knowledge or consent'.[46] Coltman was committed to the Lunatic Asylum in 1848 and died there shortly after.[47]

With only incomplete records of financial transactions, it is difficult to rebut Stevenson's comments about Robert's use of monies from the firm – rather than from his own pocket as the partnership agreement required – to put up their business premises on acre 56. However, between July 1839 and August

1842, Stevenson reported his income from the firm as £1367.[48] But Robert's must have been more as, according to their partnership agreement, Robert was entitled to rent from the firm's premises. The agreement had required him to finance the building of the firm's premises, and in return he was to receive an annual payment from the firm equal to 10 per cent of the money he had invested.[49]

Robert and Mary also received rent from the John o' Groats Inn; Mary's annuity from her father's estate; some rent from the Skippers who occupied the top floors of the stone building; as well as rent from a quarter of a town acre leased at £40 per annum. With the addition of payments to Robert for the buildings used by the firm, these sources of income probably brought in about £4 and 15 shillings per week – at the time an adequate income for a family occupying a freehold dwelling.[50] This left Robert's share of the profits from R. Thomas and Co. of £1367, plus his net return from land sales of £2150[51] for building costs. With these sums and the money brought to the colony from asset sales in England[52], it seems that, as he was required to do, Robert would have been able to meet the £4500 – which Stevenson claimed was invested in buildings on acre 56 – from his own resources. As discussed earlier, virtually all of R. Thomas and Co.'s book debts, as Stevenson listed them in his insolvency papers, were incurred between 1841 and 1842, when Robert was away from the colony. Given the depressed state of the economy during that period, debt recovery was well nigh impossible.

George Stevenson's questioning of Robert and Mary's honesty is unjustified; it would have been grossly out of character for either to have attempted to gain a benefit for themselves to the detriment of Stevenson, or any other person. Given their loyal support of Stevenson in his unrelenting editorial policy, ultimately at great personal cost, it is even more unlikely.

The *Register* continued to be printed at acre 56 for only a few months after its sale to James Allen. He moved the paper to new premises on the corner of Rundle Street and King William Street, at today's Beehive Corner.[53]

William did not remain with the *Register* after its loss, but turned to farming at his country section on the Main North Road in the vicinity of Prospect. By January 1843, he had married Mary Jane Good and their first child, a daughter, was born at the end of the year.

Mary Thomas, portrait painted by Frances Skipper (nee Thomas), c. 1834. Courtesy of V. Willington.

Above: Mary Thomas, c. 1859. Courtesy of M. Hogan.

Above right: Mary Thomas, c. 1873. Courtesy of V. Willington.

Right: Mary Skipper (nee Thomas), second wife of John Michael Skipper, thought to be her wedding portrait, c. 1856. Courtesy of E. Miller.

John Michael Skipper Australia, 1815–1883. *Artist and his wife Frances Amelia on horses*, c. 1840, Adelaide, oil on canvas mounted on masonite 109.8 x 89.5 cm. Gift of the Maughan Family 2007, Art Gallery of South Australia, Adelaide.

Left: Robert Thomas, c. 1859. In *The Diary and Letters of Mary Thomas*, W.K. Thomas and Co., Adelaide, 1925, opp. p. 91.

Below: Robert George and Charlotte Thomas (nee Tuckett). Courtesy of C. Tuckett.

Above left: William Kyffin Thomas, c. 1862. Courtesy of V. Willington.

Above: Mary Thomas (nee Good), wife of William Kyffin Thomas, and son Evan, c. 1860. Courtesy of V. Willington.

Left: John Michael Skipper, widower of Frances Skipper (nee Thomas), husband of Mary (nee Thomas), c. 1863. Courtesy of the State Library of South Australia (SLSA: B 7028).

Above: Helen Mantegani (nee Thomas), c. 1875. Courtesy of L. O'Brien.

Above right: Robert George Thomas, c. 1880. Courtesy of the State Library of South Australia (SLSA: B 9659).

Opposite page top: William and Mary Kyffin Thomas, c. 1870. Courtesy of V. Willington.

Opposite page below: The Thomas's tent and rush hut at the first settlement, by John Michael Skipper, 1836. In *The Diary and Letters of Mary Thomas*, W.K. Thomas and Co., Adelaide, 1925, opp. p. 64.

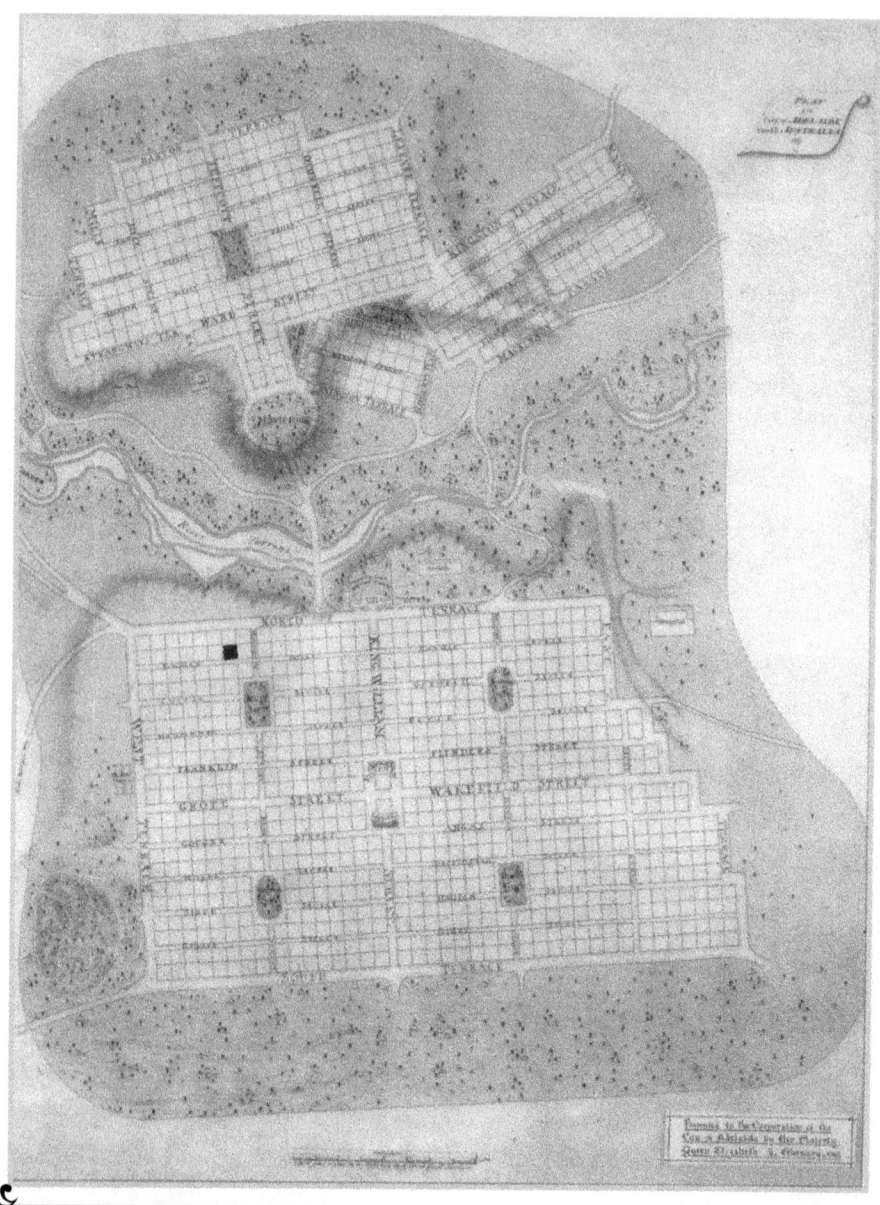

Colonel William Light's City of Adelaide plan (Acre 56 is marked). Adelaide City Archives.

Top: Residence, printing office and store (the long building), Hindley Street, 1838. In *The Diary and Letters of Mary Thomas*, W.K. Thomas and Co., Adelaide, 1925, opp. p. 107.

Above: Clarendon House (the two-storey stone building) with Rhantregwnwyn Cottage, Hindley Street, by John Michael Skipper, c. 1840. Courtesy of the State Library of South Australia (SLSA: B 4692).

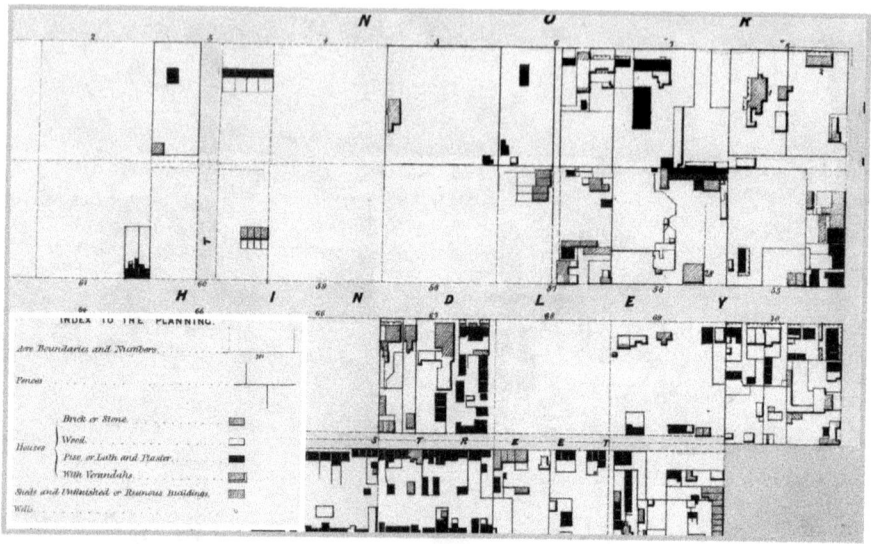

Top: Town Acre 56, Hindley Street, detail from G.S. Kingston's map of Adelaide, 1842. Courtesy of the State Library of South Australia (SLSA: Map Coll. 831.51p).

Above: S.T. Gill, Australia, 1818–1880. *Hindley Street, Adelaide, looking east*, 1845, Adelaide, watercolour on paper 27.5 x 39.6 cm. Gift of South Australian Company, 1931, Art Gallery of South Australia, Adelaide. (The first two-storey building on the left is the Thomas's 'stone house', Clarendon House.)

Top: The Queen's Theatre, Gilles Arcade, 1842. Courtesy of the State Library of South Australia (SLSA: B 4502).

Above: Rhantregwnwyn Cottage, c. 1865. In *The Diary and Letters of Mary Thomas*, W.K. Thomas and Co., Adelaide, 1925, opp. p. 150.

First edition of the *South Australian Gazette and Colonial Register,* London, 18 June 1836, in the facsimile edition of the *South Australian Gazette and Colonial Register,* 1837–1838, published by the South Australian Government Printer and the South Australian Historical Society, 1988.

Top left: The *Register* offices, Grenfell Street, 1854–1859. In *A Modern Newspaper Building*, W.K. Thomas and Co., Adelaide, 1909, opp. p. 8.

Top right: The offices of the *Register* and *Observer*, Grenfell Street, 1860–1909. In *A Modern Newspaper Building*, W.K. Thomas and Co., Adelaide, 1909, opp. p. 10.

Above: The proprietors and editorial staff of the *Register*, c. 1857; with William Kyffin Thomas second from left, back row; others include Anthony Forster, Joseph Fisher and E.W. Andrews. In Allan Sierp, *Colonial life in South Australia: 50 years of photography*, Rigby, Adelaide, 1969.

Top: Martha Berkeley Australia, 1813–1899. *North Terrace, view taken looking east s east*, 1839, Adelaide, watercolour on paper 34.2 x 45.0 cm. South Australian Government Grant 1935, Art Gallery of South Australia, Adelaide.

Above: North Terrace with the Institute Building on the right, c. 1860. Glass Negatives Collection, History Trust of South Australia.

Top: Corner of North Terrace and King William Street with Government House in the middle distance, c. 1860s. Glass Negatives Collection, History Trust of South Australia.

Middle: King William Street looking south, c. 1860s. Adelaide City Archives.

Above: King William Street looking south to the recently built Town Hall and GPO, 1872. Courtesy of the State Library of South Australia (SLSA: B 1961).

Top: Pioneers landing at Port Adelaide by John Michael Skipper, c. 1839. Courtesy of the State Library of South Australia (SLSA: B1212).

Above: Port Adelaide 1845 by F.R. Nixon. In *Twelve views in Adelaide and its vicinity South Australia*, printed by F.R. Nixon, 1845, facsimile edition (Australiana Facsimile Editions No. 186) published in Adelaide by the Libraries Board of South Australia, 1968.

Chapter 12
After the fall

Robert, having been discharged by the Insolvency (Supreme) Court, was free to apply for newly created government posts and was successful in his application for the position of inspector of weights and measures. The position was created by the *Act to Establish Standard Weights and Measures* 1843 and was intended to prevent 'the use of . . . [weights and measures that] are false and deficient'. But the state of the economy was so poor, and government funds so limited, that even at a salary of only £60 per year, the position could not be financed and his appointment did not eventuate for almost three years.[1] Robert, while waiting to take up his post, probably occupied himself by helping out on William's farm.

The colony's economic recovery, stimulated by the discovery of copper at Kapunda, some 40 miles (64 kilometres) north of Adelaide, had begun very modestly in the previous September and gradually strengthened throughout 1843.[2] Because of the fertility of the Adelaide plains, land around Adelaide was being increasingly devoted to cereal crops, and pastoralists, mainly sheep graziers, were taking up pastoral leases at greater distances from town, to the north and beyond the Barossa Valley. Shepherds picked up the first specimens of ore lying on the ground and noticed unusual outcrops as they tended their sheep. But it was generally the pastoral leaseholders who benefited, able to raise the capital to purchase the land, and so obtain the unrestricted mineral rights which accompanied freehold title at the time.

It was fitting that this rejuvenation in the colony's prospects should coincide with its first small steps toward representative government. On 10 October 1843, the new Legislative Council, which had been expanded under the British *Act for the Better Government of Australian Colonies* 1842, met for the first time. The council included the governor, three of his officials, and four colonists appointed by him.[3] South Australia's unique status as a largely self-funded colony was at an end – it had become a Crown colony and was no different in its governance from any of the other Australian colonies.[4] Legislative Council Chambers were built in North Terrace, on the site now known as Old Parliament House. They were completed in time for the new council's first session, which was witnessed by over 200 colonists who were 'crowded to the doors' of the public gallery.[5] One of the first matters the council considered was the viability of the Adelaide Corporation which, although elected in October 1840, had been unable to enforce the payment of rates during the economic downturn and was virtually extinct. The Legislative Council very quickly decided that because 'the colony was not prepared for, or in a situation to make use of a municipal corporation, its affairs must be wound up and its debts discharged'; by the end of the year, the corporation had become legally defunct.[6]

Although the colony's governance and economic health were improving and recovering, Mary Jnr's health was not. She was dogged by illness again in 1844 when she contracted another intermittent but persistent fever. On this occasion, Dr Wright ordered 'cupping', a treatment in which heated cupping glasses were applied in an attempt to relieve inflammation.[7] Charles Wright administered them to her temples, shaving off only as much hair 'as was necessary to leave room for the glasses'. The procedure was repeated the following week, and Mary Jnr commented on Charles's 'great kindness'. She remained ill for most of March, and although by the end of the month she was able to walk the block or so to Waymouth Street, she considered that 'the fever had injured her memory' and left her very thin.[8]

For the past two to three years, Mary not only had Mary Jnr ill, often for many months at a time, she also had Frances, whose health was consistently frail – especially during the final stages of her third pregnancy – in need of her care. And Frances's two children, Georgy, almost four, and Fanny, two years younger, were lively toddlers and also demanded a considerable amount of Mary's attention; she had little time for relaxation. Frances gave birth to her third daughter on 26 May 1844 and named her Helen Stark.

The financial difficulty that Mary was also experiencing is reflected in the absence of the combined party at the end of August for the birthdays of the two Marys, but, more tellingly, there was not even a single party for Mary Jnr to mark her legal majority. Mary's budget was simply too stringent to accommodate the usual gatherings for celebratory dinners. However, early in August Frances, perhaps in anticipation of Mary Jnr's 21st birthday, began a joint portrait of her with Helen using chalk as her medium. And toward the end of the year, as some consolation and as a belated birthday present, Mary Jnr sat for a portrait in oils by John Skipper. She also received by deed of conveyance, 56 acres, a gift from Robert George, and she leased part of it, which provided her with a small income.[9]

Escorted by Robert George, the girls saw the 1845 traditional New Year race meeting from a friend's home that overlooked the racecourse, and in the early evening they were at the Wrights' for tea as guests of Charles and his brothers who were all in town from Dry Creek. The Thomas girls stayed on for the party held later the same evening. Nine or 10 other friends were also invited including Captain John Holmes, his wife, Ann, and their daughter; Lucy, William Cook and William Everard. Dancing continued for several hours until a number of the young men began to entertain their friends with songs. Edward Wright joined them singing 'in Arabic while his brothers accompanied him by clapping their hands'. Mary Jnr considered it the 'most pleasant' evening she had ever spent in the colony, particularly when Charles Wright called the next day to enquire whether the girls had been tired out by the dancing. New Year celebrations continued that evening and Mary, Helen, Mary Jnr, Frances, John, and the children went out to see a display of fireworks in which 'The passion flower, among other things was represented and several rockets were thrown up'.[10]

The restrictions of their pinched circumstances must have been eased by the opportunity Mary and the girls had from time to time to visit their friends' country sections, located in some of the loveliest settings known in the colony at the time. At the end of February, with Mrs Wright, the girls were driven by Ann Holmes to the Holmes's farm on Fourth Creek, about 5 miles (8 kilometres) east of Adelaide.[11] Fourth Creek, one of a number of tributaries of the River Torrens that cross the plain east of Adelaide, descends from the Adelaide Hills by a series of waterfalls at Morialta, passing through today's Rostrevor and Hectorville before joining the Torrens at Campbelltown. The Holmes's farm may have been almost anywhere along the creek's lower reaches. In its original state, the plain was skirted by a dense forest of peppermint gums known as the Black Forest. Visible for miles as a dark, impenetrable mass, it covered the foothills in an arc to the south-east, around today's Burnside and further south toward Mitcham.[12]

Fourth Creek is now almost lost within suburban Adelaide, but in 1845, the country the girls were driven over was only partially cleared – mainly for wheat crops. Where it was used for pasture and the native vegetation had been spared, the plain's open, savannah woodland seemed like an English park, with the cattle knee deep in luxuriant kangaroo grass. Slender, elegant blue gums and the more densely crowned blackwoods, both large handsome trees, were interspersed with umbrella-like golden wattles, native cypress pines, she-oaks and the smaller native Christmas bushes. The creeks were clearly marked by giant red gums and, as the party approached them, shrubby native hops, white bottlebrush and the native cherry could be glimpsed beneath their overarching branches.[13] Bird and animal life abounded. Brilliant green, blue and red lorikeets, yellow-tailed honeyeaters, and blue wrens took nectar and insects from trees they shared with possums, while grey kangaroos, bandicoots, scrub wallabies, bettongs and echidnas inhabited the understorey.[14]

As Mary Jnr described it, 'The approach to Captain Holmes's residence was particularly good . . . owing to the splendid large gum trees that grow by the water just there'. Captain Holmes showed them his farmyards, dairy, 'brewhouse', cellar and

> good gardens filled with vines, oranges and other fruit trees . . . After tea was over we all took a walk in the bright starlight and regaled ourselves with listening to the songs and rejoicings of a wedding party in a cottage not far distant.

On another occasion, when Mary was with them, the heat was extreme and they were driven to his farm by John Holmes himself. 'We had been exposed during our drive of five miles to a hot wind', and on arrival found 'that Captain Holmes's thermometer against a wooden wall in the house registered 113 degrees'. After dinner, they were refreshed by watermelons, grapes and peaches from the garden; and captivated by the beauty surrounding them, William Cook drove Mary and the girls home by the 'light of a brilliant moon'.[15]

Despite the beauty of the countryside surrounding it, Adelaide lacked even basic sanitation – it was unsewered and its water supply was polluted. These generally unsanitary conditions were blamed for Mary Jnr's next round of health problems – fly-born infections were endemic. In March 1845, she was badly bitten on the arm by a cat as she tried to rescue it from a dog. The wound became very inflamed and would not heal; the infection was so severe that she was still having problems with it six months later.[16] Charles Wright came regularly to Rhantregwnwyn over the following weeks to treat Mary Jnr's arm, even though at the time he was coping with major problems himself. He had been called as a witness in the trial of his father being heard in the Supreme Court.[17] Dr Wright had been indicted in March 1845 on the two counts of 'administering violent medicine' and 'neglecting to watch the effect of these'. His patient, William Wilkins, on post-mortem examination, was found to have died of an overdose of morphine. Dr Wright had diagnosed chronic lunacy and prescribed the morphia in order to induce a deep sleep, as Wilkins seems to have been experiencing what today would probably be considered a severe psychotic episode. His carers, two men engaged by his wife, had had to restrain him with straps in order to prevent him from harming himself.[18]

Although Dr Wright was found to have been intoxicated when he ordered the morphia from Paxton's pharmacy, he was acquitted on a technicality as Paxton's assistant had dispensed a slightly different form of morphia from the type Dr Wright had prescribed (muriate of morphia had been dispensed rather than acetate, although the two were virtually interchangeable). Furthermore, the chemist was considered to share some of the blame because he had allowed Dr Wright's prescription to be filled, knowing that the doctor was drunk. The patient had also been attended by Charles Wright who, on his own initiative, had varied his father's orders by reducing the dosage.[19] Given these two irregularities, the court determined that Dr Wright could not be held accountable for instructions which countermanded his own. He was, however, severely reprimanded by the judge.[20]

An editorial in the *Register* not only lambasted Dr Wright for his poor professional judgement and oversight – being drunk while administering medicine – but for his over-charging to attend the patient. It was also highly critical of Charles Wright's involvement in the case: 'Who is Charles Wright that he should visit and be allowed to tamper with his father's patients?' Charles had no formal medical training, although he had acted in a position similar to that of an apprentice in his father's practice for some years. At the time, there was no other training available in the colony.[21]

Dr Wright, his wife and sons had been friends of the Thomas family since their arrival in South Australia, and probably before at the Adelphi rooms in London, and the Wrights had come out on the *Cygnet* at the same time as Robert George. Dr Wright had been given a free passage as the ship's medical officer. He had been one of the original intending settlers, along with John Morphett and others who, from 1834, had supported and assisted Gouger and the project to found the colony.[22]

Mary was not one to abandon her friends in times of trouble. With characteristic loyalty and compassion, she continued her close family friendship with the Wrights, and Dr Wright – with Charles from time to time at her request – remained the family's general practitioners. A fortnight or so after the trial, Mrs Wright, accompanied by Charles, called in their carriage to take Mary Jnr and Helen to the Wright brothers' farm at Dry Creek. The visitors had tea and damper in the brothers' hut and were shown the site for the house they planned to build. Some weeks later, toward the end of April, when Mary Jnr called on Dr Wright about her infected arm, he ordered leeches to be applied to it every other day, which Mary was eventually able to get from Moorundee (near today's Morgan on the Murray). The treatment was a form of 'bleeding' intended to reduce inflammation. After her consultation, Mary Jnr visited Mrs Wright who told her that Charles 'intended to go up to the country section at Dry Creek and remain there with his brothers', presumably having it in mind to give up medical practice and live permanently out of town.[23]

For most of July and August 1845, Mary Jnr was once more in difficulties with her health, this time over a tooth that Charles Wright had attempted to extract. He had removed a troublesome tooth for her about 12 months earlier without complications, but on this occasion she was not so fortunate. As Charles was out of town, Mary Jnr had to wait a week before he returned and could attend to her 'obstinate' tooth. It had apparently broken off at the root during its extraction some weeks earlier.[24] He checked her sore gum and thought it would settle, but reassured her that if it didn't, she could get a message to him on the following Saturday – seven days away – when he could come in again from the farm.

It continued to be extremely painful and, although Charles had not been in Adelaide for about 10 days, Dr Wright was very reluctant to attempt to intervene as her gum was inflamed. Mary Jnr had to cope with her problem tooth for a further week until Charles eventually returned to Adelaide. He called at Rhantregwnwyn just as the Thomases were sitting down to dinner and accepted Mary's invitation to share their meal of bacon and fowls.

With dinner over, he took out the remainder of Mary Jnr's tooth and 'although the operation was a very difficult one, he performed it with great deftness'. Anaesthesia was not generally available at the time and presumably unavailable to Mary Jnr, who, without it, must have suffered excruciating pain. Charles 'declined the usual fee and, after a smoke and a walk in the garden, took his leave of the family'. But there was still little relief and Mary Jnr put up with a painful gum for another fortnight before Charles was in town again. He was very surprised that there was still a piece of tooth remaining in her jaw, and 'took his lancet and drew away the skin' to find it. He 'then lanced it and fixed a hooked instrument besides using a pair of pincers, but neither would draw the piece out as it was too deeply rooted and the surface was too small to afford a hold for the instruments'. The intensity of the pain must have been indescribable, even though Charles 'was very careful to avoid giving me more pain than he could possibly help and he candidly told me that nothing but punching would be of any help'.[25] This was a horrendous option and so presumably nothing more was done.

Charles, in choosing to forgo medicine to join his brothers in their farming venture, was participating in the growing economic importance and strength of the colony's agricultural sector. As reported in the *Register*, by 1845 South Australian farmers were not only growing enough wheat to supply the colony's bread, but there was a surplus for sale overseas. Although this excess wheat accounted for only about 10 per cent of the total value of exports, virtually the whole wool clip was sold abroad, making up a further 50 per cent. And copper had its first impact that year, accounting for just under 17 per cent of the overall value of goods traded overseas. Its share would jump dramatically in 1846, when copper exports more than doubled and made up over half of external trade, easily outstripping wheat and wool combined, even though the wool clip had increased significantly.[26] In mid 1845, another copper lode was discovered at Burra, 60 miles (96 kilometres) north of Kapunda and 100 miles (160 kilometres) from Adelaide, and dubbed the Monster Mine.[27] On 2 July 1845, the *Register* reported that the

> *posses of gentlemen mining speculators [who visited the mine to inspect the newly discovered copper fields are] satisfied that there is sufficient mineral wealth on the spot to justify much more than all the proposed outlay ... and the returns are stated as likely to be immense and far exceeding any that are likely to arise from the mines at present in operation.*

And a few weeks later the *Register* enthused: 'Never since the days of the Special Survey batches has there been so much excitement as upon the subject of the Monster Mine.'[28]

Governor Grey allowed the survey to be divided into two sections: one for the 'nobs', mainly wealthy graziers and the proprietors of Kapunda, who selected the southern section and floated the Princess Royal Mining Company with 400 shares at £50 each; and the other for the 'snobs', mainly Adelaide 'shop-keeping nobodies', who got the northern half, which proved a bonanza. The 'snobs' floated the SA Mining Association with shares issued 'deliberately democratically' at £5 each.[29]

In spite of the colony's improving economic outlook, after less than three years ownership of the *Register*, James Allen also found himself in financial difficulties and sold the paper to John Stephens, the founder and proprietor of the *Observer*. By June 1845, with this change of ownership, William Thomas had rejoined the staff of the *Register* and so at least one member of the Thomas family was to continue to make a contribution to the paper.[30] Stephens moved the *Register* from the corner of Rundle Street across the road to his more spacious printing offices on the south side of Hindley Street, almost to the corner of King William Street.[31]

With a more buoyant economy, Robert also was finally able to take up employment again. His appointment as inspector of weights and measures was gazetted on the 1st October 1845[32], but, in order to start work, he had to lodge a bond of £100 with the Treasury to ensure the 'punctual performance of [his] duties and for the safety of stamps and Imperial weights and measures' – the official standards against which he checked and certified the weights and measures being used by shopkeepers. In addition to his annual salary of £60, he was to be paid all the fees and a moiety of the fines imposed by the act. Robert established his first office in the old *Register* printing office on acre 56 until the government was able to provide him with suitable accommodation.[33] The income from Robert's employment provided some relief to Mary's stringent budget and she could now look forward to the occasional small luxury and a few special treats for family birthdays and other celebrations.

Mary maintained the English tradition of roast beef and plum pudding on Christmas Day 1845 and William James, the friend and colleague of Robert George, who was absent surveying in the hills, joined the family for dinner. During the afternoon, he drove Mary and the girls to the Hawkins' hotel in the 'Stringy Bark Forest' at Crafers. The assent was very steep and both Marys and Helen walked to ease the uphill climb for the horses. To Mary Jnr's eye 'the mountain scenery was truly splendid and sublime'[34] and Mrs Hawkins invited her to stay the week, during which Mary Jnr recorded her delight in her surroundings:

> *I have seen hills, valleys and gullies till I have been bewildered by fine scenery though so much delighted that when on a rambling*

excursion I am obliged to pause at every turn in the road to admire it. Last Sunday I walked out on a bridle path cut into the slope of a hill, with a mountain rising boldly on one side, altogether forming a far more romantic view than I can pretend to describe.[35]

A party of overlanders with their cattle came through from Port Phillip Bay. Although one of them had not combed his hair for three months, Mary Jnr generously allowed him to borrow her comb! Robert was also among the visitors to the hotel during her stay – he called in on his way to Balhannah, presumably as part of his weights and measures work. Another visitor, a colleague of Robert George, left a few things for him in the hope that a passing dray might take them onto him at Mt Barker[36] (copper was reported to have been found there 'in a hundred places'[37], and Robert George was working on a special survey for the South Australian Company).

Mary Jnr returned to Adelaide by wagon, drawn by a team of six bullocks driven by a man and a boy. It had no seats, but fortunately Mrs Hawkins was able to lend her one. It took them nearly five hours to negotiate the steep descent to the plains and Mary Jnr passed the time in 'the delightful remembrance of the sublime and beautiful' vistas she had experienced during her stay.[38]

On New Year's Day 1846, Helen and Mary Jnr attended the traditional race meeting for the first time. They were taken to the track by John and Ann Holmes and their daughter, Lucy, in the Holmes's cart. The races were enjoyable, 'but the dust was so awful . . . [our] skin was covered almost as if we had worn masks'. Afterward, at the Wrights, they dined on roast beef and plum pudding, before going home to change and return for the evening entertainment. Following tea, there was dancing and singing, with most of the music provided by Charles and his brothers. It was 2 am before they were escorted home by Tom Wright. Charles, who became unwell during the evening, was too sick to accompany them.[39] Mary Jnr had 'scarcely felt any fatigue'[40], but Charles remained ill and, with either Frances or Helen or Mary, she called at the Wrights almost daily to enquire after his health.[41] He was suffering from a severe eye infection but was well again within a week.

As Mary Jnr's journal noted, Sturt's northern expedition, which had left Adelaide in August 1844, was long overdue and virtually given up for lost when news of it reached Adelaide on 14 January 1846. The expedition had returned to the Darling River with the loss of only one life, and was expected at Moorundee, on the Murray, within a day or two. '[They] had not crossed the continent as they had hoped to do, having met with a desert which, with its sandy ridges, stones and want of water, seemed altogether appalling.'[42] It was about a week later that Sturt – still suffering acutely from scurvy – arrived in Adelaide ahead of the rest of his party, to an emotional reunion with his family and very relieved colonists. Robert Black, one of the Thomas's former employees, who had joined the relief supply team for the explorers, called to see Mary at Rhantregwnwyn at the beginning of February.[43] He brought her 'several bulbs of a beautiful white lily that he had found growing wild on some sand hills', which had flowers the size of a teacup, and Mary sent one as a gift to Mrs Wright. Some weeks later, Robert, with Captain John Holmes, attended the banquet held to honour Sturt and his men.[44]

During mid February, Robert George came home from the mine site at Mt Barker where he had been surveying. Within a matter of days, he had decided to sail for England with his business partner, William James, to take advantage of the demand for surveyors there due to the railway boom.[45] The two men had worked in association since leaving George Kingston's employment some 12 or so months earlier. They booked their passages on the *Cleveland*, which was listed to leave from Port Adelaide within the next six weeks. Robert George, it seems in order to have an image of his mother as a reminder of home, accompanied Mary to Mr Goodman's studio in Rundle Street 'to have her portrait taken in daguerreotype'[46] – an early form of photography. Also intending to sail on the *Cleveland* were friends of the Skippers,

George Wilkinson with his wife and children, who had left their property, Bullaparinga, near Rapid Creek, and were in Adelaide preparing for the voyage.[47]

With the Wilkinsons and the Skippers, Mary Jnr and Helen visited the native wurlies on the banks of the Torrens in March 1846. A corroboree was to be held there and they had received an invitation to attend it from Aborigines they had known for some time. According to Mary Jnr's journal, the guests admired the splendour and primal nature of the setting. Huge trees partially lit by a circle of fires, formed the backdrop.

> The whole scene was well acted and . . . they kept such true time with foot and voice . . . [that] although I have often heard the corroboree I never discovered anything in the shape of a song so nearly like real music as that we were favoured with.[48]

George Wilkinson's *South Australia*, possibly written, at least in part, on his voyage back to England during 1846, was published in London in 1848. It was a comprehensive description of the colony's development to 1846. Robert George, a fellow passenger on the voyage with Wilkinson, was among several contributors to the book who offered schemes aimed at providing practical solutions to the difficulties faced by the Aborigines. Robert George deplored the practice of pursuing the goal of literacy when it was motivated solely by the aim of converting the Indigenous population to Christianity.

> Their education has begun at the wrong end . . . The first thing that should be taught to an Aboriginal tribe . . . is the mechanical arts and processes, the agricultural methods of their visitors . . . An education which would fit them, in the great demand for labour in a new country, to take their places beside the labourers and mechanics of the colonists, would be to them as also to their country, the greatest of blessings, and Christianity and education . . . would follow in due course . . . the missionary method of instruction so generally followed is, we think, of the worst

description . . . [and seems] systematically directed to the purpose of completely isolating the natives.[49]

Wilkinson also included in his book considerable information about Aboriginal culture, which he had observed in his association with them during his years at Rapid Creek. John Skipper illustrated the margins of his personal copy of Wilkinson's *South Australia* with painstakingly detailed miniature watercolours – many of the images portray Aborigines in contemporary settings and illustrate their customs and culture.[50]

Wilkinson praised the Aboriginal shepherds, commenting on their loyalty and honesty when they were well paid with food.[51] But he noted with sadness

> a great diminution in the number of natives, and [I] should say they were less than one third than when I first saw them about seven years before. In one part a tribe of 30 or 40 was reduced to 12 or 15, and these had joined a neighbouring tribe, so that as a distinct tribe, they were lost.[52]

There is little doubt that this level of decline was widespread, and that the Aborigines were powerless to resist their dispossession.

Robert George had left the colony in April, but Mary was unable to manage a dinner party for him and he was farewelled by his friends at the Club House, one of Adelaide's leading hotels. However, by 6 July, with some easing in her budget gained through Robert's employment, Mary was able to put on an impromptu party at Rhantregwnwyn for Helen's 21st birthday. It had been extremely wet and the streets were very muddy; nevertheless, Mary Jnr called upon Mrs Wright to invite her for the evening. She demurred, but Captain Holmes arrived just at the right time in his cart, and so she was persuaded. Captain Holmes also acted as 'coachman' for Mary Jnr to call upon other friends. John Primrose, with his wife's sister, Agnes Reid and a Mr Gibbons and a Mrs Wotherspoon also made up the party.

Elizabeth Primrose (nee Reid) had remained at home with her new baby. After tea, they spent a very pleasant evening 'in conversation, pictorial books, [and] the amusement of cake, wine and sandwiches'.[53]

Although Mary Jnr's health had seemed to stabilise for a time during the early months of 1846, she had a recurrence of her throat problems. The treatment was again almost daily cauterisation with caustic for a fortnight or so while the infection was most acute. Charles Wright also made incisions to the inside of her throat, virtually on a weekly basis until mid June, when he considered it better. Her trials, however, were not yet over.[54] A few weeks later she became acutely ill late one evening, and Dr Wright attended her and ordered medicine which was brought by Charles sometime after midnight. A severe liver complaint was diagnosed and she remained unwell until the end of August; but, much to her satisfaction, in early September she was able to announce that she 'was in very tolerable health'.[55]

Toward the end of July, Mary Jnr had recorded in her journal details of a public meeting held at the courthouse – the former Queen's Theatre – to discuss state aid for religion. It had become a burning issue in the colony during June 1846, when Governor Robe, a high churchman, introduced the subject into the Legislative Council.[56] Concerned that the churches, particularly the Anglicans, were unable to keep pace with the expanding rural populations, he proposed to apportion government aid among all the Christian sects for church building and religious education – and opened up a hornet's nest. Most Dissenters and some Anglicans believed it would inevitably favour the larger churches, particularly the Anglicans. They dreaded the linking of state and religion and saw it as preparing the way for an established church. Many considered Robe's proposal an attack upon one of the colony's founding tenets: freedom of religious worship and freedom from state intervention in religion. But Robe's determination to go ahead with funding to the churches was undeterred and state aid was proclaimed in September.

On 14 September 1846, Mary Jnr made the last entry in her journal. She described her sadness that the Wrights were moving from East Terrace and that she had paid her last visit there, 'for in that house I have passed many happy hours. It has been like a second home to me'.[57] The blossoming romance between Mary Jnr and Charles did not mature; perhaps it gradually faded as Charles spent more time with his brothers at Dry Creek. The whole Thomas family would have been saddened by the loss of their companionship with Charles Wright and his brothers.

The source for much of the information about her own health as well as that of Frances was recorded in Mary Jnr's journal, and the only text that has survived ceases in September 1846. Given the later health problems they both faced, it is unlikely that either of them enjoyed a return to complete good health over the intervening years.

By the year's end, emigration had not only recommenced but was approaching the levels achieved during the colony's first years. South Australia's population had reached almost 26,000 – boosted during the year by over 5,500 new arrivals, the largest increase through emigration since 1839 – and the colony's recovery was well under way.[58]

Part 4

Chapter 13
Endurance

Responding to pressure from Adelaide's citizens, who, after the very wet winter of 1846, were concerned about the state of their streets, the Legislative Council took over the administration of Adelaide's affairs[1] and the defunct City Corporation's debts. Included among them was an outstanding account owed to the former R. Thomas and Co., and with these funds Robert and Stevenson were able to meet some of their ex-employees' unpaid wages.[2] In taking up Adelaide's administration, the council was insistent that the owners and occupiers of land should contribute to the maintenance of roads and footpaths and levied a rate on all houses and properties. Rate assessors and collectors were appointed and along with other Adelaide property owners Mary paid rates in 1847 on an assessment taken the previous year.

Details of Mary's acre 56 on Hindley Street appear in the rate assessments for 1847 and continue in succeeding years, forming an unbroken record of her ownership of this land and the structures on it throughout her lifetime.[3] Between 1846 and 1850 there was very little change to the buildings on the acre. They included the long building at the bottom of the acre, housing the John o' Groats Inn, and what had been the old printery of the *Register* – by this time let as government offices for Robert's weights and measures work. Rhantregwnwyn was still there, of course, and the two-storey stone house. Rents from the stone house (now let as a boarding house), the old printery and the John o' Groats brought in about £3 per week.

Mary and Robert's future looked more secure as their income increased due to Robert's employment and then through the lease of the stone house as a boarding house. Despite this improvement in their circumstances, the future they had envisioned, when they abandoned their London home and made the long and dangerous journey to the new province of South Australia, was now completely beyond their reach. Their present situation fell far short of the comfortable existence that had seemed feasible, and almost within their grasp, during their first arduous years in the colony.

By now Mary was 59 and Robert 64 and with their capital exhausted they had no capacity to recover their earlier prosperity, unlike many younger colonists who, with time on their side, would rebuild their fortunes. Mary's wish to return to England with enough capital to ensure a congenial retirement was doomed. And Robert George's decision to leave the colony because he saw greater opportunities in England turned the knife in the psychological wounds which both Mary and Robert had suffered; wounds caused not only by the shattering of their dreams and hopes for themselves, but by their loss of optimism for their family's future wellbeing. Contrary to Mary's earlier hopes for Frances, colonial life had not improved her health, and child-bearing seemed to exacerbate her condition. Mary Jnr was physically very slight, perhaps as a legacy of her scarlet fever just before their departure from London, and with her frequent illnesses she required almost constant medical attention.

Mary, however, had a strong Christian faith and no ambition for colonial grandeur; as far as colonial life went, Rhantregwnwyn suited her well. Given that there was no prospect of fulfilling her dream to return to England, wealth and the associated social-standing meant little to her. She had a wry sense of humour and a well-developed sense of the ridiculous[4], which no doubt eased the rub of her reduced circumstances. Prolonged self-pity was not Mary's style – she could not afford its self-indulgence – her family had great need of not only her practical help but her emotional support.

For Robert the transition from business proprietor to unemployment must have been extremely difficult. It is now almost impossible to know what the long-term psychological consequences of the failure of R. Thomas and Co. were for him, but it is inconceivable that he was not deeply affected. Given his age and lack of capital, re-establishment of a printing business, or even a business as a stationer, was out of the question.

In the known and highly predictable business milieu of Fleet Street, Robert had achieved a modest prosperity. Perhaps it was his success as a law stationer in this well-defined sphere – with a clientele whose requirements were relatively easy to anticipate – that deluded him into believing he could succeed equally well in the unknown and totally unpredictable environment of a new and untried colony.

During the colony's first years it seemed as if he could achieve a similar, if not greater, success and in fact he very nearly did. But his inability or incapacity to supervise James Coltman in the ill-fated store left him with a significant debt totalling £1500 (which today would translate into approximately $300,000). His failure to ensure that he had, in writing, a long-term appointment as government printer and his wasted journey to London to seek redress also cost him dearly. He had too many irons in the fire to pay sufficient attention to any one of them; his responses to problems were reactive rather than proactive and his management was dictated by crises. In the unknown and unfamiliar circumstances of the new colony Robert, was out of his depth.

Many younger colonists, however, were beginning to benefit from South Australia's slow recovery, now well underway, with the Burra mine paying dividends of 400 per cent. Between June and December 1847 its dividends totalled £49,280 on the original subscribed capital of £12,320, representing a very considerable injection of much-needed capital into the colony and its economy.[5] It boosted Adelaide businesses, particularly those servicing the mines and mining communities. Primary industry also benefited from accessible capital for investment and growth. But these developments had a downside; creating labour shortages and wage and price increases. After much public pressure, assisted emigration resumed in 1846 with a trickle of arrivals. In July 1847 it was given significant impetus when '£160,000 was appropriated ... and arrangements made for the dispatch from England of one vessel per month'. Just over 3000 assisted emigrants reached the colony during the year.[6]

At the beginning of 1848 Robert applied, unsuccessfully, for the newly created government post of clerk of market – he had been hoping to augment his weights and measures work, which he considered a part-time job.[7] Later it seemed that the position of supervisor of public pounds might be offered to him but nothing came of it.[8] Nevertheless he worked assiduously in his weights and measures job, petitioning the government for a horse and cart in order to carry his standards with him. This would allow him to certify weights and measures on the spot, rather than visit premises simply to establish whether they were being used and then having to ask the storekeeper or publican to bring them to his office for certification and stamping.[9] But his pleas for transport in the cause of greater efficiency fell on deaf ears. Again in the interest of efficiency, he proposed that all makers or vendors of weights or measures should be compelled to have their products certified by him before they were sold[10], but, as with his earlier suggestion, he was unable to gain official support.

There was some better fortune for the Thomases, however, with an increase of £1 per week in Mary's income through the rental of 'additional stabling and dwelling' on acre 56.[11] It was probably for renovated yards and outbuildings associated with the John o' Groats Inn. Also, some of Robert's modest investments in allotments, particularly in newly forming villages – just beyond Adelaide at Norwood and Kensington – appreciated very rapidly. Land he bought in 1848 at Norwood for £41 he sold a year later for

£150.[12] In this instance, though, it seems to have been paid to a creditor, perhaps for the horse and cart he ultimately bought for his work.

During February 1849 the governor, Sir Henry Young, was petitioned to transfer the management of Adelaide's affairs from the Legislative Council to a new city corporation. A five-member City Commission, nominated by the governor, was appointed to act in the interim until legislation to establish a new corporation could be drawn up. The commissioners had the authority to levy rates, keep bridges and streets in order, and to construct sewers and waterworks. Later, the draft act also made provision for central and local road boards.[13]

On New Year's Day 1850, the *Register*, under the proprietorship of John Stephens, changed its format from a weekly to a daily; a further indication of the colony's increasing affluence.[14]

At about the same time, another sign of an improving economy was the licensing of the stone house, on acre 56 – formerly a boarding house – to become the Clarendon Hotel, which brought an increase in rent of 15 shillings per week to Mary.[15] By the beginning of 1850 the John o' Groats Inn and the old printery/office (the long building) had disappeared from the rate assessments and were replaced by six small brick cottages. Two were three-roomed dwellings but the other four were even smaller structures, of only two rooms. Based upon rate assessments, by 1852 Mary's income from the cottages was about £2 per week. Provided they were all tenanted, the income from them was about 7 shillings a week more than the rent had been from the now demolished John o' Groats Inn and the old offices next to it. Including rent from the Clarendon Hotel plus stabling, Mary's income was now about £4 and 7 shillings a week.

The old pioneering pisé structures – such as the long building – were gradually being pulled down throughout Adelaide, and replaced with more substantial buildings of brick, stone and timber. With their new-found wealth from the copper mines people were adding verandahs and balconies and other elaborations to the four-square plainness that had characterised even the substantially built homes of the first years. But Mary's cottages for workingmen and their families were simple structures. They were probably in a couple of terraces; one at the bottom of acre 56 in place of the long building, with the other located along part of the western perimeter of the acre and facing onto a private street.[16]

The new cottages were put up toward the end of 1849 – how and where Mary found the money for them is difficult to establish. There is no evidence of money having been borrowed, no mortgage documents have survived, but the lack of documentation is not conclusive as land transactions did not have to be lodged with the Registry Office until 1858. However, between 1846 and 1850 Mary had gained some improvement in her income, and as she had been managing on a stringent budget earlier she might have continued to do so for a time, putting the increases aside to finance the cottages. Alternatively, or perhaps as well, the profits from some of Robert's land transactions may have provided the funds. By whatever means the money was found, with rent from the cottages Mary was able to add to her family's income in the short term. It gave some small respite and eased the pressures of balancing the family budget.

While the passage by the British Parliament of the *Act for the Better Government of Australian Colonies* 1842 had promised an increased degree of representative government, there were long delays. Eventually, in September 1849, the draft of a bill, which applied to all Australian colonies, reached Adelaide. The bill's basic uniformity for all Australian colonies stimulated discussion about the possibility of an eventual Australian federation.[17]

It was not until January 1851 that news reached the colony that the *Australian Colonial Government Act* 1850 had received royal assent. South Australia was granted a Legislative Council of 24 members. Eight were to be nominated by the governor, with 16 elected in an open forum by adult males who possessed 'a small property or house qualification'. Candidates for election were to own freehold property to an annual value of £200 or a total value of £2000.[18] F.S. Dutton, for East Adelaide, was the first candidate to offer himself; and George Fife Angas, a director of the South Australian Company and a recent arrival in the colony, was persuaded to stand unopposed for the district of Barossa.[19] The new Legislative Council was inaugurated toward the end of August and its first major debate sought the abolition of state aid for religion. Although the resolution opposing it was only narrowly carried by a majority of three, the canker of state aid became a thing of the past. By year's end the council was seeking a design for a House of Assembly and had established a competition – in two separate divisions with prize money of £50 in each – that sought, as well as a building to accommodate the new council, the best design for a bridge over the River Torrens.[20] William Bennett Hayes, later to be appointed colonial architect, won the prize for the design of the House of Assembly.[21]

During August, rumours that gold had been found in Victoria began to reach Adelaide and a credible report of the discovery of gold at Ballarat was circulating by the beginning of September. At the end of October, when it was realised that the diggings could be reached overland, the exodus from South Australia, initially a trickle, increased dramatically to a torrent.[22] As a result, by the beginning of 1852 the government was experiencing financial difficulties. John Skipper was retrenched from his position of assistant clerk to the Adelaide Local Court and almost immediately applied for the post of resident commissioner on the goldfields at Mount Alexander.[23] He was unsuccessful but, undeterred, he joined the exodus anyway. He was at the diggings, at least, during the early part of 1852 – a series of signed and dated pen and ink drawings and watercolours of goldfield scenes place him at Forest Creek.[24] Whether he was there as a prospector or in an official capacity, due to a change of heart by the South Australian colonial secretary regarding his application for employment, is unknown; but the South Australian resident commissioner at the goldfields had a £3000 budget for staff, which may have included John Skipper.[25]

William Thomas was also at the diggings during these

months[26] and the brothers-in-law had probably combined forces to get to there. The quickest and least arduous route before mid 1852 was by ship to Melbourne and then by road to Ballarat. The passage cost £5 for a cabin or £2 and 10 shillings steerage[27]; the latter, at least, was well within the means of both men. Many, who went by boat, including the Thomas's friend Hiram Mildred, took horses and carts with them to carry their equipment the 75 miles (120 kilometres) from Melbourne to the 'fields. Just getting there was high adventure as Hiram recorded in his diary. After having been becalmed in St Vincent's Gulf it took he and his friends – neither John nor William was among them – 11 days just to get to an anchorage at Hobson's Bay (today's Williamstown on the outskirts of Melbourne). They docked amid 58 other vessels of all nations and all tonnages, 'most of which had been deserted by the crews for the goldfields in some instances Captain and all'. They were given only two hours to unload their luggage plus their horses and a cart into a steamer to be taken ashore.[28] The road to the diggings was crowded with 'hundreds of foot passengers . . . some dragging carts, some pushing wheelbarrows, some limping . . . but generally . . . with joyful countenances anticipating the successful realisation of fortunes in the shape of camp ovens full of gold'.[29]

At Forest Creek Hiram and his companions were 'gratified with the sight of acres of ground perforated all over, thousands of men popping up and down and going to and fro, some carrying bags, some wheeling barrows, some driving carts, both horse and bullock, loaded with the soil going to the creek to tin dish or ladle it'. There were 'tents of all sorts, sizes and shapes in every direction for two or three miles down Forest Creek'.[30] John Skipper's watercolours of Forest Creek show miners at work around a shaft and others panning for gold. The scenes in the rest of his goldfield paintings are not identified but one is of a miner, perhaps William, standing beside his bush camp.[31]

The financial difficulties created in South Australia by the exodus to the 'fields were deepening into a crisis. The colony was losing not only men but money – swift action was required. Before the end of January the *Bullion Act* 1852 was passed, which allowed the gold of individual diggers to be assayed in South Australia, stamped with its value, and used as legal tender.[32] If the gold won by South Australian miners could be brought back progressively during their time at the diggings, a way had been found to support the wives and children left at home and also Adelaide's businesses, including those like Mary's which were reliant upon income from leased housing.

By early February the first gold escort, commanded by the police commissioner, Alexander Tolmer, left Adelaide to bring back the diggers' gold, and to establish a direct overland route to Mt Alexander. The overland route, it was considered, would encourage the returning men to come directly home with their gold, rather than dissipate it in Melbourne waiting for an Adelaide-bound vessel. Tolmer was amazed and delighted at the miners' response to his offer to take their 'winnings' home to support their families. Despite concerns about possible attacks by bushrangers, he had a trouble-free return trip. As the escort made its way through the Adelaide Hills, and long before they had reached Crafers, they were cheered on by people who had come from town to welcome them.

> On the following morning March 20th ... an eager throng, mostly of women and children ... pressed forward, with faces beaming with delight, to receive their gold, packed in chamois bags containing from half an ounce and upwards.[33]

In the first escort, gold worth almost £18,500 was returned to the colony.[34]

Some Adelaide merchants began to do very well by supplying the goldfields. Through the pioneering use of paddle-steamers on the River Murray and its tributaries, they travelled almost to the heart of the diggings more cheaply and more quickly than their Melbourne counterparts.[35] The downside of these ventures was the scarcity of food in Adelaide and the consequent escalation in its cost. Meat rose from a penny a pound to 18 pence, and flour and potatoes trebled in price.³⁶ During this testing time, Mary, along with many others, had difficulty balancing the family budget. When the 1852 rate assessment was taken at the height of the exodus, three of her cottages were untenanted. It was the same everywhere. One in five of Adelaide's dwellings was unoccupied.³⁷

By this time, however, there were another three cottages on the acre and a carpenter's shop. They belonged to Helen, now aged 27. Records from the General Registry Office show that Robert sold 45 acres (18 hectares) – part of a country section – for £180 in December 1851 on Helen's behalf.³⁸ It may have been this money, with some further financing from either Mary or Robert, which enabled Helen to put up the additional buildings. Other than the rate assessment records, and Mary's letters to Helen a few years later, no documentation of her ownership survives. Perhaps it was a private family agreement and never formalised. Helen's net income from rent for these buildings, a little over 18 shillings a week, provided her with a degree of financial independence.³⁹ According to rate assessments Helen's cottages fronted onto Hindley Street, and were possibly to the west of the Clarendon Hotel.

A 'William Thomas' sent three pounds two-and-a-half ounces (troy weight) of gold (1.2 kilograms) back to Adelaide with the first gold escort.⁴⁰ For government assaying it was valued at £3 and 11 shillings an ounce⁴¹, and so these winnings were in the order of £137, indicative of a good claim. Whether the William Thomas recorded on the surviving gold receipt is the son of Mary and Robert is uncertain, but likely. The gold escorts continued until the end of 1853, but only the documents of the first and third escorts have survived. Although no William Thomas is recorded for the third, William was at the goldfields for at least several months during 1852.⁴² Not all gold came home with the escort, some was carried back by the diggers themselves. Over the almost two years of the escorts' operation, it brought nearly £2,000,000 into the colony.⁴³

Despite South Australia's difficulties, following the passage of the *Municipal Corporation Act* 1849, a new Adelaide City Corporation was eventually established with the election of four aldermen and 12 councillors from four wards, which had been named after the first four governors (Hindmarsh, Gawler, Grey and Robe). They held their inaugural meeting on 1 June 1852 and elected J.H. Fisher as mayor.[44] Electors of this new corporation comprised 'every male householder who had registered, who had property in the City and who lived in it or within seven miles of it'.[45] Although both Mary and Helen were ratepayers and property owners, as women, they were denied the vote.

The Adelaide City Corporation confronted financial problems almost immediately. The government, also facing budgetary pressures, passed part of the responsibility for the office of inspector of weights and measures, including part-payment of the salary, to the newly elected body. Unable to meet this additional cost, the corporation wrote to Robert dispensing with his services for the current year. Robert responded that he had 'prepared [himself] with a vehicle . . . at considerable expense to perform [his] duties in the country'. His letter continued:

> *I by no means desire to press my undoubted claims to consideration at such a period of the colony's distress. And therefore respectfully tender my gratuitous services for executing the duties of the office . . . If the office is abolished the poorer classes will become a prey to the unprincipled small dealer . . . justice is expected by the community.*[46]

While accepting his gratuitous services for 12 months, the corporation had no compunction in appointing a salaried officer in Robert's place once full control of the position had passed to them, and their finances had improved. Robert argued that he should be allowed to continue his work – his role was to serve the whole of the colony, country as well as city. His protestations were to no avail, and his role as inspector of weights and measures came to an end in March 1853.[47] It was a bitter blow. Robert was only a few months short of his 70th birthday and this was in effect an enforced retirement. For Mary, Robert's retrenchment and the associated loss of income was compounded by her problems in keeping her cottages occupied by tenants who paid their rent regularly.

Robert was spending most of his week at Glen Osmond by 1856, returning home only at weekends, and he had probably been doing so for some years. Following the termination of his weights and measures position, he may have obtained employment there with his old associate Osmond Gilles (the first colonial treasurer) who had various business interests. Robert clearly had some income, given his capacity to buy Burra mining shares, and Mary's resentment – expressed later in letters to Helen – that he refused to help her financially. Gilles' country section was in the foothills at Glen Osmond, about 3 miles north-east of Adelaide. Silver had been mined there during the early 1840s, but by this time the mines were no longer operating (although an attempt to reopen them was made toward the end of the 1850s). Robert may have been employed as a caretaker during the mine's closure.

By February 1853 William had returned from the goldfields to his employment at the *Register*.[48] And by May he had paid £500 (an estimated $80,000 today[49]) – perhaps helped by his winnings from the goldfields – to join a syndicate[50] and so regain part ownership of the *Register* and the *Observer*. The total amount the nine or so partners/shareholders in the syndicate paid for the papers was £11,000.[51] They held weekly meetings and a prominent syndicate member, Anthony Forster, took over the role of manager and editor[52], while William, who had been on the staff since June 1845, remained closely associated with the printing presses and the mechanical production of the papers. Within a few months of these major changes the *Register* had moved from its offices in Hindley Street, near the corner of King William Street to larger premises in Grenfell Street.[53]

William continued to live on his country section, on the Main North Road, and maintained his daily ride into the *Register* offices. By this time his family had increased to three girls and two boys, although he and his wife had suffered the grief of the death of their eldest son, aged 12 months, in 1850.⁵⁴

The return of the *Register* to the family, at least in part, gave both Mary and Robert considerable satisfaction and consolation. It made some sense of their emigration and their life in South Australia, as well as raising their level of optimism for the future. It came at a time when Robert's pleas for reappointment to his position of inspector of weights and measures had been rejected; and Frances's health was of increasing concern to Mary. William's success provided the good news that was sorely needed.

With the loss of his government appointment, Robert's occasional purchases and later profitable sales of parcels of land, mainly building allotments in the newly developing villages of Norwood and Kensington and later at Glenelg, came to an end. But he retained most of the Kensington land;⁵⁵ nine allotments in all, and built dwellings for rental on several of them.

How long John Skipper spent on the goldfields after April 1852 is unclear, but in August 1853 he was appointed clerk of the Port Adelaide Local Court, a position he held until his retirement almost three decades later.⁵⁶ Although John had a long ride to reach his employment, the Skippers remained on Robert George's country section at Islington where they had been living for some years. By this time John and Frances's family had increased with – in addition to their three older girls – Spencer's birth in 1847 and Isabel's two years later.

As is apparent in her later correspondence with Helen, Mary was very resentful that John Skipper failed to give Frances the care and consideration that, she believed, Frances's poor health demanded.⁵⁷ Despite this the Thomases had some reason to be grateful to him. When John returned from the goldfields he introduced them to Alfred Mantegani, a Swiss/Italian musician, also recently arrived in Adelaide from the diggings. Alfred became a frequent visitor at Rhantregwnwyn. He was an accomplished pianist, although, as Desmond O'Connor commented in his monograph on Alfred, 'not of the calibre of Carl Linger', his contemporary, who later composed the music for the 'Song of Australia'. Alfred was engaged in Adelaide for concerts, soirees, the 'free and easies' or sing-songs, and other entertainment, during the latter half of 1853.[58] Even though he was born in England at Wisbech, Cambridgeshire, in 1829 to Swiss/Italian parents, Alfred identified himself as Italian. His father, a jeweller, had opened a shop in Wisbech, but the family retained their links with Italy and returned each year to tend their vineyards. Although his siblings acquired positions of substance in Italy, Alfred seems to have rejected his father's guidance and came to Australia for adventure. He made contact with his family during 1854, after a silence of five years, only when he had gained recognition in Adelaide as a pianist, and had become more settled and financially secure.[59]

Alfred was warmly welcomed into the Thomas home. His attainments as a pianist and as a skilful painter matched the Thomas's interests in music and the arts. Like John Skipper, his maternal uncle was a renowned artist and a painter of frescos. Alfred was very attracted to Helen and was intent upon courting her. It was also a happy time for Mary, with some lightness and gaiety returning to her life.

Early in 1854 the Skippers shifted to Queenstown, a satellite village of Port Adelaide, to be nearer John's work. But the move did nothing to improve Frances's health. Mary considered the Skippers' new home to be a 'miserable place', not what Frances was accustomed to, and believed that on occasion John 'neglected' her.[60] Since the birth of the Skippers' first child, Mary together with Helen and Mary Jnr – when her health allowed – had been the support and mainstay of Frances in the care of her children. While the Skippers were living at Islington it was possible to walk there and Mary, with one or other of the girls, as Mary Jnr's journal records, frequently made the two-hour trip along the Main North Road to visit Frances and the children.[61]

Frances also depended upon them to shop and run errands in Adelaide for her. Frances's brief pencilled notes to Helen, or Nelly as she was affectionately called, asked for help with day-to-day household matters:

> I have sent the cheese as I promised do not forget to send the [?] other things and in addition my butter dish, which you can pack in the round basket with some hay, the bottle cleaner and Spencer's best frock and jacket as he has a dreadful finger and I must send [?] L... with him to Dr Davidson and I do not like him to go shabby. With many happy returns of the day... I am with love, in which John joins me,
> Your affectionate sister, Frances.
> P.S. How do you like your gage chamois? Is it not pretty?... Don't forget the wine. Because they are going to drink your health.
> [undated, but Helen's date of birth was 6 July]

Another undated note indicates how important Helen's practical support was to Frances:

> Dear Nelly,
> If you can possibly get out today will you call at Brays and change Spencer's shoes they are the right length but too narrow in the instep. Say they are for me as I promised to send them in today. Fanny's cloak fits beautifully and she is quite pleased and sends her love to Aunt Helen... If Mrs Groser has sent my jacket will you send it with Georgy's spelling book at the same time. John will give you Mrs Andrew's agreement... This morning I intended to go into town but I hope to during the week about my dress.
> With kind love to all...
> [undated – however the reference to Mrs Andrews, one of Helen's tenants, dates it c. 1854][62]

Helen also received Frances's confidences:

> I am going up to the Thomas's[63] on Saturday. I don't want to leave home... John will be so lonely when I am away besides I am afraid he does not think I am as ill as I feel... Morton [presumably Frances's doctor] says I must go so I will but I know it will do me

no good. I would have gone [?] tonight but feel too weak to walk and I don't like the expense for the horse . . . I shall not be in Town if I go to Salisbury so any commissions I may have I shall leave to you and Hansell [a family friend] to execute making Mary my banker . . . I don't know how I have now [?] managed to make this a long letter for I am so low spirited but it is a relief.[64]

Frances was right. Sojourns in the country with fresh country food and air, the only treatment available then for tuberculosis, did her little good despite her doctor's and her family's best intentions. Her consumption was far too advanced. Her family, however, was desperate for Frances to have breaks away from that 'miserable house at Queenstown'.

Frances's c. 1834 portrait of Mary, painted when Frances was about 14, demonstrates a considerable talent, which she developed further over the years. As mentioned in letters from the Skipper family in Norfolk, they were delighted to receive her portraits of her children and her 'delicate drawings of plants'.[65] And in 1844 Mary Jnr recorded that Frances was 'taking' her portrait in chalk for her 21st birthday, as well as that of Helen.[66] Two of Frances's works were shown in the 1847 exhibition of colonial artists held in Adelaide – a study of a Spanish boy and a sketch of the interior of a hut. Her *From Mt Lofty* c. 1840 – a watercolour sketch of a man leading a horse – is held by the Art Gallery of South Australia.[67] The 'commissions' Frances referred to in her letter to Helen were probably miniature portraits which she painted for remuneration in a semi-professional capacity.

By July 1854 Frances was being cared for by Mary at Rhantregwnwyn. Two of the younger Skipper children were also there, while 14-year-old Georgy, the Skipper's eldest daughter, with visits from Helen, was helping to look after the Queenstown home and her two other siblings. She wrote touchingly to her dear Mamma, sending her love also to Grandpa, Grandma, Aunt Helen and Aunt Mary:

I am sorry Aunt Helen could not stay. I hope you are soon better and will be able to come out. I could not find any more eggs so Mr [?] H. said he would buy some . . . [?] We are all well. Spencer has been a very good boy [?] and has said his lessons well. He was rather tiresome this morning. Aunt Helen gave us some money and so did Mrs [?] H. The goose has not laid yet the fowls do not lay much . . . Kiss baby and Nelly for me.[68]

Mary had increasing involvement with the care of the Skipper children, particularly the two youngest, Spencer and Isabel.

It was perhaps some solace to her that William was doing well. In November he introduced the colony's first steam-operated printing press for the production of both the *Register* and the *Observer*. It was set up in the basement of new premises in Grenfell Street.[69]

Alfred Mantegani remained in Adelaide and continued to visit Rhantregwnwyn and to court Helen. Throughout 1854 Alfred's name appeared regularly in advertisements in the *Register* for a variety of musical events at the long room of the Blenheim Hotel, the Rose Inn and the Royal Victoria Theatre on North Terrace. His forte was the popular songs and choruses of the day, glees and catches.[70] He also performed in a series of promenade concerts, and frequently at the Adelaide Harmonics Club and the Pantheon; for the latter he composed the *Pantheon Waltz*. And he expressed his affection for Helen by dedicating the *Helen Waltz* to her; but as with the *Pantheon Waltz*, the music has not survived.

Mary's pleasure in Helen's happiness perhaps helped her to bear her distress at Frances's rapidly deteriorating health. Frances died of 'consumption' on 27 February 1855.

Nor will that God who all our weakness knows
Who bore our sorrows and hath wept and grieved –
Who pleads for us, and sees our in-most woes,
Condemn the heart that is by tears relieved . . .[71]

Mary may have reflected upon this verse, which she had composed decades earlier. Frances did not have an easy death and Mary was haunted by it. Years later, in a letter to Helen, she recalled how 'poor Frances' had lingered for weeks when 'every moment [was] expected to be her last'.[72]

Despite her own grief, Mary had Frances's five children, ranging in age from four to 15 years, to think of and console:

And all my cares must now return to those
Who still remain . . .

She had written these lines in 1831, but they were as apposite during this time of anguish as they had been all those years before.[73]

Even when she had the help of Helen and Mary Jnr in the early months after Frances's death, Mary's time was severely stretched. She had a household of four adults and generally two and sometimes three or four children in her care. In addition she managed most of the family's property, which now included two cottages and a house at Kensington built by Robert, as well as Robert George's Waymouth Street house. Although she was in her 69th year when Frances died, and was entitled to be less energetic, there was little hope of that. But in quiet moments in the midst of her busy life Mary's recollection of her optimism in London that Frances's health would be improved by emigration must have intensified her heartache. And the death of William's daughter, barely a year old, less than six weeks after Frances's, heightened her grief.

During Mary's lifetime no more buildings were added to acre 56. Those rented out were renovated from time to time and some were extended with additional rooms, so the rate assessments are not identical year by year. The 'use' of the buildings also changed. In the rate assessment books, Mary's 'stabling and dwelling' became 'large store and shop with stables', then 'shop and stables', and later disappeared altogether, presumably demolished. Also some of Helen's leased cottages changed from 'dwelling' to 'shop and dwelling' or simply 'shop'.

By the 1855 rate assessments two of Mary's cottages had passed into Helen's ownership. With this transaction Helen now owned five cottages on the acre while Mary retained three. This transfer reduced Mary's income significantly, by almost a pound a week, but there is nothing to indicate what prompted it, other than, perhaps, to lighten her workload in managing the properties.

Alfred Mantegani continued to court Helen. His gaiety and their happiness offered Mary a welcome diversion, and eased the pain of the Thomas and Skipper families after the death of Frances and of William's baby daughter. Helen and Alfred were married in July 1855 and they left almost immediately for Ballarat and the Victorian goldfields. John Skipper, writing to Helen some months after her marriage, recalled:

> *the fun we had on Sundays when Frances was here and Mantegani. You may imagine we feel very seedy when I tell you that Georgy [his eldest daughter] and I have taken to going to the Methodist Chapel on the North Road.*[74]

It is clear from Mary's correspondence with Helen that she often had the Skipper children staying with her. She had at least two almost continuously – Spencer, aged nearly eight, and Isabel only a little over four years old, are those mentioned most frequently.

Chapter 14
Consolidation and renaissance

The marriage of a widower to his deceased wife's sister was not uncommon in the mid 19th century, particularly when there was a family of young children involved. It was not without controversy, however, as most Anglican bishops questioned its legality. The frequent early deaths of the mothers of young children meant that their single sisters were often required to undertake the care of the children and the household. Under these conditions, or something like them, the marriage of brother-in-law and sister-in-law almost inevitably ensued. Although in Mary Jnr's situation the circumstances were somewhat different, in April 1856, 14 months after Frances's death, Mary Jnr married John Skipper. But it was not with Mary's blessing as Mary told Helen, several weeks later, in her letter.

> *for you know as well as I do his [John's] temper is none of the best and I am sorry to have to say I have seen but little improvement since poor Frances's death . . . I wished . . . it be delayed until the Bill*[1] *which has been pending . . . in the British Parliament should allow a man lawfully to marry his deceased wife's sister . . . but he [John] said that he had waited so long he was determined to wait no longer . . . [John threatened] to marry some other girl, take the children away and cut the family altogether, a threat which I paid little attention to . . . [It is] decided now and I hope for the best, as*

I told John . . . if he ever married Mary and treated her or neglected her as I have known him to do Frances it should surely be the worst for him . . . and so it was done and I wish Mary may not have reason to wish it undone, but in her state of health and naturally indolent habits she is by no means fit, as I told John long ago, to undertake the management of his household . . . and above all the management of his family . . . I fear Mary will have some trouble with . . . [Georgy], little Isabel may be more tractable, the other children, of course, remain with me for the present . . . but when you write to Mary do not mention anything I have said except her marriage as I should be sorry to dishearten her . . . I cannot help but feel much anxiety on Mary's account knowing how different . . . [John's house at Queenstown] is to what she has been accustomed to . . . John says he shall . . . get a place either in town or at the Port . . . He promised poor Frances the same and I still always think that living in that miserable place was partly the cause of her death.[2]

Helen was Mary's confidant, her safety valve, and Mary often used her monthly letters during Helen's years on the goldfields as a means of relieving tension and frustration. She also expressed her concern about Mary Jnr's emotional upheaval three months before her marriage. A former suitor, with whom she seemed to have once had an informal engagement, wrote to her from New Zealand, after a long silence, offering marriage. And as Mary told Helen, Mary Jnr 'for a long time was [wavering] between the two till I believe she was half out of her mind, and almost made me so too'.[3]

It is clear that Mary had complete trust in Helen's discretion. It was, however, not only Helen's day-to-day emotional support that Mary missed but her practical help with the care of the children. The fears Mary expressed about Mary Jnr's health were well founded. Despite their gaining a stepmother, Mary remained an important mainstay for the Skipper children; she continued to have the care of the two youngest at Hindley Street and the three older girls were often with her.

Even so, Mary found the time to help William's wife, staying two nights on their country section during May. She was assisting her daughter-in-law, also Mary, to make 'some bed furniture' – possibly drapes for a four-poster bed – and intended to go again to sew some curtains.[4] She was also anxiously awaiting news of the birth of Helen's first baby, which was due in April. In early May Mary received the news from Alfred that their daughter, Victoria Theresa, had been born on the 15th April and that both Helen and the baby were well.[5]

After Helen's marriage, Mary had taken over the management of Helen's three cottages and two shops on acre 56 and so her workload had increased yet again. Altogether, she now had 13 properties to care for as her family's unpaid property manager. Mary's acquisition of the family property, albeit through trustees, and her 'hands on' management of it, making her in effect the family breadwinner, was a very unusual situation for a middle class, married woman in Adelaide in the 1850s.

Throughout Mary's life a middle-class woman's domain was considered to be solely that of home and children. In Mary's lifetime a husband was entitled, in his own right, to all of his wife's possessions, including any interest she may have in freehold estates. This was to change only in the decade after Mary's death.[6] Women in colonial South Australia, in fact British women in general, were believed to have 'natural' inabilities[7] which made them less capable than men in judging what was good for them.[8]

Nevertheless, in some families 'such as that of the Scottish Catherine Helen Spence intellectual equality of the sexes was taken for granted ... The idea of human equality appeared to marry well with the Christian ideals so dear to many who came to South Australia'.[9] It was largely through Mary's influence that this attitude, rather than the societal norm, generally prevailed within the Thomas family. Mary, well educated for her time, with some financial independence through her annuity which her father's will had specified was for her use only, ensured the education of her daughters. John Skipper, Frances's father-in-law, a distinguished member of the Norfolk legal fraternity, in writing to Frances, commented 'Your letters impress us with a strong opinion – that your mind is familiar with a variety of human knowledge'. And her brother-in-law, William, recommended Carlyle's *The French Revolution and Hero Worship* to her: 'it would delight [you] and well repay a scrutinizing perusal.'[10] Mary, also, maintained a correspondence over the years with the elder John Skipper.[11]

In her journal Mary Jnr mentions male family friends visiting Mary and the girls to seek their views on the significant events of the day. It is not the fact that male visitors sought out their opinions – although in most households this, of itself, would be unusual and worth recording – but the subject matter under discussion that Mary Jnr considered worth noting, indicating that such visits were part of their everyday life. 'Mr Solomon came into our cottage and chatted upon the affairs of the colony which are in a desperate state.' And on another occasion Charles Wright 'spent an hour talking of phrenology[12] with Mama'.[13]

Mary's domain, acre 56, was like a small village and Mary its benevolent mayor. Nine of the family properties (five cottages, three shops and the hotel) were virtually at her back door. Her tenants included a dressmaker, a carpenter, a blacksmith and a plasterer. A number of her tenants had large families and her acre was literally swarming with life and activity. She maintained the properties well and carried out improvements as she could afford them. Due to her good management, as the gold rush dwindled, she was able to keep most of the dwellings occupied, particularly those belonging to other family members. Where, through misfortune, tenants were unable to keep up with the rent she moved them to her own cottages to live rent-free.

In May 1856, Mary told Helen that a tenant, Mr Ludlow, was 'ill and out of work . . . I employ him about the premises but he is not able to do much'. And that Mrs Ludlow recently had a little girl *which makes her sixth and the eldest not so big as Fanny Thomas [William's nine-year-old daughter]. She is just getting about, and I really pity her with six young children and her husband ill and out of employment except what little I find him to do for the present. He had been employed for some time at a ginger beer warehouse at £1 and 15 per week but as soon as the hot weather ceased he with four others was discharged.*[14]

And a few months later Mary reported that Helen's tenant 'Mr May manages to keep up within five or six weeks but pleads hardness of the times, however I shall have some shoes made up for the children . . . and that will help them a little'.[15]

Despite her generosity, Mary did not shrink from dealing with one of Helen's troublesome tenants. She wrote to Helen:

I had twice given her [Mrs Harding] notice . . . I told her . . . that I should apply for a warrant of Ejectment . . . A tenant is allowed 21 days to make arrangements but Mrs Harding although she told your Papa, who foolishly interfered, that she would not go, began to think . . . that it would be better for herself to give up the house quietly than to be turned out in the street . . . and accordingly she quitted it last Monday and brought the key next morning . . . she owes £8 rent [about four months' rent] . . . but she promises to pay it by degrees and as she is not gone far . . . I shall pay her an occasional visit to remind her. All the other tenants are glad she is gone for they complained that she stole their wood and water, besides being very quarrelsome. I have not let it yet but no doubt I soon shall as it is well situated. The ceiling of the back room is so black for I find that she used to make a fire in the middle of the [presumably stone] floor . . . though Ludlow has washed and whitewashed it several times it is . . . little better but he will persevere until he makes it decent.[16]

The year 1856 had been a very difficult one for Mary. Within a matter of months of her marriage to John Skipper, Mary Jnr had suffered two miscarriages, weakening her already less than robust health, hence Mary's ongoing involvement in the care of the Skipper children.[17] With John's employment continuing at the Port Adelaide Court the family home remained at Queenstown and it was difficult, because of distance, for Mary to provide immediate help to the Skipper family in times of crisis. Mary Jnr's propensity for miscarriages, which left her unable to cope with the immediate care of the children, was a continuing source of anxiety for Mary. However, the opening in February of the first 'electric telegraph' between Adelaide and Port Adelaide, followed shortly after by a steam-powered railway to the Port (the first in the colony), improved communication with nearby Queenstown, and made life a little less stressful for both Marys.

As a treat Mary had her first train ride with Mary Jnr on 30 August 1856, their joint birthday. But she did not enjoy it greatly, preferring a coach and horse.[18]

> *I have heard loud complaints . . . that the Adelaide station . . . at the entrance of the town, has been placed much further eastward than necessary thus causing . . . [Morphett Street] which before led to North Adelaide, to be blocked up at the northern end. It has been questioned whether even the Government had a right to do this, and then terminate the line by a long flight of steps, which to ascend in the midst of a crowd is not very agreeable. More than this, the train passing Morphett Street is a serious inconvenience to residents at the west end of town . . . Surely a little courtesy might be extended to those who would gladly take the nearest road to their homes instead of being carried nolens volens a quarter of a mile further, and having to walk back again, perhaps with young children already tired or requiring to be carried.*[19]

In spite of her views, Mary was still willing to make use of the railway. She caught the train again the following month with Mary Jnr who had visited an Adelaide doctor, fearful of another miscarriage. Worried, Mary accompanied her back to Queenstown. They were able to catch the train part of the way and so shorten their journey a little, 'but it was still a long walk with a hot wind against us'. Fortunately, Mary Jnr managed the walk fairly well but Mary, who had never adjusted to Adelaide's hot summers, was 'knocked up'.[20] Mary Jnr also lost this baby[21] and she remained unwell for many months; Mary had the care of the children for weeks at a time. Her old foreboding over Mary Jnr's general health was heightened – she had already lost one daughter.[22]

During November she received news from Robert George, now in practice as a qualified architect at Newport, Wales. His wedding in September would have already taken place by the time Mary had his letter telling her of his engagement and forthcoming marriage. His wife was Charlotte Tuckett, of Clifton, at the time a town on the outskirts of Bristol. Aged 25, Charlotte was almost 10 years younger than Robert George and was the daughter of a highly regarded, though somewhat impoverished, West Country legal family. Her father, a registrar of the court, had died from a lung condition at an early age, leaving a large family.[23] Robert George was seeking to return to South Australia and had been invited to apply for the position of colonial architect by his old colleague, Boyle Travers Finniss, now a senior South Australian public servant. But these plans did not come to fruition, frustrating his return to the colony, and Mary's resulting mood was one of pessimism. She told Helen: 'it ended as I expected in the appointment of another person by the Governor in the meantime, a young man of the name of Hamilton of little experience.'[24]

Her other news from England, reported to Helen, was the death of her sister Ann. She commented that not only was she (Mary) the first born of her siblings but now the last to survive.[25]

Old wounds, dating from the loss of R. Thomas and Co., were reopened for Mary with the unexpected death, at 57, of George Stevenson, Robert's former partner and the first editor of the *Register*. He died from appendicitis 'after about a fortnight of very severe illness' – there were no surgical procedures then to cure this simple, but agonising, condition. Mary unburdened herself to Helen: 'he is gone and I hope his misdeeds have died with him'; and remarked, pointedly, that Robert did not attend his funeral.

John Skipper applied for Stevenson's position as coroner but Mary was not optimistic that he would be successful: 'I fear there is no such good luck to anyone belonging to us', and she was right.[26]

During the first week of February 1857 all of Helen's cottages were occupied at a rental of 8 shillings per week. Mary forwarded her a statement of the previous year's income; detailing rent (including rent from the shops) as £125 less expenses of £46 and 9 shillings. This left a net profit of £78 and 11 shillings. However, she explained:

> *I am indebted to you, but I candidly confess that I could not pay the whole of it now were you to demand it, without borrowing, for my own expenses last year were so heavy and having no assistance whatsoever from your Papa I was obliged though very unwilling to entrench on your money . . . although I told him repeatedly that I was compelled to do so, [?] for the necessary repairs.*

Mary continued that she had had to meet £25 for maintenance on Robert George's house in Waymouth Street, which had been left in a terrible state by a tenant. There was also the expense of repairs to Rhantregwnwyn, and though these were done at Robert's 'own suggestion and desire',

> *I might as well have appealed to a stone, not a shilling would he give me nor lend me, although he . . . has been for years living at my expense, but I am now tired of it and am fully determined that he shall do it no longer . . . I shall not hesitate to tell him as he once told me . . . that if he is not satisfied he may go elsewhere for I see no reason . . . to spend every farthing of my own money . . . [and] encroach on other people's while he is living on my means that he may hoard up all he can scrape together to buy Burra shares which in reality are as useless to himself as to others since he makes no use of the income he derives from them.[27]*

To Mary's complaints about Robert's lack of financial contribution to the home, she might, justifiably, have added complaints about his lack of emotional support to her, or practical help in the care of the children throughout this period of tribulation. Robert was 74 and, in spending most of his week at Glen Osmond, he had perhaps found a means of escape from a house full of children to a more serene environment.

It is possible to account for, although not condone, Robert's refusal to help Mary financially given her ownership (through trustees) of acre 56, and her receipt of the income from the properties on it. Once it had been his, and was transferred to Mary to avoid its loss during the bankruptcy petition against R. Thomas and Co. Did he ask for it back after his discharge by the court? And did Mary refuse? Unfortunately it is now impossible to know; however, in seeking to understand the obvious deterioration in their relationship over the years these questions need to be raised.

Mary could have returned acre 56 to Robert's ownership after bankruptcy matters were finalised but, presumably, chose not to. It seems she took the practical view that her own competence in managing their sole remaining asset was likely to be greater than his. Given the prevailing social and legal attitudes toward married women and property, in turning her back on accepted norms of behaviour, Mary showed courage, strength of mind and determination.

While Mary was meticulous in her efforts to ensure the properties of family members were occupied and producing rents, she was far less assiduous about her own; preferring, for example, that Helen's cottages should be occupied before hers. She moved Helen's tenants who had legitimate difficulties to her own cottages so that she, in good conscience, could forgive their arrears, reduce their rent, or allow them to live rent-free. Mary's potential gross income should have been in the vicinity of £4 and 7 shillings per week – £3 and 3 shillings from the Clarendon Hotel and 8 shillings per week from each of three cottages, representing a reasonable income. Mary's empathy and leniency, with those of her tenants who were in difficulties, eroded her income. She then could not stretch it to cover a household of two adults and three to four children. It is questionable whether John Skipper ever offered her any financial help with the care of his children; maybe she would have refused it anyway. Much to Mary's distress and chagrin, she found herself in debt to Helen, and very angry with Robert.

It is particularly sad that Mary and Robert's long partnership should be so diminished in its latter years. Much may be attributable to the loss of R. Thomas and Co., the loss of their capital, and above all the loss of optimism. Did Mary blame Robert for his lack of business acumen, and in particular his failure to obtain a written contract for the government printing? Did Robert blame Mary for not pressing the debtors of R. Thomas and Co. hard enough for payment during 1841–1842, while he was in England, ostensibly seeking redress? Be that as it may, their changed circumstances changed them both.

Robert's expansiveness during their early years in the colony – when in 1840 he built, apart from Government House, the only two-storey stone dwelling in Adelaide, and imported the latest printing press – had contracted to his anxious saving of every possible shilling for investment in Burra mining shares – gilt-edged securities. In contrast, Mary's careful turning over of every penny for housekeeping, and her constant worry over the high cost of food during the boom days of the early 1840s, had become a lack of concern about making and saving money. Not money due to members of her family, but a lack of concern for an adequate income of her own. To her financial detriment, she preferred to share with others, especially those in need. It is as if neither Mary nor Robert comprehended the change in the other, and their respective behaviour became mutually inexplicable. They were as strangers.

By the end of February, Helen and Alfred, with baby Victoria, were back in Adelaide. Alfred stayed only a few weeks[28] but Helen remained with Mary for the whole of 1857. After receiving Mary's letter complaining of Robert's refusal to help her, they had, within a week or so, left Ballarat for Adelaide. Was Helen's return home a response to Mary's distress, or had she planned the visit anyway?

She had been away for 18 months, and Victoria, now 10 months old, was well able to withstand the rigours of travel. Perhaps Mary's letter was the trigger that activated an already contemplated visit. Helen's decision may also have been influenced by a meeting with William, who was in Melbourne for a court case and probably visited her bringing news from home.[29]

Mary was delighted to meet her granddaughter, Victoria, and as delighted to have Helen with her for an extended period. Her presence as a confidant, her help with the Skipper children, and her resumption of the management of her own properties provided Mary with much-needed relief as well as bringing some gaiety to her and Rhantregwnwyn. Helen was described, at the end of her long life, as one 'who saw the merry side of everything' – as having always had 'the temperament of a schoolgirl'.[30] Helen's tales of the goldfields and her parody of 'A Life on the Ocean Wave' captivated the children:

> *A life on a Ballarat flat*
> *A home on Creswick Creek*
> *Where nuggets lie so pat*
> *A digger's life I seek*
> *Like a raw new chum I seem*
> *On this unchanging shore*
> *Of glittering gold I dream*
> *I stay in town no more . . . etc*[31]

By 1857, however, the gold rush was virtually over, and during the year, Alfred had opened an agency for Cobb and Co. coaches, based at the American Hotel in Cresswell.[32]

South Australia had weathered the financial crisis generated by the gold rush and had ultimately benefited from the investment of 'winnings' brought back to the colony. It was fitting that during this period of increased prosperity and confidence, elections for South Australia's first bicameral parliament took place in 1857. A South Australian constitution prepared by the partly appointed, partly elected Legislative Council had been forwarded to London, and the *South Australian Constitution Act* 1856 had been proclaimed, virtually unchanged, in October.

The lower house, the House of Assembly, comprised 36 members from 17 districts. Its representatives were to be elected through a secret ballot by adult males of British nationality with six months' enrolment on the electoral roll. No additional qualifications were asked of candidates who stood for the assembly, which was required to go to the people every third year. The Legislative Council (upper house) was made up of 18 members, with no individual district representation. Eligibility for election required: three years' residence in the colony; being at least 30 years of age; and the same property qualification as previous Legislative Councils. Elections were to be held every four years and voting rights were available to adult males who met the property qualification of: freehold estate worth £50; or leasehold, of at least three years' duration, with an annual value of £20; or the occupation of a dwelling of £25 annual value.[33] A secret ballot was also to apply, as for the House of Assembly elections.[34]

On 28 February 1857, the *Observer* reported that nominations had closed for both houses. There were 89 candidates for the 54 seats, and all but two members of the old Legislative Council had offered themselves for election. Two weeks later the House of Assembly returns were listed with approval by the *Observer*; one third of the seats had been won by members of the former Legislative Council. 'The successful list comprises some of the best names in the Colony.'[35] They assembled as the first Parliament of South Australia on 22 April 1857.

> For the first time the Governor pronounced an address for which he was not personally responsible and in which was shadowed forth the policy of a Ministry depending for its power . . . upon the representative body. Yesterday the community entered . . . the position of a free, self governed constitutional state . . . with commerce in a safe and improving condition – with agricultural, pastoral and mining [pursuits] extending operations . . . steadily and vigorously.

He reported the colony's population as 109,000 and its surplus as £300,000.[36] The old loan from 1842, now reduced to £85,000, was remitted by the British Government after a direct appeal to the Queen. This made the total cost to Britain for South Australia's foundation a modest £215,546.[37] Overall, the cost of establishing the colony had been largely met through the sale of land plus the revenues raised within it. Wakefield's systematic colonisation had succeeded in part, and his concept of the sale, rather than the grant, of colonial 'waste' land had been taken up by the British Government, and applied in the other Australian colonies. Under the new South Australian Constitution, the South Australian Government gained control over the land fund and the management of the migration of Britain's 'working poor'.

Extensions to the 1855 House of Assembly – built to Bennett Hayes's award-winning design – were made to accommodate the new parliament and were completed in time for its opening. They occupied the site of the 1843 (original) Legislative Council chamber and part of it was retained within the new structure.[38]

Although women were denied the vote, South Australians could take pride in, what was for the time, a progressive and liberal constitution – the enfranchisement of all adult males, at least for the lower house, and the introduction of the secret ballot. For Mary and Robert it provided some balm. Their aspirations for greater individual liberty and opportunity, free from nepotism, and their belief, in 1836, that their best hope for the fulfilment of them lay in emigration, was rewarded by these developments – even though they had been a long time coming.

Mary did not live to see the enfranchisement of women. She did, however, gain the vote as a ratepayer through the *Corporations Act* 1862, although not the right to stand for election to the Adelaide City Corporation.[39] But Mary's granddaughter, Rosetta Birks (nee Thomas) – William's daughter – barely three months old when the first South Australian Parliament was elected, was later to play a leading role in the campaign to secure the parliamentary vote for women, which was eventually achieved in December

1894.⁴⁰ The South Australian Parliament was the second in the world to enfranchise women, and at federation in 1901, the South Australian legislation ensured the vote for all Australian women.⁴¹ Rosetta Birks is described by Helen Jones, in her 1994 history of South Australian women (*In Her Own Name*), as having gained wide experience in the management of organisations through her work with her husband Charles Birks on various committees of the Adelaide Children's Hospital, her appointment to the council of the Women's Suffrage League, and later as a vice-president of the National Council of Women and president of the Young Women's Christian Association.⁴²

> *Essentially practical ... she had a dignified and self assured manner ... [She] prepared her speeches carefully and delivered them with an accent of sincerity and tenderness that carried her words straight to the heart ... Rosetta was a brainy, travelled, cultured woman of attractive personality and very popular.*

Mary possessed many of these qualities and by this account she had bequeathed them to her talented granddaughter. Had Mary been born at a later time, she would have been among those campaigning for votes for women.

Helen was still in Adelaide when the two Marys visited their old campsite at Glenelg, just before the celebrations to mark the 21st anniversary of the founding of the colony, but she does not seem to have been with them. Mary recalled the visit in her reminiscences:

> *I determined to visit the spot, as near as I could ascertain, where our tents had formerly stood ... to see the tree which had now become so celebrated [the tree under which the proclamation of the colony was said to have been read] ... there certainly was an old trunk ... but nothing like the flourishing tree I expected to find ... 'That the tree!' I exclaimed. 'I am certain it is not' ... it was neither the tree nor the spot where the colony was proclaimed. We had ascertained this from having on our walk discovered the lagoon near to which*

> our tents had stood . . . If the Proclamation tree were still standing, which I very much doubt, it would most likely have continued to be in full vigour, as it was in 1836 . . . the tree under notice is simply a decayed old trunk with not a branch left [which was] not far from our camp. Under it my children often played, calling it 'Temple Bar', from its similarity to an arch. How it came to be distinguished as the 'Proclamation Tree', as they call it, I cannot tell . . . the magnificent gum tree which partly overshadowed Mr Gouger's tent [where the proclamation was made] afforded . . . a natural canopy for the banquet which was held on the occasion.[43]

The official commemoration was held at Glenelg on 28 December 1857. The Thomases, as early settlers, would have been represented – probably by Robert, William and John Skipper. Mary seemed unimpressed by the preparations.[44] Nevertheless, an extract from her diary of 28 December 1836, describing the events surrounding the reading of the proclamation, and the printing of the proclamation document, appeared in the *Observer* on 1 January 1858.

Most of Adelaide's residents joined the throng making for Glenelg along the Bay Road. The *Observer* described the road as 'crowded throughout its entire length with vehicles, horses and pedestrians who poured into the village in dense unbroken masses for two to three hours'. A pavilion had been put up near the beach for the formal luncheon, and 'around it were gathered numerous booths for the refreshment and entertainment of visitors'. Various sports, horseracing, foot racing, sailing and rifle shooting were planned and by about 11 am the crowd was estimated to be 10,000. 'Hotels and booths were crowded with numerous happy and gaily dressed patrons scattered about . . . [but the] weather gave signs of a change decidedly unfavourable to holiday making, and by 12 o'clock the determined drizzle had settled in', and it became impossible to continue the sports.[45]

Those fortunate enough to be able to afford tickets to the luncheon found shelter in the pavilion. They were entertained by the Brunswick Band, until *the National Anthem . . . announced the approach of the Governor and his party . . . Everything that could be required for comfort was provided. Every delicacy of the season was on the tables but unfortunately the . . . storm had the effect of dashing the cup of pleasure from the lips of numerous guests.*[46]

While the luncheon was in progress the heavy rain did not prevent a large number of people from assembling at the 'same old tree'. They had gathered to see the unveiling of the plaque that, much to Mary's annoyance, identified it as the proclamation tree:

On this spot on the 28th December 1836 the Colony of South Australia was proclaimed and established by Captain John Hindmarsh, the Governor, acting in the name of His Majesty King William IV in the presence of the chief officers and other colonists.

A small stage with bunting and a flagpole had been erected for the governor, but he did not turn up. The loyal, drenched and long-suffering crowd, 'after waiting for about three hours', hoisted the flag 'in the absence of H. E. and a bottle or two broken by volunteer hands in honour of the occasion'.[47] The plaque was eventually attached to the tree, but in Mary's view the 'tree where the Proclamation took place was cut down . . . long before, and the plate might as well have been fixed on the old tree now standing on my acre in Hindley Street'.[48]

Alfred returned to Adelaide at the end of 1857, and Helen and baby Victoria left for Creswick with him at the beginning of the following April.[49] Mary's letter to Helen after her departure lamented that she could have spent more time with Helen on the boat, had she known it would be delayed leaving the Port. She ended on a poignant note asking Helen to tell baby Victoria 'that her Grandmother will not forget her'.[50]

Her main news for Helen was that William's wife, after a difficult pregnancy, had given birth to a son, Alfred Kyffin. Mary was called out at 7 am to assist; fortunately for Mary, William and his family were now living in Adelaide. The birth itself was uncomplicated and the new baby was healthy. With his birth, William and his wife now had six children. Also during May 1858, Mary sent her servant, Lucy, to Queenstown to assist Mary Jnr, who was again pregnant and troubled by morning sickness, but she was then without domestic help herself while caring for three children. Robert Kyffin, William's eldest son, was still with Mary after his mother's confinement, as well as Spencer and Georgy Skipper.[51] In spite of Mary's effort to spare her, Mary Jnr also lost this baby and Mary attributed the miscarriage to the shock Mary Jnr suffered when the theatre she and John had been attending caught fire.[52]

In her next letter to Helen, Mary is again resentful about Robert's lack of financial contribution to the home but on this occasion she has rather a wry laugh at having gained an advantage over him in the matter of rents. In discussing the reduction of rent for the Clarendon Hotel, by 7 shillings per week, in order to retain the Rogers who were 'good tenants', Mary told Helen:

> *I could ill afford it, but trust to Providence for it is no use trusting to your Papa. He knows all this but he has never offered me the slightest assistance, there is one thing how-ever which I get out of him, though not I believe with his own good will.*[53]

She then went on to recount that at the suggestion of one of Robert's tenants – a baker who occupied one of Robert's Kensington cottages – she accepted extra bread in lieu of rent, gaining 6 shillings per week to Robert's disadvantage. 'It is little enough but better than nothing', especially as she had one of her cottages occupied rent-free by a woman whose husband had gone to the goldfields, leaving her without an income. Mary, however, is somewhat mollified by Robert's assistance to Mary Jnr in papering the parlour at Queenstown.[54]

During August 1858 Robert was confined to bed, having come home from Glen Osmond very ill with severe asthma. Mary reported to Helen that it had developed from a cold *which everybody had [and] I could not prevail on him to buy a greatcoat although he was continually grumbling at the weather for it has been exceedingly cold . . . I sent for the doctor who told me that such attacks for a man at his time of life are very dangerous. He immediately ordered a blister for his chest and medicine for his cough . . . Should he have another such attack I will let you know immediately.*[55]

From October Robert returned to Glen Osmond for several days each week having made a good recovery. There was no good news, though, regarding Mary Jnr's health, a constant source of worry. She had become pregnant with twins soon after her most recent miscarriage but by the end of September, she had 'lost' one of the twins. Mary, no doubt, had the care of the Skipper children while she was recovering, as 'she was very weak for a long time'. In Helen's October letter Mary anticipates that the surviving baby will be born in March.[56] This was not to be, however, as this baby did not survive either.[57]

Throughout 1858 Mary forwarded Helen, on average, about £5 per month, the net income due to Helen from her properties; and Mary seemed to have had little difficulty in making these remittances regularly. But toward the end of 1858 she asked Helen, on the legal advice of John Skipper, not to agree to the request of one of her tenants for a six-year extension of a lease that still had a further 12 years to run. Because of conditions relating to the expiry of the lease, Mary seemed to be apprehensive about an extension causing complications regarding acre 56, particularly in the event of her death:

I should never consent to anything that may be likely to involve my family in disputes hereafter for I have had enough of law myself to last for twenty generations and John says it may bring on a dispute in Chancery which no one would know the end of.[58]

Mary's respect for lawyers had never been very high; she commented to George in October 1838, that the whole fraternity would promote litigation if they could.[59] Mary's earlier experience of long-standing difficulties over her annuity had made her cautious. Her concern about potential legal disputes regarding land was realistic as the lease agreement under discussion had been drawn up when documents relating to land transactions did not have to be registered, and when there was no evidence, therefore, that a title was unique.

This changed, however, with the passage of the *Real Property Act* 1858, which created a single registered land title document that ensured indisputable ownership of the land described in the document. Although it met with much opposition from the legal profession, for whom disputes over land provided a lucrative source of income, as Mary was fully aware, its passage was one of the outstanding achievements of the first South Australian Parliament. By 1864 it was the norm throughout Australia. Its author, Robert Richard Torrens – the son of Colonel Robert Torrens, chairman of the old emigration commission – became the first registrar of the new Land Titles Office and was later knighted for his services to the colony.[60] Unfortunately, the new system did not solve Mary's problems. Her land transactions predated it, and so she sought Helen's cooperation not to agree to the extension and a complication of the lease.

Over the years Mary's acre had become quite built up, and this was increasingly the case for Hindley Street. From 1855 few vacant allotments appear in the rate assessment records. When records began in 1847 there were three shops on the acre that adjoined Mary's to the east, toward Morphett Street. By 1858 these had increased to nine, while the acre still retained the warehouse, house and garden, and Joiners' Arms Tavern, all of which had been there since before records began. The acre on the other side of Mary's was divided by a roadway, Fenn Place (still there today). Ten, mostly two-roomed, cottages were built on either side of it and, as well, the Royal Oak Hotel (still trading) occupied part of this acre's Hindley Street frontage. The acre opposite Mary's had six dwellings when rate records began; one included a shop and another a workshop. Ten years on, by 1858, these had increased to nine shops including five with attached dwellings.⁶¹

During the 1850s Hindley Street remained not only the prime focus for shopping in Adelaide, with all the colour, noise and bustle that this entailed, but the courts and lanes off its main concourse were densely populated. Although Rhantregwnwyn had a sizeable garden that faced onto a private road, both providing buffers, Mary was surrounded by cottages. She was also little more than a stone's throw from the traffic in Hindley Street – not only the throngs of shoppers milling about, but bullock wagons, horses and drays and other horse-drawn vehicles. Ever present in summer were the clouds of dust, and in winter the quagmires of mud that this constant activity stirred up. Odours from the litter and refuse that accumulated in this busy thoroughfare, as yet without a system for the collection of rubbish or the cleaning of the street, were all pervasive.

While the commercial and retail focus of Adelaide continued in Hindley Street, Adelaide's centre, Victoria Square, as Light had intended, was growing in importance. The square's St Francis Xavier's Cathedral was the initiative of the first Catholic Bishop of Adelaide, Francis Murphy, based on designs prepared in England. And this major Roman Catholic building was dedicated – while partially completed – during the latter part of 1858.⁶²

Although, by year's end, Adelaide had been connected by telegraph to Melbourne and Sydney, Mary's communication with Helen remained slow. Her letters went first to Melbourne by coastal vessel and then by road to Creswick, taking many weeks. But in advising its readers of the new telegraphic links on 30 October, the *Observer* announced '[we] are within a few minutes' distance of each other'.⁶³ Newspapers were now able to report on events in other colonies within a matter of hours of their occurrence, rather than weeks.

Mary had to wait for a letter to learn of the arrival of Alfred Victor, Helen's second child, born on 13 January 1859. She was relieved and delighted to hear of Helen's safe confinement and to receive a lock of the baby's hair. 'I like his name and shall keep his hair' and then rather wistfully, 'I should like to see all of you . . . but we must wait with patience'.[64] Baby Victor was Mary and Robert's 14th grandchild: taking account of William's six children, the five Skippers, Helen's daughter and Robert George's son.[65] For the time, Mary Jnr remained without children.

In February the heat and winds were extreme; as Mary told Helen, there were

> very severe fires at Port Elliot and Macclesfield . . . destroying houses, crops and everything that came within its way, reducing many families to utter ruin . . . If a fire had broken out in Adelaide on that day much of it would have been destroyed owing to the violent north wind.[66]

Mary immediately made up a bundle of clothes for the victims of the fire; 'most people were doing the same' and she was ready to contribute £1 to the bushfire fund, despite Robert's disapproval 'although the money came out of my own pocket'.

When the appeal's collector failed to call on her, Mary gave it to William to lodge on her behalf but 'The committee mistook it for his donation' and so, as Mary recounted to Helen, she told William she did not mind that he was acknowledged in the published list of donors, but that he should put in a further £1 anonymously. 'This he refused to do as I well knew he would . . . [but] otherwise he had no right to the credit.'[67] Mary's forthrightness had not diminished with her advanced years and perhaps she was mischievously testing William's new-found religiosity. During the visit of the London-based charismatic preacher, the Reverend Thomas Binney, in September 1858, William, nominally an Anglican, had become 'a new man in Christ' and had joined the Freeman Street Congregational Church, at the southern end of Gawler Place.[68] It seems there was no Baptist congregation in the city at the time.

During April 1859 Mary, aged 72, sat for a photographer's portrait.[69] She gave copies to William and Mary Jnr, and promised

Helen one. A few months later, in July, several portraits of Robert George's wife, Charlotte, with their son, Robert, arrived with the English mail. Mary commented to Helen in her latest letter to the goldfields that she thought Robert George's son looked very like Vicky (Helen's daughter). She assured Helen that she had put aside, for her, a portrait of Robert George's wife whom she described as 'very ladylike'. Among the gifts that Robert George enclosed with the photographs were two lithographs, one of his home in Newport, Montgomeryshire, and the other of the Independent Chapel there, which he had designed.[70]

Mary Jnr's first child, Mary Elizabeth, was born on 31 July, and Mary described the baby as 'not so large a child, but a pretty little thing and seems very healthy'. She was born at about seven on a Sunday evening when the trains were not running and Mary could not be sent for but, as she recounted to Helen, 'the following morning I had notice by telegraph and went down [by train]'. Somewhat unexpectedly, 'Mary [Jnr] got over her confinement very well'.[71] The Skipper children were all still with Mary on the following Sunday (a week later) and consequently, as she confessed to Helen, she thought that 'there would be enough to fill the [Thomas] pew at church without me and therefore stayed home to write to you'. Given her large household it was probably the only time she could find to do so.[72]

The birth of Mary Jnr's little girl after so many miscarriages must have been an occasion of extraordinary joy for her parents, and for her grandparents, and also a release from longstanding anxiety for Mary. As she explained to Helen in her September letter, she answered for Helen as godmother at little Mary Elizabeth's christening. Her other news for Helen was the birth on 2 June of Robert George's daughter, Mary Annette. Mary concluded Helen's letter with mention of the older Skipper children, four of whom were staying with her, plus Mary Jnr and the baby.[73]

Throughout Mary's correspondence with Helen over tenancy matters there are indications, not only of Mary's efforts to help ill or unemployed men and their families, but also of a pattern of befriending and assisting women with young children whose husbands had left them without financial support. In October Mary had rent arrears to cope with when an out-of-work tenant, Heely, deserted his wife on the pretext of seeking employment in Melbourne on the railways.[74] Mary transferred Mrs Heely and her five children from one of Helen's cottages to her own, where she allowed them to live rent-free for many months. Mary also assisted Mrs Heely and her children with food until she was able to obtain government rations. One woman in similar circumstances to Mrs Heely, whom Mary helped to get back on her feet, ultimately established a successful small business employing several other women.[75]

In the Adelaide of her day, Mrs Heely's situation was by no means unusual. Although the *Destitute Person's Act* 1843, better known as the Maintenance Act, provided for maintenance orders and for the punishment of deserting husbands (who could be summonsed before two justices of the peace and sentenced to two months gaol for the first offence and three months for the second), most absconding husbands could not be found. Like Heely many deserted across the border, where without uniform legislation throughout Australia, South Australian law could not reach them. During the years of the gold rush this was particularly the case. These difficulties were partially resolved with federation.[76]

Mary told Helen of the death, on 7 November, of their old friend and family doctor, Edward Wright, in her last letter for 1859. He had died in the Destitute Asylum where his family had placed him for 'security for himself', perhaps because of his history of alcoholism.[77]

Chapter 15
A new prosperity

In her letter to Helen of January 1860, Mary complained about the extreme weather Adelaide was experiencing with temperatures of up to 115°F (46°C) degrees. She grumbled that it was affecting her garden, which was also suffering from 'want of proper cultivation which I cannot afford, and your Papa will not for he is more stingy and avaricious than ever, and cares for nothing but hoarding up money'.[1]

In relating to Helen the death of a neighbour and former merchant, she likened him to Robert, describing him as 'another melancholy specimen of grudging and greediness'. News had just reached Adelaide that 'old MacGeorge' had perished on board the *Royal Charles*, which had sunk en route to England. Rather than pay the small fee for a bank transfer, MacGeorge had carried a large quantity of sovereigns worth thousands of pounds with him and, as Mary told Helen, 'he and his money went to the bottom together'.[2]

MacGeorge was an atheist who had booked on the doomed ship to be able to refute the teachings of a fellow passenger, the Reverend Thomas Binney, who was returning to London from a tour of the colony. But Binney switched from the *Royal Charles* to another vessel at the last minute and Mary, relishing the irony of the situation, wondered what MacGeorge's 'thoughts were when he found himself drowning'. She considered that he had behaved irresponsibly by carrying his money with him and not protecting it, and his family's future wellbeing. She had nothing but contempt for those whose habitual meanness impacted unfairly upon their families. Mary saw Robert as being tarred with the same brush.

Her irritation was provoked by Robert's purchase of another Burra share when 'he cannot afford me half a crown a week to pay for his washing'. Although the share increased his income by another £20 a year, Mary told Helen she believed that if she died 'he would starve himself to death rather than allow sufficient to keep him'.[3]

'My eyes are so bad I can scarcely see to do anything'; and so Mary started her letter to Helen of April 1860 and continued that her eyes 'have been so for a long time. I waited a full hour to see Dr Bayer and could not wait any longer. I will try again tomorrow'.[4] Mary's time was still at a premium; notwithstanding her eye problems she had a 'full house'. Telling Helen of the arrival of her new niece, Florence Emily, William's sixth daughter, she explained that William and his wife were

> in great trouble with the sudden illness of their Governess, Miss Webb ... She was taken ill with fever which increased and then she developed a broken blood vessel ... [and] her recovery is doubtful ... She seems to linger in the same way poor Frances did.[5]

From Mary's description and her allusion to Frances's death, it seems Miss Webb had advanced tuberculosis. The doctor wanted all of the children, except the baby, sent away from home as Miss Webb was being nursed there.[6] Mary had with her Helen (14), Robert Kyffin (9) and Rosie (Rosetta) (4) as well as their cousin, Spencer Skipper who still had his home at Rhantregwnwyn. And, as if unwilling to be outdone, Mary Jnr was visiting with her baby!

It is not surprising that in June when Mary wrote again she had only just recovered from influenza, which had affected her right eye. It 'had completely deprived me of the use of [that] eye but thank God it is quite recovered and I can [now] write or read normally'.⁷ Mary was 73, but she was to have very little respite from the almost unremitting demands of her family for her help. She had no sooner recovered from the 'flu' when she was called to look after William's wife, who was in a very distressed state. Mary thought that her daughter-in-law was suffering from the shock of the illness and death of Miss Webb so soon after her recent confinement: 'I was with her every day for a week till her Mother [who was caring for another recently confined relative] could remain with her, and she got better during that time.'⁸

Then, just as Mary was relieved of her care, Robert, now 79, returned home from Glen Osmond

> *very ill with lumbago and shortness of breath which resulted in another attack of asthma . . . he talks of getting up today but he will not be able to get up very long. Dr Bayer . . . considered the danger past . . . but his age was against him . . . if you do not hear from me again in a few days you may conclude that he is recovering . . . should he be worse I will let you know as soon as possible.*⁹

Mary's marriage of 42 years came to an end on the 1 July 1860. Robert died during the afternoon, seated in an armchair, as because of the 'oppression in his chest' he was unable to lie down.¹⁰ William notified Helen by telegram and Mary wrote to her the same day:

> *You will not be surprised from my last letter . . . that your Papa is no more. He expired at four o'clock this afternoon after much suffering but sensible to the last . . . the Doctor visited him last evening, saw no hope and gave him a powder which enabled him to sleep.*¹¹

It also allowed Mary – virtually without sleep for a fortnight while nursing Robert – to rest. She woke only two hours before Robert's death and was at his side with William and William Hillier¹² when he died.

Robert had made his will a week earlier and, as Mary told Helen, she considered it to be very fair. Mary continued that in the end Robert had wished to do everything in the right way and he was very thankful when the will was read to him. Anticipating

Helen's return home, Mary closed her letter with a promise to send her £5 in the mail toward her fare.

Robert left 20 National Bank shares and 8 Burra shares to be divided into four equal parts, with one part each to Robert George, Mary Jnr, and Helen, and the last to be shared between Frances's children. William inherited the house at Kensington and Mary the two cottages and land there. Mary, however, had a life interest in the income derived from the Kensington house and also the Burra shares – so the dreaded shares were to be of some benefit to her at last, at least for a few years. Robert's estate was sworn for probate at £2000[13], which in today's values would approximate $320,000. Mary's earlier resentment that Robert was hoarding money, to her detriment at that time, was not misplaced, but she benefited from these savings after his death. It may be that Robert had been desperate to compensate for his business failure and his 'hoarding' was motivated by what he, perhaps, saw as a need to redeem himself in his family's eyes by leaving a significant estate.

He was buried on 4 July following a funeral service conducted by the Dean of Adelaide, the Reverend Farrell, at Trinity Church, where his funeral procession to West Terrace Cemetery was joined by 12 carriages. Among those at the graveside were five members of parliament, the French consul, William's partners in the *Register*, and 'numerous old colonists and other gentlemen connected with the press in South Australia'.[14] Robert's obituary in the *Register* was reprinted in the *Observer* and ran to two thirds of a column. It recorded his status as one of the first arrivals in the colony and his establishment of its first newspaper: 'Thus has the earth closed again upon one of the primary pioneers of this province, and upon one who first brought to this country that without which no country can be great, or noble or free – the printing press.'[15]

A noble monument they leave behind,
Those brave old men ...
No sculptured marble then need we uprise;
Here stand the living works of their own hand

These lines, as Mary recorded, were 'written by a member of the literary staff of the *Register*, and published in that paper on the occasion of my late husband's death'.[16]

Within a few months of her father's death, Helen returned to Adelaide with her two children to be with Mary. Alfred planned to follow Helen almost immediately, but he was delayed in Creswick, unable to sell their house and land. Nevertheless, he had managed to wind up a business partnership to establish a second Cobb and Co. booking office (to service the goldfields), entered into with the owner of the Prince of Wales Hotel as recently as March 1860. It seems that it was now Helen and Alfred's intention to make their permanent home in Adelaide. Alfred visited Helen and the children during February 1861, and went back to Creswick in April, as, although he had managed to sell a parcel of land for £14, he still hadn't been able to dispose of their home. A few weeks later he sold it for £120, enabling his return to Adelaide. But by mid May he was seriously ill and his health continued to deteriorate rapidly. Alfred died of 'heart disease' on 5 June 1861.[17] He was only 31, six years younger than Helen, and had accumulated little in the way of assets. She was left with minimal financial resources for her two young children; Vicky was only five and young Alfred just two.

It was an extraordinary coincidence that mother and youngest daughter were both widowed within a few months of each other; these unique circumstances seem to have strengthened the bond between them. Helen and her children lived at Rhantregwnwyn for many years, and after both her children had married and left the home, Helen continued to live there for the rest of Mary's life. Over the years Helen made several requests to Alfred's family in Italy for help with the expense of the children's education but these appeals were unsuccessful. She did not remarry, and although she had some income from her cottages and shops, Mary was probably her financial backstop, as Helen had been her mother's during the years when she and Alfred were on the goldfields.

South Australia's equivalent of gold was copper, and a further deposit had been discovered, toward the end of 1859, by Walter Watson Hughes on his sheep run in the northern districts of Yorke Peninsula. Hughes, with others, formed a company to work the new find, and during 1860 the Wallaroo Mine was opened. The ore body was very rich and copper once again added a much-needed boost to the drought-affected South Australian economy; fuelling development and innovation which brought not only greater efficiency for businesses but an increase in amenity for Adelaide's housewives.[18]

Although Robert had not lived to see them, Mary witnessed extraordinary advances in the technology of printing and information gathering introduced at the *Register*, largely at William's instigation as part of his responsibility for the firm's 'mechanical operation'.[19] William and his partners had previously bought a portion of town acre 141 in Grenfell Street, near King William Street on a private lane – now known as Register Street – presumably with a view to expansion; but they decided against a total rebuilding programme in 1860.[20] Instead they added a second floor to their existing offices and the necessary equipment to produce gas on the premises was included with these renovations. Gas lighting was introduced at the *Register* offices and printing works well before it was generally available in Adelaide.[21] While, as previously mentioned, two years earlier, in another advance, William had replaced the old hand-operated presses with the first steam printing press to be brought into the colony.[22]

These developments in the technology of printing and the greater convenience and superiority of gas lighting (compared with candles and oil lamps), were major innovations in the production of newspapers. They transformed the working conditions of compositors and printers and thus efficiency at the *Register*'s offices. And the 'electric' telegraph, which revolutionised the gathering of information and had already connected Adelaide with Melbourne and Sydney, continued to expand to join Adelaide to South

Australian country centres. At the close of 1860 links had been made to Kapunda, Burra and Mt Barker.[23]

Further progress in communication came in August 1860 with the completion of a rail connection between Gawler and Kapunda, and an additional extension of the Adelaide to Gawler line was planned for Burra to service the copper mines there. These were significant developments in the colony's emerging rail system.[24]

At the beginning of the year Mary and Helen, along with other residents of Adelaide, were at last able to enjoy the labour-saving amenity of having water laid onto their homes following the recent damming of the Torrens upstream to form the Thornton Park Reservoir. Because of the well in her garden Mary had been fortunate in not being dependent, as most homes were, on the polluted water drawn from the Torrens along its Adelaide reaches. Given the unregulated drainage of Adelaide's waste into the river from the first months of settlement, the water now piped to the homes of much of the city's population was their first readily available, safe drinking water in decades. The supply was also laid onto the public baths, and another boon was the opening of public drinking fountains within the city.[25]

The improving economic conditions also meant that extensions to the Treasury Building in Victoria Square, underway for three years, were completed by the end of the year. Kingston's single-storey 1839 structure was enlarged by an upper floor, and wings were added to the King William and Flinders street frontages.[26] Another significant public building finished during the latter part of 1860 was the new home of the South Australian Institute on the corner of Kintore Avenue and North Terrace. Still in use today, it was built to house the colony's subscription library, embryonic museum and art collections, and to provide lecture and meeting rooms. In the 1840s Robert had been a committee member of the organisation formed by the merging of the Literary and Scientific Association with the Mechanics' Institute. This body underwent several transformations and name changes between

1839 and 1856 when it was established by an act of parliament (*South Australian Institute Act* 1856) with a board of governors, and became formally known as the South Australian Institute. By 1859 it had merged with the Philosophical Society and the Society of Arts and was required to conduct lectures of relevance to these two groups.[27] It was the significant cultural influence in the colony – the forerunner of the State Library of South Australia, the South Australian Museum and the Art Gallery of South Australia. The Institute building was designed by the colonial architect of the day, Edward Hamilton, and in July the *Observer* gave its approval: 'It is decidedly in advance of any other building, public or private, in the colony.'[28]

By mid 1861, Robert George, with his wife and young family, had achieved his dream of returning to Adelaide and was in the process of establishing a private architectural practice. His return had probably been assisted by Mary's sale of the Kensington cottages she had inherited from Robert.[29]

The increased wealth from the copper mines, not only at Wallaroo but also those more recently opened at Kadina, plus the discovery in May of additional promising deposits at Moonta, continued to boost the economy, making further investment in public buildings possible. Adelaide was beginning to take on its enduring architectural form in which Robert George was to play a significant role. He had returned to the colony an experienced architect and a fellow of the Royal Institute of British Architects, vindicating Mary's faith in his abilities.[30] His first Adelaide commission was the Baptist Church in Flinders Street.

William, as a leading member of the Baptist Church, in 1861 decided with two other church leaders – George Fife Angas, and the Reverend Silas Mead – to build a church whose architectural significance would enhance the Baptists' presence in the city of churches. In his preparatory work, Robert George 'drew upon his deep reserves of knowledge of the Gothic Revival ... but allowed his fancy to rove free in the addition of some French and Italian elements'.[31] The foundation stone was laid on 18 December, in front of an assembly of 300, which no doubt included Mary as well as Robert George and William with their families.[32]

William, not to be overshadowed by his talented brother, was continuing to make his mark in Adelaide's business community. He and his partners expanded their publishing activities to include an evening paper. On the afternoon of 4 August 1862 the first *Evening Telegraph*, edited by Mr F. Sinnett, was on the streets. The firm was now responsible for three papers – as well as the *Register* continuing as a morning broadsheet they also put out the weekly *Observer*, with summaries of major events, mainly for country readers.[33] Barely two years later, in October 1864, William's proprietary interest in the *Register* partnership increased with the retirement of Anthony Forster, when William and his remaining partners, Andrews and Fisher, were able to acquire Forster's share. Then, sometime during the next 12 months, Fisher retired and sold his interest to John Howard Clark, who entered the partnership as editor, and the firm became known as Andrews, Thomas and Clark.[34]

Adelaide was prospering and the colony's economy was expanding. During the early weeks of 1862, the *Observer* anticipated that the extensive building works and port facilities established by Messrs Hughes and Co. at Wallaroo would 'give a considerable impulse to the commerce of the colony', and the construction of a railway between Adelaide and Wallaroo was also being contemplated.[35] In the primary sector, many who had benefited from the gold rush had 'turned away from Adelaide to invest their earnings and their energies in pushing back the frontiers of settlement'.[36] In the near north, land previously leased by pastoralists was being purchased by grain farmers; to aid them, 'Goyder's Line' was drawn on the map of South Australia to distinguish land where reliable rainfall might be expected from land unsuitable for agriculture.

Replacement for the hectares taken up by the grain farmers was sought by cattle and sheep graziers in the colony's far north and in the centre of the continent. Between 1859 and 1861, the explorer John McDouall Stuart – a member of Sturt's 1844 expedition – and others made a number of forays seeking a way into the centre around what was believed to be an impenetrable horseshoe of salt lakes. Stuart's journeys opened up vast tracts of valuable, although semi-arid, grazing land, much of it watered by natural artesian springs. For these discoveries he was awarded the 1861 Royal Geographic Society's Victoria Medal.[37] During December Stuart's expedition left Adelaide again, determined this time to cross the continent. Only a few months prior to Stuart's departure, John McKinley and his party had also set out north from Adelaide, not to find new grazing country, but in search of the missing Victorian explorers, Burke and Wills.[38]

Early in the New Year, 1862, Stuart planted his Union Jack on Central Mount Stuart, Australia's central point, having passed and named on his way the MacDonnell Ranges after the former governor, probably unaware that he had already left the colony. Stuart continued his epic trek north and, just three months later, on 24 July, reached the shores of the Indian Ocean. Without respite he and his party immediately set out on the return journey and arrived back in the 'settled districts' of South Australia in December. They had covered over 4000 miles of mostly uncharted, extremely difficult and hazardous terrain within 12 months. It was an achievement of remarkable leadership, of extraordinary physical and emotional endurance, and made without loss of life. Stuart had pioneered the track to the Indian Ocean, and South Australia claimed as her own all that land leading to the northern shores of the continent. In the centre, huge pastoral leases extending over hundreds of square miles became available to be taken up and stocked.[39] This extension of the colony's borders underpinned the government's later successful bid to build the Overland Telegraph.

Within a few months there was a further demonstration of the colony's developing confidence and maturity, this time in Adelaide. Robert George's first South Australian architectural commission, the Flinders Street Baptist Church, was formally opened in April 1863 by a visiting Melbourne Baptist preacher, the Reverend James Taylor. The ceremony was well attended by more than a capacity congregation.[40] Mary's pleasure and pride in her son must have been unbounded that morning as she sat amidst the gathering in the beautiful church he had created for them. Today the building is considered to 'admirably represent . . . the fortitude and influence of South Australia's dissenters . . . The coherence of the design is enhanced . . . by the superbly detailed porch and rose window to Flinders Street'.[41]

Only a few weeks later the foundation stone of the Adelaide Town Hall was laid by the new governor, Sir Dominick Daly.[42] Earlier proposals to put up a town hall had come to nothing, but when the builder Thomas English became mayor in 1862 he resurrected the project with a design competition which was won by Edmund Wright. Under their 1861 act, the Adelaide Corporation had the power to borrow up to £20,000 for its construction.

During June 1863, within less than two months of these initiatives, a gas supply for the general public was introduced, providing a further indication of Adelaide's sophistication, as the *Observer* editorialised[43]:

> *June 20th will be an important day in the history of the colony . . . on that day its capital was lit by gas . . . Many of the burners in the shops were lighted as early as 3 pm, some had as many as twenty to thirty lights . . . At the Register Offices, a large star . . . lit up part of King William Street as if it had been by the sun's clear light*

As yet, however, there was no gas lighting available for the streets.

Notwithstanding the progress, earlier in the decade, with water and gas laid onto its homes, Adelaide was still poorly drained and unsewered, earning it the epithet 'city of stenches'. In the early 1860s, after Robert George's return to the colony, two of his children died in infancy. No regulations existed to control noxious waste from tanneries and slaughterhouses, for example, nor to control overflowing privies and overcrowded, unhygienic dwellings; 'the hazards to life – especially young life – and health in the first three decades of the Colony, were infections of the bowel and lungs'. Infant mortality in the colony reached its peak in 1868 with 180 deaths in children under the age of 12 months, for every 1000 live births.[44] This rate would exceed that of some of the poorest Third World countries today, and at the time was the worst in Australia.[45] Perhaps motivated by the tragedies within his own family, in c. 1863 Robert George, who had qualified as a civil engineer as well as an architect, 'won an essay competition on the vexed subject of sewerage and drainage for the city'.[46] But his plan was not taken up. At the time the management of public health was in the hands of local government, which did not have the funds to tackle the problems at their source[47] – it was to be a further 10 years before Robert George's ideas would make an impact.

In January 1864 Mary mortgaged acre 56 and the properties on it for £500[48], raising the loan to assist Robert George. Of the total borrowings, Robert George was advanced £250, on which he was to meet interest set by the SA Insurance Company (the mortgagee) at 10 per cent per annum payable in quarterly instalments. Of the balance, after costs were shared equally between Mary and Robert George, £209 and 11 shillings was paid to 'Blackler', on Mary's behalf, to quit a 'former mortgage, principal and interest'[49], which she had raised toward the end of 1863. It was possibly to reimburse Helen for her investment in cottages on acre 56 as, at about the same time, Helen's name disappeared from the rate assessment records and once again Mary was listed as owning all of the properties on the acre.[50] An amount of about £200 would have approximated Helen's investment, based upon the annual value of the cottages and shops, but excluding the value of the land, which belonged to Mary. There is nothing to indicate why this change in ownership was made; perhaps it can be attributed to Mary's concern in her advancing years – she was 76 – to simplify matters regarding acre 56, and so ensure an uncomplicated settling of her estate.

It is also unclear why Robert George needed the money raised for him, but South Australia was once again beset by drought[51], which affected the availability of capital for building projects and reduced the demand for architectural services. Nevertheless, the Congregationalists announced a competition for a new church to commemorate the Reverend Thomas Quinton Stow, to be built in Flinders Street, alongside the Treasury buildings. Robert George's design was successful and he was awarded the commission.[52] He may have used the loan that Mary had raised to support his family while he prepared his competition entry.

In the meantime, work on the town hall was progressing and in January 1864 the first section of the tower was laid – but funds were running short. Eventually, at a public meeting, a further loan of £4000 was sanctioned to ensure that the face of the building would be finished with cut stone rather than the cheaper stucco suggested during funding shortages.[53]

On the first Sunday in February 1865, the foundation stone of Robert George's Stow Memorial Church was laid by Alexander Hay, a leading Adelaide businessman. His address to the congregation of nearly 800 recognised the work of the Reverend Thomas Quinton Stow who, for almost 25 years, had been identified not only with the Congregational Church, but with 'every noble philanthropic institution in the colony'. The church that Robert George described as being in the early Gothic style was designed to hold over 1000 worshippers accommodated on the ground floor and in galleries over the transepts and the southern entrance.[54]

During the early part of the year, just around the corner from the foundations of Robert George's church, Townsend Duryea, a professional photographer, took a series of panoramic views from the height of the partially completed town hall which depicted Adelaide in remarkable detail.[55] Hardly any of its buildings were more than two storeys and many, perhaps the majority, were still simple wooden structures with split-shingle roofs. Only a few of the stone buildings were finished with carved embellishments or decorative plaster work, and the more elaborate of these were in a cluster along King William Street from North Terrace to Victoria Square and the streets in the immediate vicinity of this main thoroughfare. Although Adelaide was no longer a 'forest city' there were still many large open spaces – vacant town acres either in use as the yards of builders and stonemasons, or taken up by horse paddocks for both private and commercial stables. When Duryea created his panorama, Adelaide was at the beginning of 'a remarkable transformation'; over one third of today's heritage buildings were erected between 1865 and 1884.[56]

To accommodate the developing telegraphic services, a new general post office was needed to replace the old single-storey building – now too small – and another architectural competition was announced in August. It was to be built next to the original post office, on the corner of King William and Franklin streets at the entrance to Victoria Square, almost opposite the town hall development, still in progress. Entries were required to reflect the government's optimism for the expansion and development of both its postal and telegraphic services. It was almost 12 months before the competition's winner was announced. The architect of the Adelaide Town Hall, Edmund Wright, repeated his success, this time with an associate, E.J. Woods. The runners-up were Robert George Thomas and E.A. Hamilton, in partnership.[57]

Although he was still involved in building Stow Church, during the first weeks of 1866, Robert George was offered the position of assistant government architect, 'perhaps with the implication that when Hanson [the architect-in-chief] retired in the near future he would be promoted'. Robert George began work in June and over the next six months he was directly involved (probably with the assistance of William McMinn) in the design and supervision of the Local and Insolvency Court in Victoria Square – now the old Supreme Court.[58]

Also during the early months of the year, before Robert George's government appointment had been formalised, William and his partners had sought his help. The *Register*, and its sister papers, the *Evening Telegraph* and the *Chronicle*, were all developing rapidly and Robert George designed large additions to the rear of their existing premises to accommodate their continuing growth. At last in her final years Mary could feel that her confidence in her sons' abilities was bearing fruit. She had maintained in 1838 that 'neither of my boys is deficient in genius or education'.[59] Her family was beginning to prosper again.

The Adelaide Town Hall was opened on the 20 June with an inauguration ceremony, a banquet and a ball, which together occupied several days of almost nonstop celebration. Although he served only one term, William, as a former city councillor for Grey Ward, was listed among the 800 male guests who took part in the banquet. Female guests, as the convention of the time demanded, watched from the balcony![60] In 1866 'it was . . . the most significant structure in King William Street, the tallest, the grandest and most expensive'.[61] But its pre-eminence was not to last for long.

At William's behest, during the early months of the year, Mary began to edit the diary of her voyage to South Australia on the *Africaine* from her original pencil text and to write her reminiscences. It was largely due to Evan, William's last child, who was born just a few months before Mary began this task[62], that *The Diary and Letters of Mary Thomas* was first published by W.K. Thomas and Co. in 1915. However, for now, with Evan's birth in 1866, William and his wife had a family of seven daughters and three sons.

Two of the Thomas family's old friends had died during 1866. The death of Dr John Woodforde, who had visited Frances and Mary Jnr, professionally, and was also a regular guest at Rhantregwnwyn, had occurred in April – he was only 57. In September, Robert's old friend, Osmond Gilles, who was the first colonial treasurer and a founder of the National Bank, died aged 79.[63]

Stow Church was completed during the early weeks of 1867, and dedicated on 12 April. Stow's inaugural service was conducted by the Reverend A.M. Henderson, a highly regarded preacher from Melbourne.[64] Its total cost of £11,000 was considered a 'princely sum for those days'[65] and as the *Observer* commented:

> *The exquisite beauty and chasteness of the Church have been the subject of remark for sometime past . . . The building . . . does great credit to the architect who designed it, to the builders who erected it, and to the congregation who have been spirited enough to carry it out.*[66]

Today's assessment, by the authors of *Heritage of the City of Adelaide*, is that:

> *The building is of intrinsic merit . . . It justifiably won the acclaim of critics and remains significant to the historical development of the Congregational Church and the quality of architecture in South Australia at a time when the colony was gaining confidence and prosperity.*[67]

Robert George was a skilled exponent of the highly fashionable Gothic Revival style.[68] Although both his churches were designed in this genre, their interiors are markedly different. The Baptist Church has a light and spacious simplicity, while Stow (now Pilgrim) Church gives a sense of imposing mass and formal solemnity – each nicely judged to suit its congregation's respective sensibilities toward worship.

Robert George's success, emphasised by the opening ceremonies of public worship, was undoubtedly a great source of contentment, happiness and quiet pride for Mary. Seated in Stow Church she would have experienced light flooding through the southern rose window making visible the details of the interior enrichments and seeing it as Robert George intended.[69] She would have recognised and silently applauded her son's creative versatility – his capacity to design two quite unique places of worship for two very different congregations. On the retirement of William Hanson, during 1867, Robert George was promoted to architect-in-chief, on a salary of £600 per annum.[70]

Mary celebrated her 80th birthday on the 30 August 1867 surrounded by her family who were now all living in South Australia. It must have been a joyous and probably a very noisy occasion, with ages ranging from her 80 years down to the few months of her youngest great-grandchild. Her family included 25 grandchildren – Frances's five, Robert George's five, William's 10 and Helen's two. Mary Jnr now had three children; two sons, Walter Charles in 1862 and Henry Robert in July 1864, had followed the birth of Mary Elizabeth.

Mary could also count nine great-grandchildren; among them were the five children of Frances's three eldest married daughters. Similarly, William's two eldest married daughters had four children between them.[71] In all, she had 41 living descendants.

She had witnessed not only the growth of her own family but the growth of the colony's population from the few hundred of 1836 to 109,000 at the introduction of representative government in 1857; and by 1867 its further increase to almost 163,500.[72] And she had watched the development of Adelaide from little more than a tiny bush settlement to a city with elegantly designed public buildings and broad thoroughfares; a city well able to host a royal visit.

Like Mary, most South Australians were avowed royalists. The visit of Prince Alfred, Duke of Edinburgh and son of Queen Victoria, in November 1867, sparked unprecedented demonstrations of loyalty, and aroused enormous outpourings of affection for him and the sovereign, from this 'most English' of the Australian colonies. After his arrival at Glenelg on the *Galatea*, the prince was accompanied by a ceremonial procession of loyal officials to Adelaide where he was met at the intersection of South Terrace and King William Street by the mayor and the Adelaide City Corporation. The procession then moved onto Victoria Square and along King William Street toward Government House. In acknowledgement of the visit, a continuous line of decorations, which included gas piping to provide night-time illumination, had been put up, festooning the front of the buildings along King William Street. These were not, however, to the taste of the *Observer*'s columnist:

> *This street in its natural state is the finest in the city, and contains the choicest buildings . . . During the past three years King William Street has been adorned with warehouses, banking offices, insurance offices, etc, among which may be traced the latest modifications of Lombard Street Palladian. The South Australian Insurance Office, Murray's warehouse, the Bank of Australasia, and the National Bank would in their natural state have done more credit to the city . . . Fortunately the noblest of all – our new Town Hall – was left comparatively undisfigured. It decided at a glance the character of the street, and attested the high point to which our municipal enterprise had developed itself.*

Mary given her loyal devotion to the monarchy, is certain to have braved the crowds, even at her advanced years, with Helen to watch the royal procession. The *Observer* described how its progress was slow, impeded by the throngs surrounding the royal carriage and 'there were [also] crowds of heads in balconies and knots of heads at windows'.[73]

Earlier, opposite the town hall where the procession had paused briefly, 4000 children sang the national anthem. They were from 35 interdenominational churches. Assembled under the supervision of Mary's son William, they were massed on the tiered seating set up on the site for the new General Post Office. Their order 'was a contrast to the seething restless multitude beneath'.[74]

Prince Alfred laid the foundation stone of the new post office during his visit 'watched by thousands of citizens. Adelaide's "elite" filled the dress circle of the temporary stands, erected for the occasion' and reserved second-class seating was also provided 'for lesser folk'.[75] Robert George's position as colonial architect-in-chief would have made it possible for him to ensure a seat for Mary, and given its royal nature she would have accepted the invitation. Prince Alfred graciously gave consent for the proposed sister towers, on either side of King William Street, marking the entrance to Victoria Square to be named Victoria (General Post Office Tower) and Albert (Adelaide Town Hall Tower).

The foundation stone of the Wesleyan College at Kent Town was also laid during the royal visit and was subsequently known as Prince Alfred College. It was the second boys' school opened in Adelaide based on the English public school system.[76] (The Anglican St Peter's College had been established in 1847.) The prince left Adelaide for Melbourne in the *Galatea* on 21 November with pressing invitations to return, which he did, briefly, before leaving Australia.

Chapter 16
Last years and requiem

Construction work on the new post office reached a stalemate during 1869 when disputes over the foundations and the quality of the building stone led to delays and a parliamentary inquiry. Fresh plans were called for and it fell to Robert George to resolve the difficulties. He 'made some radical modifications including greatly reducing the proposed height of the tower ... [and] brought the expected cost back to £50,000'. Although it was to come in at about £53,000, only slightly over budget, it would be 'the most expensive building constructed by the Government to that date'.[1] Its tower was to mirror that of the town hall but would be higher; also its two frontages, on King William Street and Franklin Street, were larger than the town hall's and designed to accommodate comfortably the two separate functions of General Post Office and the Central Telegraphic Office. The *Register* described the elevations as imposing and 'in the Anglo-Italian style'.[2]

It was an extraordinary experience for Mary to see, what was for the time, this large and imposing building going up and to recollect that less than 30 years earlier, in December 1836, she had used her tent at the settlement at Glenelg as a post office for the first collection of letters to be sent from the colony:

> *A ship was about to sail for Sydney ... Accordingly, many availed themselves of the opportunity, and brought their communications*

to us, all of which I enclosed in a brown holland bag ... Being carefully sealed, it was sent to Sydney, thence to be conveyed to England.[3]

Robert George continued his supervision of the rising walls of the post office, but was also directly involved with the design and management of a number of other notable buildings during his time as architect-in-chief. Among those now demolished were the Government Printing Offices on King William Road, the Magill orphanage, later reformatory, and the Prince Alfred Sailors' Home at Port Adelaide – whose foundation stone had been laid by the Prince on his second brief visit to the colony in February 1868. The central block of Glenside Hospital, formerly the Parkside Lunatic Asylum, is, architecturally, the most important of Robert George's buildings to have survived and has been described as 'perhaps the most magnificent Italianate building in South Australia'.[4] His government appointment had come at the beginning of a decade, the last of Mary's life, that heralded an unprecedented upsurge in civic building which, with some pauses due to financial constraints, went on to span the next 20 years. There has been nothing like it since.

The year 1869 was also the year in which the foundation of St Peter's Cathedral was laid on land purchased seven years earlier at North Adelaide. Its design was based on a church in Scotland, with the plans modified by the architect E.J. Woods whose firm supervised the construction.[5]

The three years of Robert George's tenure as the government's architect-in-chief had been 'solidly productive'. Expenditure on public buildings totalled £343,000 and 'his department was very fully occupied on work in the city and the country'. He prided himself on keeping within estimates, and building costs 'during his tenure had been as low as sixpence per square foot (per 929 square centimetres)'.[6]

But by the early months of 1870 the government faced acute budgetary problems due to 'the depressed state of commerce in the colony'. Reductions in expenditure, including cutbacks in the public service, had been under discussion since the preceding September.[7] Robert George was retrenched toward the end of 1870 and his department was placed under the control of the engineer-in-chief. In his final report, he defended his department and his employment:

> *In every case the most important buildings have been constructed within the estimates accompanying the plans laid before parliament . . . the government have had their money's worth beyond all doubt while my remuneration . . . has certainly not been on the side of excess.*[8]

During this lean time Robert George had little alternative but to return to private practice. Among his commissions would have been designs for the homes of some of Adelaide's wealthier citizens[9], and probably included William's two-storey mansion on the South Esplanade at Glenelg. Although completed in 1878, after Robert George had returned to government service, it has survived to the present and is now known as Albert Hall. In 1872 Robert George also won the design competition for the new Port Adelaide Institute Building.

From a series of letters that Mary wrote to Robert George as her eldest son and head of the family, it is clear that by March 1870 she had begun to contemplate her death and had started to put her affairs in order. Whether this was precipitated by serious ill health or simply her advanced years is not clear. Her will, made earlier in 1848, required that the proceeds of the sale of acre 56 be divided equally between her five children, and should any predecease her, for that share to be divided among their children 'share and share alike'.[10] All of the trustees appointed by her father's will to administer her annuity had died by 1867, and subsequently Mary was able to arrange for the £1000 principal, on which it was based, to be shared equally among her children (or their offspring) according to the terms of her father's will.[11] Now, in 1870, she began to work out how the contents of Rhantregwnwyn, and her personal possessions, clothing and linen should be distributed within her family.

A codicil of 28 March[12] shared most of her household silver, most of the furniture and all of her clothing between Helen and Mary Jnr. She had put a great deal of thought into ensuring that this apportioning was fair – Mary Jnr gained three pieces of silver and Mary's gold chain and eyeglass while Helen's share approximated four pieces of silver. There was no mention of jewellery, and Mary may have already given it to them, or perhaps had disposed of it years ago during difficult times.

Robert George was bequeathed six silver forks and William was to have 'the clock which is in my kitchen, and I wish him to keep it as a relic of olden times, it being, I believe, the first clock of the kind in the colony'. She identified 'drawers' which she had already promised to Isabel Skipper, Frances's youngest daughter. Her books and paintings were to be 'divided among all my children', with some exceptions – an ivory miniature portrait of 'my little Alfred (deceased)' to William's wife, as it bore some resemblance to her youngest son Evan. Robert George was to have her folio Bible and Stowe's *History of England*, and to Mary Jnr she left 'my Pictorial Prayer Book given to me by poor Frances'. Mary made these arrangements as she did 'not wish any public sale to take place, but if they wish to exchange or dispose of any part of it to do it privately'.

Concerned that Helen would need accommodation and an income after her death, Mary made provision for her to remain living at Rhantregwnwyn, rent-free, for three months or until her portion of the estate was available to her. Additionally, during that time, Helen was to receive 'rent from the cottage at the bottom of the acre, and half the rent from the Clarendon Hotel'. She also asked that Robert George and William be fully reimbursed for any money she owed them, and requested as soon as possible after her death that Mary Jnr and Helen should each have access to £10 to buy mourning clothing for themselves and their children. And for the same purpose, Spencer Skipper and Isabel were each to have £5. It seems rather out of character for Mary to be such a stickler for formality at her funeral; perhaps she was trying to compensate those whom she knew could ill afford to go into mourning, but who would nonetheless feel obliged to do so. She also left to Isabel the three volumes of her *Pictorial Bible* 'that she may keep it for my sake, and continue . . . a faithful member of the Church of England to her life's end'. Mary's codicil went on to request that any debt owed by John Skipper should be forgiven, as she had named him with Robert George and William as an executor of her estate, 'as his advice and assistance may be of great service'.[13]

Her attitude toward John Skipper had softened over the years – from her earlier resentment expressed in letters to Helen that he 'neglected Frances', so contributing toward her early death – to seeing him as having her family's interests at heart, and a sound source of advice. John Skipper, the lawyer, had highly regarded skills as a mediator in the sphere of what we would now call dispute resolution. His obituary described him as having

> *a total disregard for money . . . He was a model Local Court clerk, and . . . in the early years of the Port Police Court he was virtually the magistrate, little being done by the nominal S.M. without consulting him . . . Mr Skipper was what might be called the public lawyer at Port Adelaide for many years. Many assault cases and other grievances used to be laid before him by the parties concerned, who requested his advice . . . He thus often healed breaches which might have only been widened by the regular lawyers.*[14]

To what extent, over the years, Mary's values and attitudes influenced those of John Skipper is a matter for conjecture. However, given that he was barely 21 when his romance with Frances on board the *Africaine* first drew him into Mary's close-knit family circle, it is likely to have been considerable.

By the end of the year the *Deceased Wife's Sister Act* 1870, which legalised marriage between a widower and the sister of his deceased wife gained royal assent on its fifth attempt, and at last

Mary's worries over Mary Jnr's marriage to John Skipper could be put to rest. The act was passed by a majority of 26 in the Legislative Assembly and equally as strongly by the Legislative Council.[15]

Mindful of her own difficulties over her annuity Mary was at great pains to set her wishes down in considerable detail. However, she also asked that the codicils she had made be considered only informally, as transactions within the family, and not submitted with her will when it was officially 'proven'. During the latter half of 1871 she added another codicil[16], which specified that both Mary Jnr and Helen were to receive £50 for the education of their children. She also noted that she owed John Skipper £70 as he had paid arrears due to the South Australian Insurance Company – presumably the interest on her half of the £500 mortgage she shared with Robert George. She asked that William be given £100 in recompense for sums he had paid on her account at various times, and that Robert George should repay only £130 of the £250 which was his share of the mortgage with the South Australian Insurance Company. The balance, she considered she owed him in return for services rendered to her.

Mary also wished to honour a promise she had made to Isabel:

it was my intention to make my grand daughter ... Isabel ... a present of a pianoforte as soon as I could spare the money, but losing the Burra dividends[17] put ... it wholly out of my power to do so, I hereby give ... £30 for [it] ... to be bought if such to be had of Mr Platts according to the tone and durability, but I do not limit the price so that it be a good one, more for music than for show.[18]

Apart from problems with her eyes that had plagued her for almost 20 years and, now, deteriorating eyesight, Mary had remained in reasonable health. She had the occasional cold and influenza, but seemingly nothing more serious until the beginning of 1872 when she had some months of severe illness. In September she wrote to Robert George telling him she believed she would not live long and did not expect to reach her 85th year. She asked him to arrange a burial plot to replace the one next to Robert that had been used for the burial of one of Robert George's children. She wished to be buried as near to Robert as possible, and allowing for the child's grave, she wished to have

> the next [plot] and I wish a stone to be put up for your sister Frances, who died . . . in the 37th year of her age, and another to your Father, who died . . . in the 79th year of his age, and on that same you may put my name and age, but no epitaph except it be Resurgam – and let the whole be fenced in.[19]

During her 'long illness' her granddaughter Isabel had cared for her and she was anxious to thank her. In March 1873 Mary wrote to Isabel's sister, Nelly, whose husband, Alfred Sawtell, was a jeweller. She asked Nelly to bring several gold brooches to her at Hindley Street for Isabel to choose one. 'She has been very kind and attentive to me at all times, but specially since I have been ill, and I believe has often put herself to inconvenience to oblige me . . . and let it be handsome.'[20]

Twice over the next 12 months in notes to Robert George, Mary instructed that further gifts were to be made from her estate – bequeathing a silver watch to Robert George's eldest son, and another to her eldest great-grandchild, Thomas Sherman Marshall – the son of Georgy Marshall (nee Skipper).[21] Mary had coped well with the task of putting her affairs in order, but the 1874 City Corporation's rate assessment records indicate that the management of her properties on acre 56 had now passed to property management agents, Simms and Chapman.[22] Seemingly, she was becoming too frail or too ill to maintain her 'hands on' involvement. Nevertheless, she was capable enough during the latter months of the year to write to Robert George twice with requests that additional gifts be bought after her death. She added a mourning ring for Thomas Marshall, the father of her eldest great-grandchild, to the list of five she had already set down and asked that a gold chain and a brooch be purchased for William's wife 'who has been very kind to me in my long illness'.[23]

In May 1870 South Australians had elected a new government,

but the ministry it formed lasted only a few weeks and within a month a new ministry had been sworn in. One of its first actions was to approve work on the possible development of an overland telegraph. (Queensland was competing with South Australia for the project and there had been no time to lose.) It was to connect Adelaide, by means of Stuart's overland track, to South Australia's far-flung outpost at Port Darwin, and through a cable laid on the seabed, to the rest of the world. The South Australian Government was awarded the right to build the line and undertook to complete it by 1 January 1872, giving the supervision of the project to Post Master General Charles Todd. Its cost was estimated at £120,000 or £80 per mile (1.61 kilometres).[24]

The first party contracted for laying the northern-most part of the line left Adelaide for Port Darwin on the steamer *Omeo* in August 1870, and by the beginning of September two more government parties had been dispatched overland to construct the central section.[25] Only a week or so later, in a ceremony at Port Darwin, the first pole of the Overland Telegraph was 'planted' by the daughter of the government resident.[26] By the end of October 1871 the central part of the telegraph was well advanced and Todd had sent out the operators for the four telegraph stations north of Beltana – one of the most significant of this central group was to be Alice Springs, named after Todd's wife.[27]

By December 1871 news from Batavia (Jakarta), in Indonesia, was received in Adelaide advising that the steamer *Investigator*, which was carrying the cable to be laid between Java and Darwin, had arrived there and was due to leave within a matter of days to lay the shore-end of the cable at the southern tip of Java.[28] Although the contractors operating out of Darwin were replacements for the original team, which had proved incompetent, they were still making little progress due 'to the swampy and flooded state of the country' and Todd sent large reinforcements to their aid[29] – increasing the cost of the project significantly. Overland telegraph communications were opened from Adelaide as far as the Alice Springs station on 3 January 1872, and the following day

Charles Todd, now designated superintendent of telegraphs, sailed for Darwin.[30]

As a further indication of the colony's progress, in May 1872 the General Post Office was opened to acclaim. The *Observer* reported that a white ensign was flown from Victoria Tower in honour of the event and that 'The people who flocked throughout the day into the spacious hall were struck by its proportions and style'.[31] Mary's serious illness during the early part of 1872 meant that she was probably unable to join the throngs visiting the new building, but she would have been kept informed and up-to-date by the reports in the *Register* and the *Observer*.

The telegraph office, located in the new building, had been finished just in time to receive the first message from Darwin by the Overland Telegraph. It was received on the 22 August 1872 when 'the Town Hall bells rang, flags were hoisted, government offices were closed, the day was generally devoted to rejoicing, and hearty congratulations were sent to Mr Todd . . . on the successful and satisfactory completion of his gigantic and important undertaking'. A break in the submarine cable between Darwin and Java prevented messages being sent to Europe, but by 20 October it had been repaired, and the first message from London was received in Adelaide, which 'was followed by congratulatory telegrams from all parts of the world'.[32]

This overseas connection made a massive difference to the range of sources that could be tapped for international news and the speed at which news could be garnered. And for readers of daily newspapers, the immediacy with which events as such wars and natural disasters could now be reported heightened their dramatic impact. For William's firm of Andrews, Thomas and Clark, this development was of great significance, given that they were publishing both a morning and an evening paper. From now on communication with London and other overseas centres was a matter of minutes from Adelaide, and most of the rest of Australia. It made Australia part of the world, rather than – as Mary had known it less than 40 years before – that remote continent at the ends of the earth.

The laying of the line across the continent had been a huge undertaking for a colony with a relatively inexperienced parliament, and a small population. Incredibly, it was achieved in little more than two years, through some of the most remote and inhospitable land in Australia. There were no roads, and most of the supplies – materials for the work and food for the men – were shipped halfway around the continent from Adelaide to Darwin. Once there, supplies were trans-shipped to work camps via uncharted rivers, subject to massive flooding during the monsoonal season. Todd described the complexity of the task in his speech at his celebratory banquet. It also helps to explain the massive increase in the project's cost – three times more than the 1870 estimates.

> *to cart building materials, instruments, batteries, and other stores for stations; to build a stone station of twenty-two rooms at Port Darwin, stone or wooden stations of seven or eight rooms at eight other places; to sink wells, establish depots, and a variety of other things [involved] great labour and thought.*[33]

Meanwhile in Adelaide communication between its northern and southern parts had been improved during 1870 with the completion of the Morphett Street Bridge. It spanned the railway yards and connected with the Victoria Bridge across the Torrens, re-opening the direct route from Morphett Street to North Adelaide via Montefiore Hill and Jeffcott Street. Elegant footbridges from North Terrace gave access to the footpaths on the main span.[34] The closure of Morphett Street at North Terrace due to the railways, which had annoyed Mary for a decade, had been overcome. By this time, however, Mary may have been too frail to mount the several steep flights of stairs to the footbridge and walk across the new structure to savour its amenity. Nevertheless she very likely recalled that the new bridge was close to the spot where she had crossed the Torrens by means of a fallen log just 30 years before when setting out to visit a friend at North Adelaide, and had passed by a hundred or so Aborigines camped on the banks of the Torrens.[35]

It is sad to contemplate that in her declining years Mary was subject to the uncontrolled noxious odours and effluents emanating from the industries beginning to establish themselves in the western end of the city. She blamed the railways for some of these problems, complaining that they had 'injured' her part of town.[36] But she did not budge and join the retreat to the south-eastern part of the city or to the suburbs. Much to her displeasure the railway yards were absorbing increasing amounts of land near the north-western corner of the town as rail networks continued to develop to Glenelg and to near country areas. In Hindley Street, a brewery and other industries were replacing commercial and retail trades, which were moving further east toward Rundle Street. The proximity to rail transport and the decline in land values were encouraging manufacturing activity.

At the end of 1872 William was appointed to a committee – drawn from a number of the nonconformist churches – to initiate discussions to establish a tertiary theological college. They approached the copper magnate W.W. Hughes who offered the very generous endowment of £20,000. The committee 'patriotically' considered that such a large sum should be devoted to the founding of a university, and so a University Association, led by the Anglican prelate, Bishop Short, was formed.[37] Its preliminary meeting, attended by 11 clergymen from all denominations, decided that a university should be available to all students irrespective of creed and that the support of the general public should be invited.[38] In January 1873 Walter Hughes signed a deed of gift – his endowment was to become available only in 10 years but, in the interim, an annual interest on it of 5 per cent was to be paid to the association.[39] With basic funding assured, the efforts to found the University of Adelaide could now be accelerated.

Some six months later the association approached the government for assistance, but its response was parsimonious in comparison to the government funds that had been made available to found Sydney (1850) and Melbourne (1853) universities. The South Australian Government did, however, introduce a bill of incorporation for the university and provided a building site on North Terrace for its future construction. It also offered a single lump sum grant of £10,000 plus an annual amount equal to the income, which would accrue on other donations at an interest rate of 5 per cent.[40]

The *Adelaide University Incorporation Act* 1874, passed in October, granted the University Council – to be nominated by the governor – the power to confer degrees, and by 1880, women had been granted admission alongside men. As well as the building site of 5 acres (2 hectares), the act endowed a further 50,000 freehold acres (20,200 hectares), and confirmed the already agreed lump sum grant plus interest on funds donated by the public. Within days of its passage the university's financial situation was consolidated by a gift of £20,000 from the pastoralist and merchant, Thomas Elder, and, including the dividends that would accrue from it, the university could now anticipate an annual income from all sources of £6000.[41]

At the University Council's first meeting held in December 1874, the chief justice, Sir Richard Hanson, was appointed chancellor and Bishop Short vice-chancellor. Committees were formed to develop a scheme of professorships and lectureships and to negotiate with the commissioner of crown lands regarding the appropriation of the endowed land.[42] Arrangements were also underway to establish evening classes to bridge the gap between ordinary schooling and the training to be undertaken for a first-class degree.[43]

And during the preceding year, there had been other developments in Adelaide's intellectual and cultural life. Still in private practice, Robert George had won the design competition for the redevelopment of the South Australian Institute, which had outgrown the building, opened just 12 years before, that housed its circulating library, and embryonic museum and art collections. His design was set aside, however, when the government, with the possibility of a 'national' reference library in mind, ordered an inquiry.[44] The inquiry, headed by Sir Richard Hanson, reported in April 1874.

Its findings supported the institute's focus on fostering the objects of societies that encouraged the arts and the study and discussion of philosophy, and also its work 'as a parent body to country Institutes'. The commission recommended that the institute expand these activities to include lectures on scientific topics. It also wanted to see an extension of the museum's available space and resources, and advocated the immediate development of two new facilities – an art gallery and a free reference library. Funding of up to £25,000 was to be made available for a building to house these initiatives.[45] Adjustments were made to Robert George's winning design for what ultimately was to become the Jervois Building, and it is not clear how much of his design was left intact in the final development.[46]

But in spite of these advances, Adelaide was still without a sewerage system or adequate drainage. The *Observer* commented in December 1871 that public health had not received much attention during the recent parliamentary elections. 'Year by year the accumulations of decomposing animal and vegetable matter . . . are storing up sources of poison and miasma . . . Many lives are lost annually entirely through preventable causes.'[47] The *Public Health Act* 1873 was eventually passed in August, effective from the New Year, which established a central board, whose main function was to direct and supervise municipal councils, and their local boards of health, including that of the Adelaide City Corporation.

> *[The] legal responsibilities and duties [of municipal councils] so far as sanitary matters are concerned, will be materially increased, and at the same time the law will afford them greater means of protection against annoyance and noxious trades and ill kept premises in their neighbourhood.*[48]

Regulations detailed standards for the provision of properly constructed privies and the disposal of wastes. Inspectors were empowered to take both legal and, where appropriate, practical action against offenders, who were then required to pay for any work begun or ordered to be undertaken by inspectors; 'the Act introduces no reform that will prove a hardship to householders who keep their premises with due regard to cleanliness and health'.[49]

Robert George took up an appointment as secretary to the first Central Board of Health at the beginning of the year thus returning to government service. His second qualification as a civil engineer now stood him in good stead, and over the years he had maintained a general interest in public health, having written a prize-winning essay on the subject. The six-member board included, besides Robert George, two doctors – Charles Gosse and Allen Campbell (who would be instrumental in founding the Adelaide Children's Hospital) – and they met for the first time on 13 January.[50] A return to prosperity meant that the necessary expenditures on long-delayed projects for improvements in public hygiene, and subsequently health, were more feasible.

In March the *Observer* congratulated the new central board, noting the commendable energy and focus it had shown in having 'recently issued a code of directions for the guidance' of local boards to ensure that they 'properly discharge the functions entrusted to them'. A number of local boards had already been set up, for example at Hindmarsh, West Torrens and Moonta.[51]

In a companion article the same *Observer* commented that the Adelaide City Corporation's Local Board of Health had 'issued a code of regulations for the sanitary government of the city' that had been 'drawn up under ... the Public Health Act and ... assented to by the Central Board' and which possessed 'all the force of law'.[52] Whilst praising their extent it also noted that they were by no means exhaustive as, for example, they had not made adequate provision for the collection of rubbish, or 'scavenging' as it was called then. Many also considered that the city's problems could not be cured without a waterborne sewerage system.[53]

By the end of the 1874 the Adelaide City Corporation had, at last, resolved to begin to tackle the city's drainage problems. The efforts of Robert George and the central board were making an impact and plans for the drainage of the eastern portion of the city were put on display for public comment at Green's Exchange.[54]

But there was neither the political will nor the money to resolve the problems faced by the Aborigines. During the 1860s and 1870s the remnant populations were swept up into missions at Poonindie, near Pt Lincoln (where groups from Adelaide were placed) at Point McLeay on Lake Alexandrina, and at Point Pearce on Yorke Peninsula.[55] Later, missions would be established in the far north. The alienation of Aborigines from their lands was complete – Aborigines were placed in the care of missionaries, and out of sight was out of mind.

Although Mary had witnessed the establishment of tertiary education in South Australia, she did not live to see the passage of the *Education Act* 1875. She would have, given her liberal views and concern for those less well off, applauded its introduction of free, compulsory and secular elementary education for all children.[56]

In January 1875 the weather was extreme, with hot winds and temperatures of up to 109°F (42°C). A ring of fires encircled Adelaide – at Walkerville, Mitcham, Fifth Creek and the Reed Beds. And the hills between Cherry Gardens and Clarendon were ablaze.[57] The city was engulfed in smoke.

Mary had always found it difficult to bear the heat of South Australia's summers and she died on 10 February 1875 at Rhantregwnwyn cottage, aged 87 years. Spencer Skipper, for whom she had cared with his sister Isabel for many years from early childhood, and to whom she was more like a mother than a grandmother, composed, an *In Memoriam: Those Women Pioneers*. It is a heartfelt and fitting tribute to Mary from a loving 'son':

> *They are leaving us, those brave kind hearts,*
> *So patient firm and true*
> *Those noble women pioneers,*
> *Who dared all we dared do,*
> *Whose faithful, all-enduring love*
> *Outlived the constant toil . . .*
> *And now the land they helped to win*

Receives embalmed with tears,
The bravest of that sisterhood
Of Women Pioneers[58]

Her obituary, in the *Register*, of 13 February 1875 was repeated in the *Observer* of the following weekend:

Another of the pioneer colonists of South Australia passed away on Wednesday, February 10th . . . Mrs Robert Thomas . . . the widow of the founder of the 'Register' and therefore of the press in South Australia . . . In 1831 she published, at the earnest request of her friends, a collection of 'serious poems,' which bore evidence of her ability and originality of thought, and she was also the author of many meritorious contributions to the Press of this colony. Her living descendents all of whom are residents in South Australia number 56, viz, 4 children, 27 grandchildren, and 25 great-grand-children . . . The burial rites were performed by the Rev. R. Reid, of Trinity Church . . . The remains were followed to West Terrace Cemetery by her sons . . . and grandsons . . . [and] E. Sawtell and C. Birks [connections by marriage, and also] . . . Dr Gosse and several Gentlemen . . . [partners and associates of] the 'Register'.

And the *Register*, of 15 February, reported the sermon of the Reverend Reid at Trinity Church on the following Sunday:

The death of [Mrs Mary Thomas] . . . was very feelingly alluded to . . . [The Reverend Reid also] alluded to her devout attendance there up to a very recent period, when the infirmities consequent on her advanced age (87) prevented its continuance. He had visited her for 16 years in the course of his parochial duties, and always found her of a kind, loving, and Christian disposition – in truth a God-fearing woman. Some four years ago, whilst discussing the various writings and periodicals of the day, she had given him a book of her own composition, which he characterised as bearing evidence of great mental ability, and the stamp of true piety. He valued it most highly.[59]

Mary was a significant presence at the birth of the press in South Australia. In his unpublished 'History of the Register' William Sowden, a former editor of the paper, refers to her as having taken

> so active and useful a part in the journalistic department that she might well have been classed as one of the firm of Robert Thomas and Co ... Mr Thomas and his partner had to do the best they could with the limited staff they had, assisted by the lady members of the family.[60]

Overall, her presence as a knowledgeable, reliable and capable additional pair of hands was an invaluable asset.

Mary's other significant legacy to the press in South Australia is that, with Robert, she initiated a family engagement with newspapers, both as proprietors and editors, which was maintained for four generations. Their son William, a proprietor of the firm Andrews, Thomas and Clark, was largely a self-taught master of the technical printing processes.[61] Two of William's sons, Robert and Evan, continued the association as proprietors (with others) of W.K. Thomas and Co. Evan was also an editor with Register Newspapers Ltd and Robert was knighted for services to the press as the chairman of the overseas delegates to the 1909 Imperial Press Conference in London.[62] Later, Evan's son Archer, who had also worked on the *Register* (and then as managing editor of the Melbourne *Herald and Weekly Times*) became chairman of Australian Associated Press.[63] For Mary and Robert, as for many of the first pioneers, 'Wakefield's promises were not for them but their children's children'.[64]

As Mary had willed it, acre 56, her sole asset, was sold off after her death. When application was made by her executors in September 1875 to register the title of acre 56, it was valued at £3000, and the mortgage of January 1864 was discharged as part of the 'winding up of her estate'.[65]

Within seven months of her death, Rhantregwnwyn and the cottages, which stood where the original printing offices had been, were demolished.[66] William survived his mother by just three years, and by the end of 1883, both Mary Jnr and John Skipper were dead. Robert George lived only a few months longer and died in April 1884.

When the first of her children was born Mary was 32, yet, apart from Helen, she very nearly outlived them all. Within a few years of her death all those other family members from the *Africaine*, who on 10 December 1836 had set foot with her into an unknown wilderness, had perished. It was as if they had lost their mainstay, their ever-present help in troubled times.[67] Of them it was left to Helen to carry their story into the 20th century.[68]

Acknowledgements

No project such as this comes to fruition without the help of many people and I owe a particular debt of thanks to a number of the descendants of Mary Thomas.

Chief among these was her great-great-granddaughter, Mrs Joan Kyffin Willington, and Joan's husband Victor. Their kindness, encouragement and generosity in giving me access to and permission to quote from their family papers – including Mary Thomas's manuscript book – have been invaluable. Access to and their permission to use family portraits is also appreciated. Sadly, Mrs Willington's death occurred before the book could be published.

I thank Victor Willington for permission to quote extensively from the original transcript of Mary Thomas's diary of the voyage to South Australia, and the original transcript of her letters to her brother George Harris. Both are held in the archives of the State Library of South Australia. Although these transcripts were edited and published in a single volume (E.K. Thomas, *The Diary and Letters of Mary Thomas*, W.K. Thomas and Co., Adelaide, 1925), I have used the original versions throughout as a number of significant comments made by Mary, about her sister, Ann, and about South Australian colonial officials, have been edited out of the published letters. To maintain consistency, I have also used the original transcript of the diary.

I thank Mrs Lyn O'Brien, another of Mary Thomas's great-great-granddaughters, who has been similarly helpful and generous in allowing me to quote extensively from Mary Thomas's letters between 1855 and 1860 to her daughter Helen. These letters are held in the archives of the State Library of South Australia. Mrs Mary Hogan, also a great-great-granddaughter has offered encouragement and has made family portraits available for the book.

One of the unexpected pleasures of this project was the discovery of a branch of the Thomas family in Western Australia, and I am grateful to the Reverend Edward Miller and Mrs Johannes McManus for their permission to quote extensively from the journal of Mary Skipper (nee Thomas). An edited transcript of the journal is held in the archives of the State Library of SA.

Both the general staff and the archival staff of the State Library have provided invaluable suggestions and research help with unfailing courtesy and promptness. In particular, the assistance of Ms Prue McDonald is much appreciated. I also thank the Library for permission to quote from the Proceedings of the Royal Geographical Society of South Australia. The staffs of State Records of South Australia, the Adelaide City Archives and the General Registry Office have been similarly helpful and I thank these organisations for permission to quote from their collections. My thanks are also due to the Dixon Library of the State Library of New South Wales for permission to quote from the journal of emigration agent, John Brown. A copy of this document is held in the archives of the State Library of South Australia. The assistance of the staff of the Southampton Archives, United Kingdom, in researching the early years of Mary Thomas has also been invaluable.

I also express my gratitude to the Pioneers' Association of South Australia for permission to quote from their publications.

My immediate and extended family and a number of friends have maintained a continuing interest in this undertaking and I am very appreciative of the faith they have shown in it and their ongoing encouragement. I would also like to thank my one-time fellow student and now friend Sandra Lindemann, for her commentary on the manuscript at various stages and for her proofreading.

This project owes its origins as part of the final year of the Advanced Diploma in Professional Writing undertaken at the Adelaide Institute of TAFE, and I acknowledge the input, in its early stages, of Roger Zubrinich. The project has also been supported by a grant from the History Trust of South Australia.

I would also like to acknowledge the input and guidance of my editor Ms Kathy Sharrad.

Appendix A
Descendants of Robert and Mary Thomas to 1875

Mary Thomas at the time of her death had four surviving children, 26 grandchildren and an estimated 25 great-grandchildren.

Dates of births, marriages and deaths have only been recorded where they occurred before 1875, except for the first generation – the children of Mary and Robert.

Robert THOMAS
Son of John Thomas and Mary (nee Davis)
b. 16.11.1782, Rhantregwnwyn, Wales
d. 1.7.1860, Adelaide, SA

married
8.1.1818, Southampton, UK

Mary (nee HARRIS)
Daughter of George Harris and Mary (nee Batchelor)
b. 30.8.1787, Southampton, UK
d. 10.2.1875, Adelaide, SA

---

(1) Frances Amelia
b. 14.11.1818, London
d. 27.2.1855, Adelaide, SA
m. 28.12.1839, Unley, SA
John Michael SKIPPER
b. 12.7.1815, UK
d. 7.12.1883, Adelaide, SA

(2) Robert George
b. 16.2.1820, London
d. 14.4.1883, Unley, SA
m. 16.9.1856, UK
Charlotte Annette (nee TUCKETT)
b. 17.7.1826, UK
d. 17.11.1901, Adelaide, SA

(1) Jane Georgiana KYFFIN
b. 16.10.1840
m. 3.10.1860
Thomas B. MARSHALL
Offspring:
 Thomas 1861
 Amelia 1863
 Arthur 1868
 Ella 1870
 Spencer 1867 (died in infancy)
 Herbert 1872

(2) Frances Mary
b. 10.10.1842
m. 13.11.1863
William JONES (killed 1868)

(3) William Kyffin
b. 4.11.1821, Newport, UK
d. 4.7.1878, Glenelg, SA
m. 28.1.1843
Mary Jane (nee GOOD)
b. 17.7.1826, UK
d. 17.11.1901, Adelaide, SA

(1) Robert George Shum
b. 30.7.1857

(2) Mary Annette
b. 2.6.1859

(3) Kyffin Michael
b. 1861
d. 1862

(4) Jessie Kate
b. 1862
d. 1863

(5) Clara Eliza
b. 1864

(6) Llewellyn Shum
b. 1865

(7) Arthur Churchill
b. 1867

(4) Mary
b. 30.8.1823, London
d. 28.4.1883, Kent Town, SA
m. 28.4.1856, Pt. Adelaide, SA
John Michael SKIPPER
b. 12.7.1815, UK
d. 7.12.1883, Adelaide, SA
Widower of Frances Amelia (14.11.1818–27.2.1855)

(1) Mary Elizabeth
b. 31.8.1859

(2) Walter Charles
b. 5.4.1862

(3) Henry Robert
b. 22.7.1864

(5) Helen
b. 6.7.1825, London
d. 17.8.1921, Adelaide, SA
m. 25.6.1855, Adelaide, SA
Alfred MANTEGANI
b. 5.10.1829, Wisbech, UK
d. 5.6.1861, Adelaide, SA

(1) Victoria Theresa
b. 15.4.1856

(2) Alfred Victor
b. 13.1.1859

(6) Alfred
b. 22.2.1827, London
d. 26.6.1828, London

Mary Maria
b. 19.11.1843
m. 13.9.1866
Charles BIRKS
Offspring:
 Mary 1867
 Ellen 1869
 Edith 1871

Helen Rosetta
b. 30.8.1845
m. 28.1.1863
George Napier BIRKS
Offspring:
 Helen 1863
 George 1866
 Emily 1867
 Florence 1870
 Charles 1871
 Alfred 1874

Descendants of Robert and Mary Thomas to 1875

Offspring:
Isabelle 1864
m. c. 1875 (second marriage)
Rev. Benjamin Gilbert EDWARDS

(3) Helen Stark
b. 26.5.1844
m. c. 1864
Alfred Edwin SAWTELL
Offspring:
Edith 1865
Clara 1867
Alfred 1869 (died in infancy)
Esther 1870
Millicent 1873
Margaret 1874

(4) Spencer John
b. 21.5.1847

(5) Isabel Margaret Gower
b. 17.9.1849
m. 1871 Richard ROBINSON
Offspring:
Percival c. 1872
Eleanor c. 1874

(8) Ernest Shum
b. c. 1867

(9) Laura Henrietta
b. 1871

(3) Frances
b. 9.10.1847
m. 29.10.1867
William NEILL
Offspring:
Frances 1870
Florence 1873

(4) William James
b. 11.10.1849
d. 30.10.1850

(5) Robert Kyffin
b. 19.8.1851

(6) Catherine Louise
b. 8.3.1854
d. 30.3.1855

(7) Rosetta Jane
b. 3.12.1856

(8) Alfred Kyffin
b. 31.5.1858

(9) Florence Emily
b. 28.3.1860

(10) Margaret Edith
b. 28.2.1862

(11) Annie Isobel
b. 19.6.1864

(12) Evan Kyffin
b. 17.7.1865

Appendix B
Serious Poems

In 1831 Mary collected her writings together as *Serious Poems*. This 270-page, octavo-sized volume containing 58 poems was published in London by Whittaker and Treacher of Ave Maria Lane, near St Paul's Cathedral. They were written, Mary says in her preface, 'without the smallest idea of them ever appealing to the public, but with a sole view to the instruction and amusement of my own family . . . some of the pieces were written expressly for children'. She published them at the urging of friends: 'they fancied they could see a merit in my production' and she was hopeful that the views she espoused would help the 'rising generation'.[1] The longest poem, 'The Village Sabbath', occupies 28 pages:

> *And now the lanes, the fields, and meadows throng*
> *With cheerful villagers who trip along*
> *In the same paths which their fathers' trod*
> *And which will lead them to the house of God.*

Mary's most effective poems are her simplest, for example in 'To the Robin', whom she feeds with bread crumbs.

> *And all the recompense I ask*
> *Is to perform thy daily task*
> *With thy sweet warbling throat.*

For nature's music is to me
Beyond the studied harmony
Of viol, harp or lute.
(*Serious Poems*)

For the biographer the merit of her poetry lies in what can be construed about Mary's ethical and religious values – her emphasis upon the love of God and upon truth, loyalty, compassion and contentment – and her belief in liberty, equality and justice before the law for all humankind. The poems also give an insight into aspects of her life in London, the loss of her youngest child, the deaths of friends, and her thoughts about emigration.

Other than Mary's statement in a letter to her brother George that 'some pieces ... have been considered by good judges as not unworthy of publication', there is no indication of any contemporary review or assessment of her poetry.[2] Kathleen Kyffin Thomas, Mary's great-granddaughter, in reflecting upon *Serious Poems*, commented during a radio broadcast in 1960:

> *They certainly are serious poems. The first one is entitled 'The Churchyard' and runs to 26 pages; the second 'The Balm of Grief', and another 'The Village Sabbath'! I therefore much prefer to think of my great-grandmother as the settlement's diarist than as its poetess, for her records have a real historical interest and reveal her own personality, whereas the poems are certainly of doubtful value!*[3]

Nevertheless, Mary's fellow colonists thought of her as a poet, as, in the same broadcast, Kathleen Kyffin Thomas commented: 'In an account of those early days written by another hand, she is described as the "capable Mrs Thomas, the poetess of the settlement", who is known to be keeping a record of events in her diary – a fitting wife for a printer and publisher and again, as "a friendly person, busy about her tent".' A copy of Mary's *Serious Poems* is held by the State Library of South Australia.

Manuscript Book

Mary's manuscript book contains 54 poems as well as a transcript of her diary from the *Africaine*. Both are in her hand. Her poems, as with the diary, were probably transcribed from another source in 1866. None of the poems published in *Serious Poems*, 1831, are duplicated in the manuscript book. However, several poems in the manuscript book date from before 1831 and the publication of *Serious Poems*. Most, however, were composed between 1832 and 1835. The only poem for 1836, 'Adieu', was written on board the *Africaine*. Mary's manuscript book is in the family papers of Victor Willington.

Style

Mary's poetry reveals her as an 'exceedingly well educated'[4] woman, with an extensive vocabulary and a familiarity with classical mythology. She was adept at using stanzas of varying length, of up to nine lines, and she also experimented with rhyming patterns and varied both length of line and metre from poem to poem.

Her compositions include narrative, descriptive, didactic and lyric poems, as well light and humorous verse. Some of Mary's most successful are her humorous verses.[5] A series of parodies written in 1835 are the last compositions in her manuscript book and were probably intended to be recited as part of a skit. There are 15 of well-known persons including, William IV, the Duke of Wellington, Sir Robert Peel, Lord Brougham, the Duchess of Kent, the Princess Victoria and Mrs Fry, a Quaker.

Themes

Mary was a child of the Age of Reason who grew to adulthood and maturity in the Romantic era. In general, she eschewed the Romantics, adopting in her more solemn verse the emotional restraint and ordered self-control of the late Augustan poets as exemplified by Pope.

Her two major themes are: God as love encapsulating a faith in redemption and eternal life; and God the creator of both mankind (all men are equal) and of nature (all nature is infused by joy as the creation of God's love).

Mary looks back beyond Pope to Milton regarding the central place that God occupies in her poetry and in the maintenance of the Puritan imperative to elevate God as the central theme of literature. Her emphasis upon charity as well as upon hope and faith and her belief in man's capacity to appeal immediately, without an intercessor, to God for salvation are both very Protestant themes. Enlightenment values – liberalism and individual rights, both directly related to the Protestant ethos – also inform Mary's work. They are linked to the Evangelical Movement, the Established Church's answer to Methodism and a reaction to the materialistic values of the late 18th and early 19th centuries. A theme deriving from this is her support in *Serious Poems* for the anti-slavery movement with which prominent Evangelicals such as William Wilberforce were involved.

The Christian theme that all men are equal in the sight of God appears frequently in her verse.

> *The human race are brethren all,*
> *The children of one sod,*
> *Dispers'd throughout this earthly ball.*
> *Our Father is our God.*
> ('A Farewell to England' – manuscript book)

Despite the morbidity of some of Mary's poems (death, pestilence, wars), a characteristic not uncommon in the poets of her era, hope and optimism are ultimately pivotal. In the end worldly troubles melt away in the bliss of eternal life; and in this world charity and compassion should dictate the relationships between person and person.

> *But let all those possessing ample store*
> *Ne'er rest with wishes to the needy poor,*
> *For as they from abundance give*
> *So double blessings shall we all receive.*
> ('On Charity' – manuscript book)

Mary's poems expressing her love of nature and the countryside record an idealised nature rather than, as in the poems of Goldsmith, the contemporary countryside. She does not mention the decline of much of the rural population into landlessness and poverty, a result of the enclosures, or the rioting of agricultural labourers against increases in food prices, although both were happening around Southampton in Mary's childhood and early adult years.

> *The rustics prepar'd the summons to obey,*
> *To join their praise to Heaven in full choir;*
> *Declare their hope of eternal rest,*
> *And shew that poverty with content is blest.*
> ('The Village Sabbath' – *Serious Poems*)

Similarly her love of England is expressed not only in her idealised countryside but in her idealising of the laws of England based, as she considered, upon a love of peace, truth and equality for all under the law. At a time when the movement for parliamentary reform was active all around her she saw them as, unequivocally, the most advanced of any nation.

> *Thou land of my fathers, where freedom was nourished,*
> *Where each noble virtue grows up to its prime.*
> ('Adieu' – *Diary and Letters of Mary Thomas*)
> *
>
> *And freedom was our Country's proudest boast*
> *And England envied by each distant coast*
> ('On Beholding the Demolition of the Ancient London Bridge, January 1832' – manuscript book)

It is in the poems in which she expresses intense grief at the death of her infant son and at the deaths of friends that she seems more modern, more like the early Romantics.

> *...fancy paints thy smiling image,*
> *With its little hands held forth for aid,*

> *And hears thy lisping tongue repeat our names*
> *And making artless efforts to express*
> *Its wants; . . .*
> ('A Fragment' – *Serious Poems*)

This is also apparent when, in her poems about emigration, she voices the depth of her emotional loss.

> *Farewell to the shades of my infancy's dwelling*
> *Farewell to the spot where I first drew my breath!*
> *My eyes fill with tears, and my bosom is swelling*
>
> *As I take a last view of Town, Meadow and Heath.*
> ('Farewell to Southampton' – *Diary and Letters of Mary Thomas*)

Mary uses no unexpected or unusual similes or metaphors that render, in a new light or from a new perspective, the religious faith espoused in her poems. Her poetic style and manner, like the simple beliefs expressed, are orthodox and traditional, almost formulaic. There are no new insights.

She has a deft turn of phrase and a ready wit in her lighter verses, but these are less than a third of her work overall – the epitaphs of Leonard and Robert Baugh, 'The Lame Man, the Blind Man and the Oyster', 'Celebs in Search of a Wife', and the parodies, for example, from her manuscript book.

The underlying and frequently central theme of all her other poems is the redemption available to the faithful through a merciful God who reduces the terrors of death.

> *On him then call, and cast your care,*
> *Whose mercy never fails;*
> *With whom the humble, contrite prayer*
> *Assuredly prevails.*
> ('The Evening Star' – *Serious Poems*)

Mary's vision of nature infused by joy as a creation of God's love was a product of the idyllic English countryside.

> *. . . rejoice! ye snowy flocks . . .*
> *Join with the lowing herd, and harmonize*
> *Your bleatings to the song of praise, until*
> *Mountain answers mountain and hill and dale*
> *Re-echo with the sound of universal joy*
> ('Evening' – *Serious Poems*)

Even the pangs of grief and loss should be accepted as an expression of faith that is uncomplicated and in which there is no questioning of the role of God in poverty, wars or pestilence. How Mary's faith changed and increased in complexity and matured as the result of confronting adversity in South Australia is unknown. No poetry written after 1836 has been discovered. That her faith did survive, however, is clear from the eulogy preached by the rector of Trinity Church on the Sunday after her funeral. She was characterised as a 'devout' and 'God-fearing woman' whose writings bore 'evidence of great mental ability and the stamp of true piety'.[6]

Charity, given Mary's relationships with those in need, was still central to her faith, but there was less hope, less optimism; and probably less joy. It would have been difficult to see the drought-stricken South Australian landscape with its emaciated and starving sheep and cattle, or a bushfire devastated, blackened countryside as infused by the joy of God's creative love.

It is very unfortunate that Mary's South Australian poems, presumably destroyed, are not available to indicate how her faith – an almost childlike simplicity of belief commonplace among women of her time and social class – was transformed to encompass the harsh realities of colonial life.

References

Abrams, M.H. (ed.), *The Norton anthology of English Literature* (5th ed.), W.W. Norton and Co., New York, 1986

Bloom, H., *The Western cannon*, Harcourt Brace and Co., USA, 1994

Evans, B.I., *A short history of English literature*, Pelican, United Kingdom, 1951

Holmes, R., *Coleridge selected poems*, Harper Collins, London, 1996

Ricks, C. (ed.), *The Oxford book of English verse*, Oxford University Press, United Kingdom, 1999

Russell, B., *History of Western philosophy*, Allen and Unwin, London, 1961

Stillman, F., *The poet's manual*, Thames and Hudson, London, 1985

The Modern Library, *William Wordsworth selected poetry*, Random House, 1950

The Wordsworth Poetry Library, *The works of Alexander Pope*, Wordsworth Editions Ltd, United Kingdom, 1995

Thomas, E.K. (ed.), *The Diary and Letters of Mary Thomas*, W.K. Thomas and Co., Adelaide, 1925

Thomas, M., *Serious Poems*, Whittaker, Treacher and Co., London, 1831

Notes

Key to notes
Abbreviations
SLSA   State Library of South Australia
PRG   Personal Records Group (SLSA)
SRSA   State Records of South Australia
GRG   Government Records Group (SRSA)
GRO   Government Registry Office (Old Land Titles Office)
ACA   Adelaide City Archives

Archival Sources, SLSA
Thomas Family, SLSA PRG 1160
    Diary of Mary Thomas (original and transcription), 1836, 1160/1
    Mary Thomas to George Harris, 1160/2
    Robert Thomas to Colonial Office 1836 (ms), 1160/4
    Journal of Mary Skipper (nee Thomas) (Mary Jnr's journal), 1160/6
    Commonplace Book of Mary Thomas, 1160/7
John Brown, diary, SLSA PRG 1002/2
Violet De Mole, papers, SLSA, PRG 39
Everard Family, letters, SLSA PRG 208, Special List, 1/5-10
A.W. Gliddon, letters, SLSA D3227 1-2(L)
Robert Gouger, correspondence, SLSA PRG 1012/5
Mantegani Papers, SLSA PRG 106
    Letters from Mary Thomas to Helen Mantegani (nee Thomas), 106/1
    Letters from Frances Skipper (nee Thomas) and others, 106/3
    Real estate transactions of Alfred Mantegani, 106/8/1-2
    D. O'Connor, monograph on Alfred Mantegani, 106/10
Mildred Family, Hiram Mildred goldfield's diary, SLSA PRG 307
Skipper Family, letters, SLSA PRG 242
J.M. Skipper, vols 1 and 2, South Australian Historical Pictures Index
W. Sowden, papers (history of the *Register*), SLSA PRG 41
Survey of Adelaide's Buildings, G.S. Kingston's 1842 map

PART 1
Chapter 1

1. 'Farewell to Southampton' in E.K. Thomas (ed.) *The Diary and Letters of Mary Thomas*, W.K. Thomas and Co., Adelaide, 1925, p. 139.
2. Letter from Mary Thomas to George Harris Jnr., 14 October 1838, SLSA PRG 1160/2
3. C. Tomalin, *Jane Austen: a life*, Viking, London, 1997, pp. 196, 202. Castle Square where Jane lived was within easy walking distance of High Street and the Dolphin Inn.
4. Tomalin, *Jane Austen*, pp. 207–208.
5. All Saints Church Register, Southampton Archives.
6. Southampton Rate Books, March 1787–December 1801, Southampton Archives.
7. The International Genealogical Index (IGI) suggests George Harris was born to John and Sarah Harris on 18 February 1847 at Downton near Salisbury. Mary Batchelor was born in South Stoneham, a Southampton parish, to Thomas and Sarah (nee Bowles) Batchelor on 17 June 1750.
8. Holy Rood Register, Southampton Archives. Although Holy Rood records show Mary's baptism as 22 August, the journal of Mary Thomas Jnr (later Skipper) and other family papers refer to their joint birthday as 30 August.
9. Mary Harris Snr died on 29 July 1899. (Thomas (ed.), *The Diary and Letters of Mary Thomas*, footnote on p. 165.)
10. Holy Rood Register, Southampton Archives.
11. Southampton Rate Books, 1801–1807, Southampton Archives; George Harris, Counterpart Leases, also Rate Records, Southampton Archives. The rates for these premises were 2/3 of those paid on the inn, indicating that for a shop they were sizeable with ample room for a dwelling. There is no record of rates being paid on a separate dwelling.
12. Southampton Rate Books, 1801, 1806 and Poll Book, 1806, Southampton Archives.
13. *Hampshire Chronicle*, 6 August 1804, in A. Temple Patterson, *A history of Southampton, 1700–1914*, vol. 1, Southampton University Press, 1971, pp. 101–102.
14. Temple Patterson, *A history of Southampton*, vol. 1, p. 15.
15. There is no conclusive evidence to suggest that these premises were the same as those from which George Snr operated his High Street business, but it is almost certainly the case. There is no record of any other land transactions in High Street. (George Harris, Counterpart Leases, Southampton Archives.)
16. George Harris, Counterpart Leases.
17. The announcement of Mary's marriage in a Southampton newspaper of 10 January 1818 states that she is the 'eldest daughter of George Harris Esq. of Ashfield Lodge near Romsey'. (Willington Family papers.) There is no indication that the family lived anywhere else in the years between 1808 (when George Snr left his High Street business) and 1818.
18. J. Duthy, *Sketches of Hampshire*, Jacob and Johnson, Winchester, 1836, pp. 405–407.
19. Mary sent Ann's eldest daughter, Elizabeth, a copy of her *Serious Poems* in 1831. (14 October 1838, SLSA PRG 1160/2.) Assuming Elizabeth was at least 14, an appropriate age for her to have the book, her parents' marriage would have taken place no later than c. 1816. A search of the IGI for the date of Ann's marriage was unsuccessful.
20. Letter from Robert Thomas to Evan K. Thomas, 11 August 1909, Willington Family papers.
21. Robert may have served an apprenticeship with a master stationer and then had employment as a journeyman. It was not possible to trace him through records of the Stationers' Company held in the Matheson Library, Monash University. Part or all of an apprenticeship may have been served in Wales before he settled in London.
22. Obituary, *Observer*, 7 July 1860.
23. *Observer*, 10 July 1920; Tallis's Panorama of Fleet Street (endpaper), in W.G. Bell, *Fleet Street in Seven Centuries*, Isaac Pitman, London, 1912.

24 Willington Family papers.
25 E.B. Chancellor, *The Annals of Fleet Street: Its Traditions and Associations*, Chapman and Hall, London, 1912, p. 194.
26 'A Hymn Written at the Consecration of the New Church of St Dunstan's in the West' in Mary Thomas, manuscript book, Willington Family papers.
27 'Early 19th century London', Proceedings of the Old Bailey, http://www.oldbaileyonline.org.
28 R. Porter, *London: a social history*, Hamish Hamilton, London, 1994, pp. 242–243.
29 'Early 19th century London', Proceedings of the Old Bailey.
30 Petition to the House of Commons, 1827, in Porter, *London*, p. 265.
31 Porter, *London*, p. 260.
32 'A Fragment' in M. Thomas, *Serious Poems*, Witttaker, Treacher and Co., London, 1831.
33 J. Summerson, *Georgian London*, Penguin, London, pp. 200–201, 208.
34 E.B. Chancellor, *The London of Thackeray*, Grant Richards, London, 1928, pp. 121–122.
35 'Reminiscences' in Thomas (ed.) *The Diary and Letters of Mary Thomas*, p. 77.
36 Mary Thomas, manuscript diary, late February 1836, SLSA PRG 1160/1.
37 The more pretentious households of wealthy tradesmen and merchants included a cook, a housemaid, a nursery maid and a footman. (D. Cruikshank and N. Burton, *Life in the Georgian City*, Viking, London, 1990, p. 27.) Mary, however, in addition to her sole live-in servant, may have had other domestic help who came in as required, e.g. a laundress and a woman to do the 'heavy' cleaning.
38 Cruikshank and Burton, *Life in the Georgian City*, pp. 30–36.
39 'Lines on the Death of a Beloved Friend' in Mary Thomas, manuscript book.
40 Letter from Mary to George, 29 March 1840, SLSA PRG 1160/2. George Harris's Will, 1831, is in Hampshire Records Office.
41 A document relating to the mortgage arrangements for the High Street, Southampton premises dated 1 June 1821, refers to George Harris of Hill, gent. (Solicitors' Collections, Southampton Archives.)
42 Millbrook Parish Register, Southampton Archives.
43 Temple Patterson, *A history of Southampton* vol. 2, p. 2.
44 Thomas (ed.), *The Diary and Letters of Mary Thomas*, footnote on p. 165.
45 At the time married women could not own property in their own right. This was altered by a series of statutes from 1860. (D.M. Walker, *The Oxford companion to law*, Clarendon Press, Oxford, 1980, p. 1306)
46 Mary's epitaph engraved on her parents' gravestone. (Thomas (ed.), *The Diary and Letters of Mary Thomas*, p. 166.)
47 'Tribute to Two Much Respected Brothers' in Mary Thomas, manuscript book.
48 'Verses on the Death of a Friend' in Mary Thomas, manuscript book.
49 'Lines on the Death of a Beloved Friend' and 'Verses on the Death of a Pious and Much Lamented Friend' in M. Thomas, *Serious Poems*, 1831.

Chapter 2

1 Letter from Mary to George, 14 October 1838, SLSA PRG 1160/2.
2 E.K. Thomas (ed.), *The Diary and Letters of Mary Thomas*, W.K. Thomas and Co., Adelaide, 1925, footnote on p. 138.
3 Letter from Mary to George, 14 October 1838.
4 Ibid.
5 Gouger, correspondence 1834–1835, SLSA PRG 1012/5.
6 E.G. Wakefield, *The New British Province of South Australia*, C. Knight, London, 1835, chaps 1–5 and conclusion passim.
7 D. Pike, *Paradise of dissent: South Australia, 1829–1857*, Melbourne University Press, Melbourne, 1967, p. 114.

8   Ibid.
9   Ibid., pp. 68–69.
10 John Brown's diary, 4 May 1835, SLSA PRG 1002/2.
11 Letter from Mary to George, 14 October 1838.
12 A preliminary land order originally bought 80 acres (32 ha) for £80, i.e. land was being sold at £1 per acre (per 0.4 ha). However, Angas negotiated a price of 12 shillings per acre (per 0.4 ha). To compensate those who had already bought preliminary land orders, the original 80 acres (32 ha) was increased to 134 acres (54 ha). (Pike, *Paradise of dissent*, p. 121.)
13 William was apprenticed to Mr Baugh of Leighton and Murphy, Fleet Street, who later became Mary's London agent. ('William Kyffin Thomas' in D. Pike, *Australian Dictionary of Biography*, vol. 1851–1890, Melbourne University Press, Melbourne, 1966, p. 264; letter from Mary to George, 14 October 1838.)
14 Letter from Mary to George, 14 October 1838.
15 Ibid.
16 John Brown's diary, 4–16 September 1835.
17 Ibid., 16 December 1835.
18 Ibid.
19 Letter from Robert Thomas to the under secretary of state for the colonies, 16 January 1836, SLSA PRG 1160/4.
20 John Brown's diary, 22 January 1836.
21 Ibid., 2 February 1836.
22 D. Elder (ed.), *William Light's brief journal*, Wakefield Press, Adelaide, 1984, pp. 28–29.
23 Mary's manuscript diary, 20 March 1836, SLSA PRG 1160/1
24 Ibid., 2 February 1836.
25 Letter from Mary to George, 14 October 1838.
26 Mary's manuscript diary, late February 1836.
27 *Observer*, 28 October 1902.
28 Mary's manuscript diary, 24 March 1836.
29 John Brown's diary, 17 May, 23 May 1836.
30 Letter from Mary to George, 14 October 1838.
31 Ibid.
32 Ibid.
33 Ibid.
34 R. Thomas and G. Stevenson, Partnership Agreement, Willington Family papers.
35 Pike, *Paradise of dissent*, p. 104.
36 de Mole papers, family recollections, SLSA PRG 39.
37 Ibid.
37 Sowden's unpublished 'History of the *Register*', SLSA PRG 41; 'George Stevenson' in Pike (ed.) *Australian Dictionary of Biography*, 1788–1850, pp. 481–482; 'Robert Thomas' in Pike (ed.), *Australian Dictionary of Biography*, 1851–1890, pp. 263–264; B.W. Pratt (ed.), *The Australian Encyclopaedia*, Grolier Society, Sydney, 1983, p. 484.
39 Mary to George, 14 October 1838 and 27 December 1840; *Register*, 14 November 1840.
40 *Gazette and Register*, 18 June 1836.

Chapter 3

1   Letter from Mary to George, 14 October 1838, SLSA PRG 1160/2.
2   Diary entry of R. Gouger, 30 June 1836, in P. Hope, *The voyage of the Africaine: a collection of journals, letters and extracts from contemporary publications*, Heinemann Educational, Australia, 1968, p. 38.
3   Mary's diary, 5 July 1836, SLSA PRG 1160/1.
4   Letter from Mary to George, 14 October 1838.

5   Ibid.
6   Mary's diary, 5 July 1836.
7   This appears to be a slight exaggeration on Mary's part. According to the earlier entries in her diary, it was probably 3–4 days.
8   Mary's diary, 24 August 1836.
9   Letter from Mary to George, 14 October 1838.
10 Mary's diary, 5 July 1836.
11 Ibid., 2 July 1836.
12 Ibid., 30 June 1836.
13 Ibid., 2 July 1836.
14 Letter from Mary to George, 14 October 1838.
15 R. Parsons, *Migrant ships of South Australia, 1836–1860*, Gould Books, Gumeracha, South Australia, 1988, pp. 55–136
16 G. Stevenson, 'Extracts from his Journal, from the original in the Papers of George Fife Angas', *Royal Geographical Society of South Australia*, vol. 30, 1928–1929, p. 31.
17 Hope, *The voyage of the Africaine*, p. 33.
18 Letter from A. Gliddon to his brother, 18 September 1836, SLSA D3227/1-2.
19 Letter from Mary to George, 1 March 1840.
20 Mary's diary, 5 July 1836.
21 Ibid., 20 October 1836.
22 Hope, *The voyage of the Africaine*, p. 32 and Appendix 2, pp. 164–166.
23 G.B. Wilkinson, *South Australia*, SLSA facsimile of 1848 edition, p. 36.
24 Mary's diary, 24 August 1836.
25 Ibid., 5 July 1836.
26 Memorandum of Agreement re *Africaine*, 14 May 1836, John Brown's papers, SLSA PRG 1002/1. This was the rate negotiated by Gouger and would have been paid by the South Australian commissioners for his passage and that of Brown, and probably their families. (SLSA PRG 1002/1, 14 May 1836.)
27 Hope, *The voyage of the Africaine*, p. 19. Intermediate passengers were required to provide their own bedding, linen and eating utensils as well as chests or cupboards in which to secure them in their cabins. They also had to have enough clothing and linen to last the voyage as they were given no allowance of water for laundering. (Wilkinson, *South Australia*, p. 37.)
28 Mary's diary, 24 August 1836.
29 Diary entry of R. Gouger, 13 July 1836 in Hope, *The voyage of the Africaine*, p. 40.
30 Ibid., p. 44.
31 H. Hussey, *More than Half a Century of Colonial Life and Christian Experience: With notes of Travel, Lectures, Publications, etc.*, Hussey and Gillingham, Adelaide, 1897, p. 19.
32 Mary's diary, 24 August 1836.
33 Ibid., 1 July 1836.
34 Ibid., 20 October 1836.
35 Ibid., 11 December 1836.
36 Ibid.
37 Diary entry of R. Gouger, 10 July 1836 in Hope, *The voyage of the Africaine*, pp. 39–40.
38 Mary's diary, 2 August 1836.
39 Ibid., 14 August 1836.
40 Ibid., 24 July 1836.
41 Ibid., 14 August 1836.
42 Ibid., 18 August 1836.
43 Ibid., 27 July 1836.
44 Ibid., 14 August 1836.

45   Ibid., 22 August 1836.
46   Diary entry of R. Gouger, 24 August 1836 in Hope, *The voyage of the Africaine*, p. 50.
47   Mary's diary, 6 August 1836.
48   Ibid., 20 September 1836.
49   Ibid., 21 September 1836.
50   Ibid., 21 September 1836.
51   Ibid., 21 September 1836.
52   Ibid., 30 September and 4 October 1836.
53   Ibid., 12 October 1836.
54   Ibid., 29 October 1836.
55   Ibid., 31 October 1836.

Chapter 4

1   Mary's diary, 2 November 1836, SLSA PRG 1160/1.
2   *Gazette and Register*, 8 July 1837.
3   G. Sutherland in P. Hope, *The voyage of the Africaine: a collection of journals, letters and extracts from contemporary publications*, Heinemann Educational, Australia, 1968, p. 10.
4   Mary's diary, 2 November 1836.
5   Ibid.
6   Mary says this was on the 2 November, but she was confused about the date. As well, her diary seems to imply that the trekkers set out from Nepean Bay, which clearly was not the case. See Mary's diary, 2 and 3 November 1836.
7   Ibid., 2 November 1836.
8   R. Taylor, *Unearthed*, Wakefield Press, Adelaide, 2002, pp. 45–46, 84–85.
9   Mary's diary, 3 November 1836.
10 Ibid.
11 Ibid., 6 November 1836.
12 Taylor, *Unearthed*, p. 72.
13 D. Pike, *Paradise of dissent: South Australia, 1829–1857*, Melbourne University Press, Melbourne, 1967, pp. 134–135.
14 Mary's diary, 6 November 1836.
15 D. Elder (ed.), *William Light's brief journal*, Wakefield Press, Adelaide, 1984, p. 75.
16 Ibid.
17 Mary's diary, 11 November 1836.
18 Letter from Mary to George, 14 October 1838, SLSA PRG 1160/2.
19 Mary's diary, 16 November 1836.
20 Elder (ed.), *William Light's brief journal*, pp. 78–79.
21 Sowden's unpublished 'History of the *Register*', SLSA PRG 41, p. 14.
22 Diary entry of R. Gouger, 9 November 1836 in E. Hodder (ed.) *The founding of South Australia as recorded in the journals of Mr Robert Gouger*, Sampson Low, Marston and Co., London, 1898, p. 199.
23 Mary's diary, 16 November 1836.
24 'South Australia's 21st Birthday' in E.K. Thomas (ed.) *The Diary and Letters of Mary Thomas*, W.K. Thomas and Co., Adelaide, 1925, p. 85.
25 Diary entry of R. Gouger, 14 December 1836 in Hodder (ed.) *The founding of South Australia*, p. 201.
26 Letter from William Everard to friends in England, April 1838, Special List 1/5-10, SLSA PRG 208.
27 'Reminiscences' in Thomas (ed.) *The Diary and Letters of Mary Thomas*, p. 69.
28 Diary entry of R. Gouger, 19 November 1836 in Hodder (ed.) *The founding of South Australia*, p. 199.

29 Letter from Mary to George, 14 October 1838, SLSA PRG 1160/2.
30 Mary's diary, 14 December 1836.
31 Ibid., 11 December 1836.
32 Ibid.
33 *Gazette and Register*, 12 August 1837.
34 Mary's diary, 11 December 1836.
35 Ibid., 25 December 1836.
36 Ibid., 20 December 1836.
37 Ibid., 25 December 1836.
38 Diary entry of R. Gouger, 29 December 1836 in Hodder (ed.) *The founding of South Australia*, p. 204.
39 Sowden's unpublished 'History of the *Register*, p. 14.
40 G.B. Wilkinson, *South Australia*, SLSA facsimile of 1848 edition, p. 338.
41 F.T. Whitington, *Augustus Short, First Bishop of Adelaide: The Story of a Thirty Four Years' Episcopate*, Wells Gardner, Darton and Co., London, 1887, p. 87.
42 Stevenson, 'Extracts from the Journal of G. Stevenson in the papers of George Fife Angas', RGSSA 30, p. 56
43 See Chapter Two, pp. 19–20 of this book re Robert's Letter to Sir George Grey.
44 Letter from Robert Thomas to Colonial Office, 16 January 1836, SLSA PRG 1160/4.
45 Diary entry of R. Gouger, 1 December 1836 in Hodder (ed.) *The founding of South Australia*, p. 200.
46 Letter from Mary to George, 17 February 1839
47 Mary's diary, 1 December 1836.
48 'Reminiscences' in Thomas (ed.) *The Diary and Letters of Mary Thomas*, p. 69.
49 Mary's diary, 1 December 1836.
50 Ibid.
51 Pike, *Paradise of dissent*, Appendix A.
52 Elder (ed.), William *Light's brief journal*, pp. 90, 92.
53 Stevenson, 'Extracts from the Journal of G. Stevenson in the papers of George Fife Angas', RGSSA 30, p. 59.
54 Journal of Mary Skipper (nee Thomas) (Mary Jnr's journal), preface, SLSA PRG 1160/6.
55 'Reminiscences' in Thomas (ed.) *The Diary and Letters of Mary Thomas*, p. 74.
56 Ibid., pp. 71–72.
57 Letter from Mary to George, 17 February 1839.
58 H. Mantegani (nee Thomas), 'Recollections of the Early Days of South Australia from 1836', *Royal Geographical Society of South Australia*, vol. 5, 1902, p. 71.
59 Journal of Mary Skipper (nee Thomas), preface.

PART 2
Chapter 5
1 'Reminiscences' in E.K. Thomas (ed.) *The Diary and Letters of Mary Thomas*, W.K. Thomas and Co., Adelaide, 1925, p. 65.
2 *Register*, 13 February 1875.
3 Sowden's unpublished 'History of the *Register*', SLSA PRG 41, p. 14.
4 *Gazette and Register*, 3 June 1837.
5 G.H. Pitt, *The press in South Australia, 1836 to 1850*, The Wakefield Press, Adelaide, 1946, p. 8.
6 'Letters to the editor', *Gazette and Register*, 8 July and 29 July 1837.
7 Editorial, *Gazette and Register*, 29 July 1837.
8 Letter from Mary to George, 30 July 1839, SLSA PRG 1160/2.
9 *Gazette and Register*, 16 September 1837.

10 Gouger left the colony almost immediately, and after spending some time in Hobart Town, he arrived back in London in July 1838 where he was exonerated and reinstated as colonial secretary, returning to the colony in June 1839. However, he never returned to his previous levels of energy or efficiency, and transferred to the position of colonial treasurer and a lighter workload. He resigned in 1844, citing ill-health and returned to England where he died in 1846. (D. Pike (ed.), 'Robert Gouger', *Australian Dictionary of Biography*, vol. 1788–1850, Melbourne University Press, Melbourne, 1966, pp. 462–463.)
11 *Gazette and Register*, 16 September 1837.
12 *Gazette and Register*, 3 June 1837.
13 D. Pike, *Paradise of dissent: South Australia, 1829–1857*, Melbourne University Press, Melbourne, 1967, Appendix A.
14 'Shipping intelligence', *Gazette and Register*, 11 November 1837.
15 Letter from Mary to George, 14 October 1838.
16 A. Ridley, *A backward glance: The story of John Ridley, Pioneer*, James Clark and Co., London, 1904, p. 58.
17 Letter from Mary to George, 6 November 1838.
18 K.T. Borrow, *Government House 1837–1901*, Pioneers Association of South Australia, Adelaide, 1982, p. 2.
19 R. Gouger, *South Australia in 1837*, Harvey and Darton, London, 1838, p. 72.
20 *Gazette and Register*, 8 August 1837–20 January 1838 and 3 February-10 March 1838 (advertisements).
21 James Hawker quoted in Borrow, *Government House*, 1982, p. 11.
22 J. Watt, *Family Life in South Australia Fifty Three Years Ago from October, 1837*, W.K. Thomas and Co., Adelaide, 1890, p. 37.
23 R. Thomas, Index of Memorials, book 3, no. 495 (11 January 1838), GRO.
24 Indenture, 29 March 1839, Acre 56 Envelope, GRO.
25 Letter from Mary to George, 14 October 1838.
26 Ibid.
27 *Gazette and Register*, 18 August 1838.
28 *Gazette and Register*, June 1837–September 1838 (advertisements).
29 *Gazette and Register*, 9 March 1839.
30 *South Australian Almanack*, 1839 (facsimile), SRSA.
31 *Gazette and Register*, 19 May 1838.
32 *Gazette and Register*, 30 June 1838.
33 *Gazette and Register*, 23 June 1838.
34 Letter from Mary to George, 30 July 1839.
35 D. Elder (ed.), *William Light's brief journal*, Wakefield Press, Adelaide, 1984, p. 41.
36 *Register*, 10 August 1839.
37 Sturt was replaced in September 1839 when the commissioners' appointment, Lt. Edward Frome, arrived in the colony. Sturt was appointed to the position of assistant commissioner for lands. (Pike (ed.), *Australian Dictionary of Biography*, vol. 1788–1850, p. 497)
38 Light was suffering from advanced tuberculosis and died on 5 October 1839. After a service at Trinity Church he was buried in Light Square. (E. Hodder, *The History of South Australia from its Foundation to the Year of its Jubilee: With a Chronological Summary of all the Principal Events of Interest up to date*, vol. 2, Samson Low, Marston and Co., London, 1893, p. 150.)
39 Pike, *Paradise of dissent*, p. 176.
40 Letter from Mary to George, 14 October 1838.
41 Ibid.
42 Ibid.
43 Ibid.
44 Ibid.

45 Ibid.
46 Ibid., 6 November 1838.
47 Ibid., 7 April 1839.
48 Ibid., 11 August 1840.
49 Journal of Mary Skipper (nee Thomas) (Mary Jnr's journal), explanatory epilogue, 27 February 1946, SLSA PRG 1160/6.
50 Letter from Mary to George, 1 March 1840.
51 H. Hussey, *More than Half a Century of Colonial Life and Christian Experience: With notes of Travel, Lectures, Publications, etc.*, Hussey and Gillingham, Adelaide, 1897, p. 29.
52 Letter from Mary to George, 17 February 1839.
53 Ibid.
54 Ibid., 14 October 1838 and 25 June 1839.
55 Ibid., 30 July 1839.

Chapter 6

1 *Gazette and Register*, 30 March 1839.
2 J. McLellan, *Adelaide's early inns and taverns*, Pioneers Association of South Australia, Adelaide, 1941, p. 12.
3 Journal of Mary Skipper (nee Thomas) (Mary Jnr's journal), 21 February 1842, SLSA PRG 1160/6.
4 'Reminiscences' in E.K. Thomas (ed.) *The Diary and Letters of Mary Thomas*, W.K. Thomas and Co., Adelaide, 1925, p. 70.
5 *Register*, 22 February and 15 August 1840.
6 McLellan, *Adelaide's early inns and taverns*, pp. 7–8.
7 Ibid., pp. 1–2.
8 Letter from Mary to George, 17 February 1839, SLSA PRG 1160/2.
9 Ibid., 7 April 1839.
10 'The South Australian record', *Gazette and Register*, 2 March 1839.
11 The purchaser of a special survey paid £4000 to select 15,000 acres (6000 hectares) outside of the general survey's defined districts. It was marked out in 80 acre (32 hectare) sections for the purchaser to choose 4000 acres (1600 hectares). The remaining sections were then available to the public at £1 per acre (0.4 hectare). (D. Pike, *Paradise of dissent: South Australia, 1829–1857*, Melbourne University Press, Melbourne, 1967, pp. 177–178.)
12 Thomas (ed.), *The Diary and Letters of Mary Thomas*, footnote on pp. 143–146.
13 *Southern Australian*, 8 May 1839.
14 Thomas (ed.), *The Diary and Letters of Mary Thomas*, footnote on pp. 143–146.
15 'Supreme court – criminal side', *Gazette and Register*, 1 June 1839.
16 Letter from Mary to George, 11 September 1839.
17 'G.M. Stephen – perjury', *Gazette and Register*, 8 June 1839.
18 'To our readers', *Gazette and Register*, 22 June 1839.
19 *Register*, 29 June 1839.
20 'Mr. George M. Stephen', *Register*, 13 July 1839.
21 'The Milner estate hoax once more', *Register*, 27 July 1839.
22 Letter from Mary to George, 30 July 1839.
23 Ibid., 11 September, 1839.
24 'Progress of the colony', *Register*, 17 August 1839. The population at the end of 1838 was 6000. (Pike, *Paradise of dissent*, Appendix A.)
25 'Progress of the colony', *Register*, 17 August 1839.
26 *Register*, 10 August 1839.
27 Pike, *Paradise of dissent*, p. 176.
28 Pike, *Paradise of dissent*, pp. 176–177, 185; 'Taxation', *Register*, 21 December 1839.

29 Letter from Mary to George, 17 February 1839.
30 'Execution of the two native murderers', *Gazette and Register*, 1 June 1839.
31 'Public meeting – the natives', *Gazette and Register*, 18 May 1839.
32 'Transactions of the Statistical Society', *Register*, 8 January 1842.
33 Mary Jnr's journal, 12 and 16 August 1839.
34 John Brown's journal, 19 May 1836, SLSA PRG 1002/2.
35 Letter from Robert Gouger to R. Giles, 28 November 1834, SLSA PRG 1012/5.
36 Pike, *Paradise of dissent*, p. 114; E.G. Wakefield, *The New British Province of South Australia*, C. Knight, 1835, Introduction and p. 141.
37 Pike, *Paradise of dissent*, p. 504.
38 *Register*, 16 November and 14 December 1839.
39 Mary Jnr's journal, 13 and 27 September 1839.
40 Ibid., 14 October 1839.
41 *Register*, 8 and 15 February 1840 (advertisements).
42 Mary Jnr's journal, 20 February 1840.
43 *Register*, 12 October 1839.
44 Ibid., 18 July 1840.
45 L.J.T. Ewens, *The establishment of Trinity Church Adelaide*, Pioneers Association of South Australia, Adelaide, 1953, p. 8.
46 Pike, *Paradise of dissent*, p. 487.
47 *Gazette and Register*, 6 January 1838.
48 *Register*, 22 February 1840 (advertisement); Mary Jnr's journal, 27 March 1840.
49 *Register*, 4 and 11 January 1840 (advertisements); and 'Progress of the colony', *Register*, 2 January 1841.
50 'Reminiscences' in Thomas (ed.) *The Diary and Letters of Mary Thomas*, 1925, p. 68.
51 Ewens, *The establishment of the Trinity Church*, p. 8.
52 D. Langmead, *Accidental architect: the life and times of George Strickland Kingston*, Crossing Press, Sydney, 1994, p. 246; Mary Jnr's journal, 19 October 1839.
53 Mary Jnr's journal, 28 December 1839.

Chapter 7

1 Letter from Mary to George, 1 March and 11 August 1840, SLSA PRG 1160/2; Journal of Mary Skipper (nee Thomas) (Mary Jnr's journal), 5 July 1840, SLSA PRG 1160/6.
2 Letter from Mary to George, 1 March 1840; Mary Jnr's journal, 28 December 1839.
3 'His father is also in the law and a Proctor in Doctors' Commons'. (Letter from Mary to George, 1 March 1840.)
4 'John Michael Skipper' in D. Pike (ed.) *Australian Dictionary of Biography*, vol. 1788–1850, Melbourne University Press, Melbourne, 1966.
5 Mary Jnr's journal, 28 December 1839.
6 Ibid., 28 December 1839.
7 Letter from Mary to George, 1 March 1840.
8 Mary Jnr's journal, 2 January 1840; Letter from Mary to George, 1 March 1840.
9 Sowden's unpublished 'History of the *Register*', SLSA PRG 41, p. 39.
10 Letter from Mary to George, 1 March 1840.
11 J.M. Skipper, *Clarendon House*, South Australian Historical Pictures Index, SLSA.
12 S. Pikuska, *The Adelaide House 1836–1901*, Wakefield Press, Adelaide, 1986, pp. 30–31.
13 Codicil to the will of Mary Thomas, 28 March 1870, Willington Family papers.
14 'An Old Timepiece' in E.K. Thomas (ed.) *The Diary and Letters of Mary Thomas*, W.K. Thomas and Co., Adelaide, 1925, p. 95.
15 *Observer*, 25 October 1902. The clock is now in the keeping of Victor, the husband of the late Mrs J. K Willington, Mary's great-great-granddaughter. The table passed to one of Frances's

daughters and is now in the possession of Mrs Mary Hogan, also a great-great-granddaughter.
16 Letter from Mary to George, 1 March 1840.
17 Ibid.
18 Mary Jnr's journal, 4 and 8 March 1840.
19 Ibid., 6 and 10 March 1840.
20 Letter from Mary to George, 1 March 1840.
21 The belongings of the apprentice printer who perished on Kangaroo Island that Mary returned to his father in London.
22 Letter from Mary to George, 1 March 1840.
23 Mary Jnr's journal, 16 and 31 March 1840.
24 Ibid., 13 May 1840.
25 Letter from Mary to George, 25 June 1839.
26 Ibid., 1 March 1840.
27 Ibid., 6 April 1840.

Chapter 8
1 Letter from Mary to George, 6 April 1840, SLSA PRG 1160/2.
2 Ibid., 1 March 1840.
3 G.H. Pitt, *The press in South Australia, 1836 to 1850*, The Wakefield Press, Adelaide, 1946, p. 60.
4 Letter from Mary to George, 1 March 1840, SLSA PRG 1160/2; Journal of Mary Skipper (nee Thomas) (Mary Jnr's journal), 24 March 1840, SLSA PRG 1160/6.
5 Letter from Mary to George, 1 March 1840.
6 *Register*, 30 May 1840 (advertisement).
7 Mary Jnr's journal, 4 August 1840.
8 Letter from Mary to George, 11 August 1840.
9 *Register* and Supplement, 1 August 1840.
10 Letter from Mary to George, 11 August 1840.
11 *Register*, 5 September 1840.
12 'Report of Major O'Halloran', *Register*, 12 September 1840.
13 Letter from Mary to George, 11 August 1840.
14 'Report of Major O'Halloran', *Register*, 12 September 1840.
15 *Register*, 19 September 1840.
16 Ibid.
17 Letter from Mary to George, 11 August 1840.
18 'To the public: letter 17 September 1840', *Register*, 14 November 1840.
19 *Register*, 22 June 1839.
20 'To the public: letter 17 September 1840', *Register*, 14 November 1840.
21 'Summary execution of the natives', *Register*, 3 October 1840.
22 'Letters to the editor: The natives', *Register*, 3 October 1840.
23 D. Pike, *Paradise of dissent: South Australia, 1829–1857*, Melbourne University Press, Melbourne, 1967, p. 206. Under Governor Grey's administration the South Australian Company agreed to a grant of land at Dry Creek in lieu of the annual interest payment.
24 Pike, *Paradise of dissent*, p. 206.
25 Mary Jnr's journal, 14 October 1840.
26 'Opening of the new port', *Register*, 17 October 1840.
27 Mary Jnr's journal, 14 October 1840.
28 *Register*, 3 October 1840.
29 'Summary execution of the natives', *Register*, 24 October 1840.
30 'To the public: letter 29 October 1840', *Register*, 14 November 1840.

31 Letter from Mary to George, 27 December 1840.
32 Ibid., 27 December 1840.
33 'To the public: letter 4 November 1840', *Register*, 14 November 1840.
34 Letter from Mary to George, 27 December 1840.
35 Ibid., 1 March 1840.
36 D. Langmead, *Accidental architect: the life and times of George Strickland Kingston*, Crossing Press, Sydney, 1994, pp. 119, 121–123, 142.
37 J. McLellan, *Adelaide's early inns and taverns*, Pioneers Association of South Australia, Adelaide, 1941, pp. 3, 10.
38 'State of the colony', *Register*, 11 July 1840.
39 Letter from Mary to George, 27 December 1840.
40 Mary Jnr's journal, 16 October 1840.
41 Letter from Mary to George, 27 December 1840.
42 Mary Jnr's journal, 6 January 1841.
43 *Register*, 26 September 1840 (advertisement).
44 'Financial position of the government', *Register*, 21 November 1840.
45 Letter from Mary to George, 27 December 1840.
46 Ibid., 27 December 1840.

PART 3
Chapter 9

1 G.L. Fischer, 'The Queen's Theatre Adelaide 1841–1842', Pioneers Association of South Australia, Adelaide, no. 13, 1957, p. 3.
2 *Gazette and Register*, 23 November 1839 (advertisement).
3 Fischer, 'The Queen's Theatre', p. 1.
4 Ibid.
5 Ibid., p. 2.
6 Journal of Mary Skipper (nee Thomas) (Mary Jnr's journal), 11 January 1841, SLSA PRG 1160/6.
7 Fischer, 'The Queen's Theatre', pp. 3–4.
8 *Register*, 23 January 1841.
9 *Register*, 9, 23 and 30 January 1841 (advertisements).
10 Letter from Mary to George, 28 March 1841, SLSA PRG 1160/2.
11 *Register*, 9 January and 20, 27 March 1841 (advertisements).
12 Letter from Mary to George, 11 August 1840.
13 Ibid., 28 March 1841.
14 'Governor Gawler's unauthorized expenditure', *Register*, 13 February 1841.
15 'Governor Gawler's explanation', *Register*, 20 February 1841.
16 'Address to Governor Gawler', *Register*, 27 March 1841.
17 'Recall of Governor Gawler', *Register*, 3 April 1841.
18 Mary Jnr's journal, 25 February 1841.
19 *Register*, 27 February 1841; Mary Jnr's journal, 1 March 1841.
20 Letter from Mary to George, 28 March 1841.
21 Ibid., 28 March 1841.
22 Mary Jnr's journal, 4 November 1839 and 16 February, 5 July, 31 August 1841.
23 Ibid., 1 January 1841.
24 Letter from Mary to George, 28 March 1841. By comparison with food prices in her letters of 14 October 1838 and 25 June 1839.
25 'The second year's husbandry', *Register*, 4 April 1840; 'Flour mills', *Register*, 8 August 1840.
26 Mary Jnr's journal, 20 April 1841.
27 'The financial crisis', *Register*, 1 May 1841.

28   D. Pike, *Paradise of dissent: South Australia, 1829–1857*, Melbourne University Press, Melbourne, 1967, pp. 230–232, 235.
29   'Arrival of Governor Grey', *Register*, 15 May 1841.
30   *Register*, 19 June 1841.
31   'Farewell to Colonel Gawler', *Register*, 19 June 1841.
32   Mary Jnr's journal, 12 May 1841.
33   Letter from Mary to George, 20 May 1841.
34   Mary Jnr's journal, 12, 14 and 16 May 1841.
35   Ibid., 31 May, 11 June and 11 September 1841.
36   Ibid., 17 August and 9 September 1841.
37   Ibid., 8, 10 and 20 May 1841.

Chapter 10

1   *Register*, 5, 12, 19 and 26 June and 3, 10 and 17 July 1841 (advertisements).
2   *Register*, 24 July and 28 August 1841.
3   *Register*, 12, 19 and 26 June 1841.
4   Journal of Mary Skipper (nee Thomas) (Mary Jnr's journal), 8, 10, 14, 19 and 28 June 1841, SLSA PRG 1160/6.
5   'The natives and their protector', *Register*, 6 February 1841.
6   'The Milmenrura murders', *Register*, 24 April 1841.
7   Ibid.
8   'The natives: Dr Penny's lecture', *Register*, 26 June 1841.
9   Mary Jnr's journal, 25 June 1841.
10   Letter from Mary to George, 28 July 1841, SLSA PRG 1160/2.
11   C. Tomalin, *The invisible woman: the story of Nelly Ternan and Charles Dickens*, Penguin Books, London, 1990, p. 16.
12   Mary Jnr's journal, 29 July 1841.
13   Ibid., 16 and 17 August 1841.
14   Ibid., 18 June and 12, 17 July 1841.
15   *Register*, 31 July 1841 (advertisement); Mary Jnr's journal, 15 September 1841.
16   'Labouring emigrants', *Register*, 16 October 1841.
17   'State of the working classes', *Register*, 25 September 1841.
18   'Fatal encounter with Murray natives', *Register*, 11 September 1841.
19   M. Steiner, 'Matthew Moorhouse: a controversial colonist', *Journal of the Historical Society of South Australia*, no. 31, 2003, pp. 59–60.
20   'Inquiry into killings of Murray natives', *Register*, 25 September 1841.
21   Stevenson in Steiner, 'Matthew Moorhouse', p. 60.
22   D. Pike, *Paradise of dissent: South Australia, 1829–1857*, Melbourne University Press, Melbourne, 1967, p. 291.
23   *South Australian Government Gazette*, August–October 1841; Pike, *Paradise of dissent*. p. 192.
24   Mary Jnr's journal, 27 September 1841; *Register*, 15 January 1842 (advertisement).
25   Mary Jnr's journal, 7, 14 October 1841; *Register*, 16 October 1841 (advertisement).
26   'The new marriage bill', *Register*, 16 October 1841.
27   Mary Jnr's journal, 1 November 1841.
28   Ibid., 17 and 19 December 1841.
29   Ibid., 21, 22, 23 and 24 December 1841.
30   Ibid., 25 December 1841.
31   Ibid., 26 December 1841.
32   Ibid., 16 and 19 January 1842.
33   Ibid., 19, 22, 25 and 26 January 1842.
34   *Register*, 22 January 1842.

35 Mary Jnr's journal, 8 April 1841.
36 *Register*, 9 April 1842.

Chapter 11

1 Journal of Mary Skipper (nee Thomas) (Mary Jnr's journal), 10 March 1842, SLSA PRG 1160/6.
2 Ibid., 30 March 1842.
3 Ibid., 4–26 April 1842, passim.
4 Ibid., 15 May 1842.
5 Ibid., 2 and 23 May 1842.
6 Ibid., 25, 26 June and 4 July 1842.
7 *Register*, 18 June 1842.
8 D. Pike, *Paradise of dissent: South Australia, 1829–1857*, Melbourne University Press, Melbourne, 1967, p. 304.
9 *Register*, 9 July 1842.
10 Mary Jnr's journal, 12 July 1842.
11 Indenture, 13 July 1842, Town Acre 56 Envelope, GRO.
12 Mary Jnr's journal, 29 and 30 July 1842.
13 R. Thomas and G. Stevenson, Register of Insolvencies, SRSA GRG 66/1, no. 63, 1842.
14 *Register*, 6 August 1842.
15 G.H. Pitt, *The press in South Australia, 1836 to 1850*, The Wakefield Press, Adelaide, 1946, p. 30.
16 The transfer of property to the court until a decision is made as to who has the right to it (D.M. Walker, *The Oxford companion to the Law*, Clarendon Press, Oxford, 1980, p. 1132); Mary Jnr's journal, 29 and 30 July 1842.
17 O. Skipper, 'Reminiscences of fifty two years', *Journal of the Royal Geographical Society of South Australia*, vol. 7, 1904, p. 48.
18 A document relating to this real estate is in Adelaide in the Willington Family papers, and is unlikely to have been brought to South Australia if sold before emigration. Mary makes no mention of it in her letters during the early years of the colony, although she does mention the disposal of other property.
19 O. Skipper, 'Reminiscences', p. 48.
20 G. Stevenson, Schedule of Estates, SRSA GRG 66/6, no. 86, 1843.
21 Ibid.
22 R. Thomas, Indenture, 9 January 1841, Index of Memorials, book 28, no. 76, GRO.
23 Thomas and Stevenson, Register of Insolvencies.
24 In the Schedule of Estates (SRSA GRG 66/6, no. 86, 1843) relating to his personal bankruptcy (August 1843), Stevenson advises that of his 10 cattle company shares valued at £840, he had used four to obtain a loan of £80 from the Bank of South Australia and six to obtain a loan of £300 from the South Australian Insurance Company. His 720 acres in the Barossa survey, for which he originally paid £900, had been used as security for cash credit with a balance due of £1300. Shares held in the South Australian Insurance Co. he listed as worthless.
25 Plan of City of Adelaide – town acres allotted to holders of preliminary land orders; purchasers of town acres at auction 27 March 1837 (M. Sherrah, government photolithographer, SRSA); Plan of Country Sections, District of Adelaide, with owners' names attached (J. Arrowsmith, 1838, from a survey of Colonel Light, SRSA).
26 Memorials of Robert Thomas, GRO; *Register*, 10 August 1839 and 11 July 1840; Letter from Mary to George, 14 October 1838, SLSA PRG 1160/2; Willington Family papers.
27 Thomas and Stevenson, Register of Insolvencies.

28 Estimates based upon assessed land values in City of Adelaide Rate Records and details of profits of R. Thomas and Co. from George Stevenson's Schedule of Insolvency.
29 Mary Jnr's journal, 26 September and 5 October 1842.
30 A. Ridgeway (ed.), *Everyman's encyclopaedia*, vol. 1, J.M. Dent and Sons, London, 1932, vol. 2, p. 2.
31 Mary Jnr's journal, 5 November and 25 October 1842.
32 Ibid., 13 December 1842 and 10 October 1842.
33 Fischer, 'The Queen's Theatre', pp. 8–9.
34 Mary Jnr's journal, 23 December 1842.
35 Ibid., 16, 17 December 1842.
36 Ibid., 24, 25 December 1842.
37 Ibid., 26 December 1842.
38 Ibid., 23 December 1841.
39 Ibid., 28 January 1843.
40 H. Mantegani, 'Recollections of the early days of South Australia from 1836', *Journal of the Royal Geographical Society of South Australia*, vol. 5, 1902, pp. 74–75.
41 D.M. Perry, *The place of the waters*, Glenelg Council and the National Trust of South Australia (Glenelg Branch), 1993, p. 33.
42 R. Thomas, Index of Memorials, book 2, nos. 410, 411, 413, 28 January 1843, GRO; Deposit and Enrolment Index, no. 364, 1858, GRO.
43 Stevenson, Schedule of Estates.
44 Thomas and Stevenson, Partnership Agreement, 1836, Willington Family papers.
45 R. Thomas, Indenture, 9 January 1841.
46 Letter from Mary to George, 14 October 1838.
47 Letter from the family of James Coltman to the colonial secretary, SRSA GRG 24/6, A(1849) 2131.
48 Stevenson, Schedule of Estates.
49 Thomas and Stevenson, Partnership Agreement.
50 Approximately John o' Groats (estimate from rate assessments) £1 and 5 shillings; Mary's annuity (from her father's will) £1 pound; rent from Skippers (estimated, 1 floor 'stone' building) 5 shillings; rent from Register buildings, fixtures and fittings (estimated) £1 and 10 shillings; rent from one quarter of a town acre 15 shillings. Total £4 and 15 shillings.
51 Total return from land sales between October 1838 and July 1940 was £2650 from which Robert met the mortgage from January 1838 of £500, leaving net £2150. His proceeds of £1500 from sale of a country section plus several town acres in January 1841 was used to clear debts from the failed store of Messrs Coltman and Co. (Memorial, book 28, no. 76, GRO).
52 The business in Fleet Street, the house at Hill, Southampton, inherited from Mary's father, and the sale of leases of cottages in Clerkenwell. There may have been other assets, the records of which have not survived.
53 Pitt, *The press in South Australia*, p. 33.

Chapter 12

1 Letter from colonial secretary to R. Thomas, SRSA GRG 24/4 H(1844) 369.
2 W. Prest, K. Round and C. Fort (eds), *The Wakefield companion to South Australian history*, Wakefield Press, Adelaide, 2001 p. 356; E. Hodder, *The History of South Australia from its Foundation to the Year of its Jubilee: With a Chronological Summary of all the Principal Events of Interest up to date*, vol. 2, Sampson Low, Marston and Co., London, 1893, p. 163.
3 Those appointed were Major T.S. O'Halloran, John Morphett, Captain G.F. Dashwood and Thomas Williams. (D. Pike, *Paradise of dissent: South Australia, 1829–1857*, Melbourne University Press, Melbourne, 1967, p. 247.)

4   E. Hodder, *The History of South Australia*, pp. 161, 162.
5   S. Marsden, P. Stark and P. Sumerling (eds), *Heritage of the City of Adelaide: an illustrated guide*, Corporation of the City of Adelaide, Adelaide, 1990, pp. 245–246.
6   T. Worsnop, *City of Adelaide*, J. Williams, Adelaide, 1878, pp. 68 and 75.
7   Ridgeway (ed.), *Everyman's encyclopaedia*, vol. 4, J.M. Dent and Sons, London, 1932, p. 586.
8   Journal of Mary Skipper (nee Thomas) (Mary Jnr's journal), 5, 8 and 31 March 1844, SLSA PRG 1160/6.
9   Ibid., 8, 30 August, 17 October, and 14 November 1844.
10 Ibid., 1 and 3 January 1845.
11 Ibid., 27 February 1845.
12 D.N. Kraehenbuel, 'Flora of the Adelaide Plains' in J.W. Warburton (ed.) *Five creeks of the River Torrens*, Adult Education, University of Adelaide, Adelaide, 1977, p. 11.
13 Ibid., pp. 11–17.
14 J. Paton, 'Birds of the Torrens and its Tributaries' and C.H.S. Watts, 'Mammalian Fauna' in Warburton (ed.) *Five creeks of the River Torrens*, p. 18–24.
15 Mary Jnr's journal, 7 January 1846.
16 Ibid., (undated) March and 7 October 1845.
17 Ibid., (undated) March 1845.
18 'Supreme Court: Dr Wright', *Register*, 15 March 1845.
19 Charles Wright had instructed that the morphia be given every two hours rather than the hourly dose his father had ordered. His intention was probably to lessen the impact.
20 'Supreme Court: Dr Wright', *Register*.
21 Ibid.; at the time, a Medical Board was being formed and the question of medical practitioners' qualifications was under scrutiny generally. (Pike, *Paradise of dissent*, pp. 508–509.)
22 Pike, *Paradise of dissent*, pp. 113–114; prior to 1834, Wright had spent some time in Syria where he had known John Morphett. He had left England due to his discharge from the medical staff of Bethlehem (Bedlam) Hospital for misconduct, although he was later cleared of wrongdoing. (Pike, *Paradise of dissent*, pp. 113–114.)
23 Mary Jnr's journal, 26 March and 21 April 1845.
24 Ibid., 13 July 1845.
25 Ibid., 6 July–28 August 1845, passim.
26 Pike, *Paradise of dissent*, p. 324.
27 Ibid., p. 333.
28 'The monster mine', *Register*, 13 August 1845.
29 Pike, *Paradise of dissent*, pp. 332–333.
30 Inferred from comments in Sowden's unpublished 'History of the *Register*', SLSA PRG 41, p. 21; H. Hussey, *More than Half a Century of Colonial Life and Christian Experience: With notes of Travel, Lectures and Publications, etc.*, Hussey and Gillingham, Adelaide, 1897, p. 95.
31 G.H. Pitt, *The press in South Australia, 1836 to 1850*, Wakefield Press, Adelaide, 1946, pp. 3–8.
32 *South Australian Government Gazette*, 2 October 1845.
33 Letters from R. Thomas to colonial secretary, SRSA GRG 24/6 A(1845) 1175 and 1218.
34 Mary Jnr's journal, 25 December 1845.
35 Ibid., 25 and 30 December 1845.
36 Ibid., 26 and 28 December 1845.
37 Pike, *Paradise of dissent*, p. 334.
38 Mary Jnr's journal, 31 December 1845.
39 Ibid., 1 January 1846.
40 Ibid., 1 January 1846.
41 Ibid., 5–12 January 1846.

42 Ibid., 14 January 1846.
43 Ibid., 5 February 1846.
44 Ibid., 20 February 1846.
45 Ibid., 26 February 1846.
46 Ibid., 16 February 1846.
47 Ibid., 7 March 1846.
48 Ibid., 31 March 1846.
49 G. Wilkinson, *South Australia*, SLSA facsimile of the 1848 edition, pp. 363–365.
50 Ibid., pp. 15–26.
51 Ibid., pp. 318–319.
52 Ibid., p. 322.
53 Mary Jnr's journal, 6 July 1846.
54 Ibid., 22 January–21 June 1846, passim.
55 Ibid., 6 August–2 September 1846.
56 Prest, et al. (eds), *The Wakefield companion*, p. 465; Hodder, *History of South Australia*, p. 171.
57 Mary Jnr's journal, 14 September 1846.
58 Pike, *Paradise of dissent*, Appendix A.

PART 4
Chapter 13
1 T. Worsnop, *History of the City of Adelaide*, J. Williams, Adelaide, 1878, pp. 85–87.
2 Letter from R. Thomas and G. Stevenson to colonial secretary, SRSA GRG 24/6, A(1846) 1166.
3 Rate assessment records for town acre 56, (C5) Assessment Books, (S5) vols 1–2, 1846–1849; (S6) vols 1–3, 1849–1853; (S34-54) vols 1–22, 1854–1874, ACA.
4 Many poems in Mary's published *Serious Poems* indicate her religious faith. 'To an Infant Sleeping: May truth and justice be thy guide, Honour direct thy way, Religion o'er thy heart preside, And God thy surest stay.' Fortunately she was often amused by the incongruities in their day-to-day life, in getting by with makeshift arrangements during the early years in the colony.
5 'The Burra Burra and its directors', *Register*, 20 April 1850.
6 E. Hodder, *The History of South Australia from its Foundation to the Year of its Jubilee: With a Chronological Summary of all the Principal Events of Interest up to date*, vol. 2, Sampson Low, Marston and Co., London, 1893, p. 173; D. Pike, *Paradise of dissent: South Australia, 1829–1857*, Melbourne University Press, Melbourne, 1967, Appendix A.
7 Letter from R. Thomas to colonial secretary, SRSA GRG 24/6 A(1848) 138.
8 Ibid.
9 Ibid.
10 Ibid.
11 Rate assessment records for town acre 56, (C5) Assessment Books, (S5), 1848, ACA.
12 R. Thomas, Index of Memorials, 11 September 1848, book 12, no. 283 and 9 December 1849, book 18, no. 390, GRO.
13 Worsnop, *History of the City of Adelaide*, pp. 91–92
14 G.H. Pitt, *The press in South Australia, 1836 to 1850*, Wakefield Press, Adelaide, 1946, p. 44
15 The building survived until 1920 when it was demolished. It traded for 70 years as the Clarendon. (J.L. Hoad, *Hotels and publicans in South Australia*, part 3, Gould Books, Adelaide, 1986, pp. 110–111.)
16 Rate assessment records for town acre 56, (C5) Assessment Books, (S6) 1850–1852, ACA.
17 *Register*, 20 August 1849; W. Harcus, *South Australia: Its History, Resources and Productions*, Sampson Low, Marston, Searle and Rivington, London, 1876, p. 31; Hodder, *The History of South Australia*, p. 178.

18 Harcus, *South Australia*, p. 31
19 'Electioneering Progress', *Register*, 1 March 1851; Hodder, *The History of South Australia*, p. 185.
20 Editorial: 'Opening of the Legislative Council', *Register*, 20 August 1851; Hodder, *The History of South Australia*, p. 186.
21 S. Marsden, P. Stark and P. Sumerling (eds), *Heritage of the City of Adelaide*, Corporation of the City of Adelaide, Adelaide, 1990, p. 246.
22 Pike, *Paradise of dissent*, p. 443.
23 Letters from J.M. Skipper to colonial secretary, SRSA GRG 24/6, A(1852), 1375 and 1376.
24 J.M. Skipper, South Australian Historical Pictures' Index, SLSA.
25 Pike, *Paradise of dissent*, p. 448.
26 'William Kyffin Thomas' in D. Pike *Australian Dictionary of Biography*, vol. 1851–1890, Melbourne University Press, Melbourne, 1966, p. 264.
27 Pike, *Paradise of dissent*, p. 443.
28 Hiram Mildred's diary, early February 1852, SLSA PRG 307.
29 Ibid., 20 February 1852.
30 Ibid., 25 February 1852.
31 Skipper, South Australian Historical Pictures' Index
32 'The Assay Office', *Register*, 10 February 1852; Hodder, *The History of South Australia*, pp. 187–188.
33 A. Tolmer, *Reminiscences of an Adventurous and Chequered Career at Home and at the Antipodes*, vol. 1, Sampson Low, Marston, Searle and Rivington, London, 1882, pp. 138–139.
34 Pike, *Paradise of dissent*, p. 449.
35 Ibid., pp. 452–453.
36 Ibid., p. 456; Hodder, *The History of South Australia*, p. 188.
37 Pike, *Paradise of dissent*, p. 456.
38 Thomas, Memorial, 23 December 1851, book 38, no. 482, GRO.
39 Rate assessment records for town acre 56, in ACC, (C5) Assessment Book (S6) 1953. (On an assessment taken in 1852.)
40 W. Thomas, Gold Receipt no. 883, March 1852, SRSA GRG 45/43 was consigned to William Johnstone – William's home was out of Adelaide, and it is likely he arranged for a friend to collect it for his wife.
41 *Register*, 6 April 1852.
42 'William Kyffin Thomas' in Pike (ed.) *Australian Dictionary of Biography*, p. 264.
43 Hodder, *The History of South Australia*, p. 191.
44 By 1845 Fisher had been officially vindicated from the charges of corruption during his term as resident commissioner, although he did not escape with a 'spotless reputation'. (Pike, *Paradise of dissent*, p. 230.) He later became an MP and president of the Legislative Council and died in Adelaide on 28 January 1875. (Hodder, *The History of South Australia*, p. 268.)
45 Worsnop, *History of the City of Adelaide*, p. 99–100.
46 Letter from R. Thomas to colonial secretary, SRSA GRG 24/6, A(1852) 689.
47 Letter from R. Thomas to colonial secretary, SRSA GRG 24/6, A(1853) 632, 655; and letter from colonial secretary to R. Thomas, SLSA GRG 24/4, U(1853) 220–1.
48 H. Hussey, *More than Half a Century of Colonial Life and Christian Experience: With notes of Travel, Lectures, Publications, etc*, Hussey and Gillingham, Adelaide, 1897, p. 119.
49 Barbara Rennie personal communication re extracts from the diary of E.W. Andrews.
50 The exact number seems a matter for debate. W.K. Thomas, Anthony Forster, E.W. Andrews, Joseph Fisher, Alexander Hay, F.H. Faulding, Thomas Magarey, J.H. Luckling have been mentioned as part of the original syndicate. (*A Modern Newspaper Building*, W.K. Thomas and Co., Adelaide, 1909.) According to Sowden (unpublished 'History of the *Register*', SLSA PRG 41, p. 25), there may have been as many as 10. He says,

however, 'some soon dropped out'. He mentions Anthony Forster, Edward Andrews and Joseph Fisher. Edward Andrews was also on the editorial staff at this time and was later editor.
51 Diary of G.F. Angas, 10 June 1853, SLSA PRG 174/17 (microfilm).
52 Sowden, 'History of the *Register*', p. 25.
53 *The Register's 75th Birthday*, W.K. Thomas and Co., Adelaide, 1911, p. 3.
54 Willington Family papers.
55 R. Thomas, Memorials, 1 March 1848, book 120, no. 190, 3 July 1856, book 104, no. 2, GRO.
56 Letter from J.M. Skipper to colonial secretary, SRSA GRG 24/6 A(1853), 2089.
57 Letter from Mary to Helen Mantegani (nee Thomas), 6 May 1856, SLSA PRG 106/1.
58 D. O'Connor, *A home away from home*, Flinders University Monograph, 1992, SLSA PRG 106/10; *Register*, 23 August 1853 (advertisement for Grand Vocal and Instrumental Concert and Alfred Mantegani's solo, *The Helen Waltz*).
59 O'Connor Monograph, SLSA PRG 106/10; D. O'Connor, *A home away from home*, 1992.
60 Letter from Mary to Helen, 6 May 1856.
61 Journal of Mary Skipper (nee Thomas) (Mary Jnr's journal), 13 September 1846, SLSA PRG 1160/6.
62 Letter from Frances Skipper (nee Thomas) to Helen, undated, SLSA PRG 106/3.
63 Possibly William Rodolph Thomas, a fellow artist – not related on the Thomas side – but who, in 1850, had married William Kyffin Thomas's sister-in-law, Maria Caroline Good. Although an exhibited artist, W.R. Thomas was employed as a law clerk, and may also have known John Skipper in that capacity. (Willington Family papers.)
64 Letter from Frances to Helen, undated.
65 Letter from Julia Stark to Frances, January 1845, SLSA PRG 242; William Skipper to his sister-in-law, Frances, 1 December 1841, SLSA PRG 242.
66 Mary Jnr's journal, 8 August 1844.
67 Joan Kerr (ed.), *The dictionary of Australian artists*, Oxford University Press, Australia, 1992, p. 729.
68 Letter from Georgiana Skipper to her mother, Frances, 24 July 1854, SLSA PRG 106/3.
69 *The Register's 75th Birthday*, pp. 3, 5.
70 O'Connor Monograph.
71 M. Thomas, 'Verses on the Death of a Friend' in Manuscript Book, Willington Family papers.
72 Letter from Mary to Helen, 17 April 1860.
73 M. Thomas, 'On the Death of an Infant' in *Serious Poems*, Whittaker, Treacher and Co., London, 1831.
74 Letter from J.M. Skipper to Helen, 1 March 1856, SLSA PRG 106/3.

Chapter 14

1 Mary had cause for concern. Between this time and 1870–1871, the South Australian Parliament passed five acts to legalise the marriage of a man with his deceased wife's sister. Only the last was allowed by the Crown; the earlier delay occurred mainly because such legislation had not reached the English Statute Books due to the bishops' opposition. Even in South Australia, the Anglican Bishop of Adelaide argued that 'since the Reformation such a marriage had been null and void by the law of England and offspring of such a marriage illegitimate'. (H. Jones, *In her own name: a history of women in South Australia from 1836 including the story of women's suffrage*, Wakefield Press, Adelaide, 1986, revised and updated 1994, pp. 19–21.)
2 Letter from Mary to Helen, 6 May 1856.
3 Ibid.
4 Ibid., 25 June 1856.

5   Ibid., 6 May 1856.
6   Jones, *In her own name*, pp. 2–3. The *Married Women's Property Act* 1883 was passed when married women were deemed capable of acquiring holding or disposing of any real or personal property. (Jones, *In Her Own Name*, p. 17.)
7   S. Magarey, *Unbridling the tongues of women: a biography of Catherine Helen Spence*, Hale and Iremonger, Sydney, 1985, p. 174.
8   Jones, *In her own name*, p. 16.
9   Ibid., p. xii.
10 Letter from J.M. Skipper Snr to Frances, 1 December 1841; letter from her brother-in-law William Skipper to Frances, undated, SLSA PRG 242.
11 The only letters to have survived were those written to Frances.
12 Phrenology is based upon the assumption that 'faculties' are localised in the brain and that those areas are in evidence on the skull. This view was first put forward by Dr J.F. Gall in 1796 with a 'map' of 30 'faculties'. It had a considerable following, but also many detractors throughout the 19th century. (A. Ridgeway (ed.), *Everyman's encyclopaedia*, vol. 10, J.M. Dent and Sons, London, 1932, p. 243.) Dr Edward Wright, the Thomas family's medical practitioner had been president of the Phrenological Society in London. (D. Pike, *Paradise of dissent: South Australia, 1829–1857*, Melbourne University Press, Melbourne, 1967, pp. 113–114.)
13 Journal of Mary Skipper (nee Thomas) (Mary Jnr's journal), 23 July 1841 and 12 April 1846, SLSA PRG 1160/6.
14 Letter from Mary to Helen, 6 May 1856, SLSA PRG 106/1.
15 Ibid., 13 September 1856.
16 Ibid.
17 Ibid.
18 Ibid.
19 'Reminiscences' in E.K. Thomas (ed.) *The Diary and Letters of Mary Thomas*, W.K. Thomas, Adelaide, 1925, pp. 81–82.
20 Letter from Mary to Helen, 26 October 1856.
21 This is assumed. Mary's letters to Helen cease for over 12 months from February 1857, whilst Helen was in Adelaide, but there is no later indication that this pregnancy resulted in a live birth.
22 Letter from Mary to Helen, 13 September and 26 October 1856.
23 Ibid., 31 November 1856.
24 Ibid., 26 October 1856.
25 Ibid., 26 October 1856.
26 Ibid., 26 October 1856.
27 Letter from Mary to Helen, kept in Mary's Commonplace Book, February 1857, SLSA PRG 1160/7.
28 Shipping Intelligence, passenger lists, *Register*, 25 February and 20 March 1857.
29 Letter fromWillliam Thomas to Helen, February 1857, SLSA PRG 106/3.
30 Obituary, *Register*, 18 August 1921.
31 Mantegani papers, SLSA PRG 106/4.
32 O'Connor Monograph, SLSA PRG 106/10.
33 W. Harcus, *South Australia: Its History, Resources and Productions*, Sampson Low, Marston, Searle and Rivington, London, 1876, pp. 31–33.
34 Pike, *Paradise of dissent*, p. 480.
35 'The House of Assembly', *Observer*, 14 March 1857.
36 Editorial: 'The first South Australian Parliament', *Observer*, 25 April 1857; 'The Governor's speech', *Observer*, 25 April 1857.
37 T. Worsnop, *History of the City of Adelaide*, J. Williams, Adelaide, 1878, p. 90.

38 S. Marsden, P. Stark and P. Sumerling (eds), *Heritage of the City of Adelaide*, Corporation of the City of Adelaide, Adelaide, 1990, pp. 245–246.
39 Jones, *In her own name*, p. 125.
40 Ibid., pp. 101–103.
41 The first was New Zealand's, which passed the legislation in 1893. (Jones, *In her own name*, pp. 146–147.)
42 Jones, *In her own name*, p. 46, pp. 101–102.
43 'South Australia's 21st Birthday' in E.K. Thomas (ed.) *The Diary and Letters of Mary Thomas*, W.K. Thomas and Co., Adelaide, 1925, pp. 84–86.
44 John Healey in 'Not the proclamation and not the tree', *HSSA Newsletter*, 162, September 2002 quotes Mary's doubts about the Old Gum Tree, and also quotes Dr Peter Howell's assessment that South Australia was 'proclaimed by the King by the Letters Patent dated 19th February 1836 . . . The first of Hindmarsh's proclamations, by contrast, was simply an announcement about law'. It was James Hurtle Fisher and other prominent legislators who, on the inauguration of responsible government, thought it necessary to identify an official birthday for South Australia, and persuaded their contemporaries that Hindmarsh's first proclamation 'was the crucial instrument in the colony's foundation'. Perhaps Mary was aware of these facts, which may have affected her enthusiasm.
45 'The majority of the colony', *Observer*, 1 January 1858.
46 Ibid.
47 Ibid.
48 'SA's 21st Birthday' in Thomas (ed.) *The Diary and Letters of Mary Thomas*, p. 86.
49 'Shipping Intelligence', passenger lists, *Register*, 1 January 1858, 10 April 1858.
50 Letter from Mary to Helen, 2 June 1858.
51 Ibid., 2 June 1858.
52 Ibid., 17 October 1858.
53 Ibid., 15 July 1858.
54 Ibid., 15 July 1858.
55 Ibid., 9 August 1858.
56 Ibid., 17 October 1858.
57 Mary Jnr must have lost the second twin quite soon after Mary's October letter to Helen; and then once more, become pregnant almost immediately, as her daughter was born at the end of the following July. Mary does not mention this pregnancy specifically to Helen until she tells her on the 7 August 1859 that Mary Jnr has not yet been confined. Helen no doubt knew of it through direct correspondence with Mary Jnr herself.
58 Letter from Mary to Helen, 11 November 1858.
59 Letter from Mary to George, 14 October 1838, SLSA PRG 1160/2.
60 E. Hodder, *The History of South Australia from its Foundation to the Year of its Jubilee: With a Chronological Summary of all the Principal Events of Interest up to date*, vol. 2, Sampson Low, Marston and Co., London, 1893, p. 20l; 'Mr Torren's Lecture on Real Property', *Observer*, 21 May 1859; 'The Real Property Act in Sydney', *Observer*, 23 August 1862.
61 Rate assessment records for town acres 55, 56, 57 and 69, (C5) Assessment Books (S5), 1847; (S35), 1855; (S38), 1858, ACA.
62 Marsden et al. (eds), *Heritage of the City of Adelaide*, p. 179.
63 *Observer*, 30 October 1858.
64 Letter from Mary to Helen, 1 February 1859.
65 As there is no mention in Mary's letters to Helen of the birth of Robert George's son on 30 July 1857, the news must have arrived while Helen was in Adelaide.
66 Letter from Mary to Helen, 18 February 1859.
67 Ibid., 23 March 1859.
68 Sowden, unpublished 'History of the *Register*', SLSA PRG 41, pp. 55, 59.

69 Letter from Mary to Helen, 25 April 1859.
70 Ibid., 14 July 1859.
71 Ibid., 7 August 1859.
72 Ibid., 7 August 1859.
73 Ibid., 12 September 1859.
74 Ibid., 15 November 1859.
75 Ibid., 4 January and 1 February 1859
76 Jones, *In her own name*, pp. 4–5.
77 Letter from Mary to Helen, 15 November 1859.

Chapter 15

1   Letter from Mary to Helen, 26 January 1860, SLSA PRG 106/1.
2   Ibid., 26 January 1860.
3   Letter from Mary to Helen, kept in Mary's Commonplace Book, 4 March 1860, SLSA PRG 1160/7.
4   Letter from Mary to Helen, 17 April 1860.
5   Ibid., 17 April 1860.
6   If all the children but the baby were being sent away to escape the infection, this is quite prescient. The baby would have been protected by the antibodies in her mother's breast milk.
7   Letter from Mary to Helen, kept in Mary's Commonplace Book, June 1860.
8   Ibid.
9   Ibid.
10 Letter from Mary to Helen, 1 July 1860.
11 Ibid., 1 July 1860.
12 William Hillier was probably the son of the schoolteacher and Mary's friend, Mrs Jane Hillier. As well as being a long-time friend of William Thomas, and previously employed by R. Thomas and Co., he had married Catherine S. Good, the sister of William Thomas's wife.
13 Will of Robert Thomas, Probate Registry, Adelaide.
14 Report of funeral, *Register*, 5 July 1860.
15 Obituary, *Observer*, 7 July 1860.
16 'The Pioneers' in E.K. Thomas (ed.) *The Diary and Letters of Mary Thomas*, W.K. Thomas and Co., Adelaide, 1925, pp. 91–92.
17 O'Connor Monograph, SLSA PRG 106/10.
18 R. Gibbs, *A history of South Australia: from colonial days to the present*, Southern Heritage Press, Blackwood, South Australia, 1984, pp. 102–103.
19 Sowden's unpublished 'History of the *Register*', SLSA PRG 41, p. 47; *Register's Birthday*, p. 3.
20 The Register offices eventually moved into a new building on this site in 1909. (*A Modern Newspaper Building*, W.K. Thomas and Co., Adelaide, 1909.)
21 'Adelaide lit by gas', *Observer*, 27 June 1863.
22 *Register's Birthday*, p. 3.
23 E. Hodder, *The History of South Australia from its Foundation to the Year of its Jubilee: With a Chronological Summary of all the Principal Events of Interest up to date*, vol. 2, Sampson Low, Marston and Co., London, 1893, pp. 203, 205, 210, 214–215; During the next four years the 'electric' telegraph stretched to Queensland and New South Wales via Overland Corner and Wentworth. Connections in South Australia had also reached Gumeracha, Normanville, the Barossa Valley, Watervale, Port Wakefield and Moonta, and as far north as Port Augusta. (Hodder, *The History of South Australia*, pp. 214–215.)
24 'Railway from Gawler to Kapunda opened', *Observer*, 18 August 1860.

25 Editorial: 'Public baths', *Observer*, 12 January 1861; Hodder, *The History of South Australia*, p. 211.
26 S. Marsden, P. Stark, P. Sumerling (eds), *Heritage of the City of Adelaide*, Corporation of the City of Adelaide, Adelaide, 1990, p. 170.
27 D. Pike, *Paradise of dissent: South Australia 1829–1857*, Melbourne University Press, Melbourne, 1967, p. 504; Marsden et al. (eds), *Heritage of the City of Adelaide*, p. 260.
28 Marsden et al. (eds), *Heritage of the City of Adelaide*, pp. 260–261; *Observer*, 28 July 1860.
29 Robert George left London in early February 1861 – seven months after the death of his father. (Letter from Robert George to Mary, 8 February 1861, SLSA PRG 106/3.) Mary inherited two cottages at Kensington from Robert in July 1860. Although there is a record of these properties, there is no record of Mary's ownership. (Discussion with Norwood, Payneham and St Peters Council historian, January 2003.) She may have sold them immediately, at a time when council records were just beginning to be kept and are patchy. It is likely that through the sale of these cottages she assisted Robert George's return to Adelaide.
30 E.J.R. Morgan and S.H. Gilbert, *Early Adelaide architecture 1836–1886*, Oxford University Press, Melbourne, 1986, p. 154.
31 M. Page, *Sculptors in space: South Australian architects 1836–1886*, Royal Australian Institute of Architects (South Australian Chapter), Adelaide, 1986, pp. 35–36.
32 'Baptist Chapel, Flinders Street', *Observer*, 21 December 1861.
33 Hodder, *The History of South Australia*, p. 214.
34 *Register's Birthday*, p. 3.
35 *Observer*, 25 January 1862.
36 Pike, *Paradise of dissent*, p. 460.
37 'Royal award to Mr Stuart', *Observer*, 25 January 1862.
38 Hodder, *The History of South Australia*, p. 212 and p. 211.
39 W. Prest, K. Round, and C. Fort (eds), *The Wakefield companion to South Australian history*, Wakefield Press, Adelaide, 2001, pp. 521–522; Hodder, *The History of South Australia*, pp. 214–215.
40 'The Baptist Chapel, Flinders Street', *Observer*, 9 May 1863.
41 Marsden et al. (eds), *Heritage of the City of Adelaide*, pp. 132–133.
42 'The Town Hall – laying the foundation stone', *Observer*, 9 May 1863.
43 'Adelaide lit by gas', *Observer*, 27 June 1863.
44 P. Woodruff, *Two million South Australians*, Peacock Press, Adelaide, 1984, pp. 27, 11, 37.
45 P. Morton, *After Light*, Wakefield Press, Adelaide, 1996, p. 133.
46 Page, *Sculptors in space*, p. 36.
47 Editorial: 'Public health', *Observer*, 9 December 1871.
48 Town Acre 56 Envelope, GRO.
49 'R.G. Thomas in account with Mrs Thomas', 21 January 1864, Willington Family papers.
50 Rate assessment records for town acre 56, (C5) Assessment Book (S43), 1865, ACA. (On an assessment taken in 1864.)
51 Hodder, *The History of South Australia*, p. 218.
52 Page, *Sculptors in space*, p. 36.
53 Marsden et al. (eds), *Heritage of the City of Adelaide*, p. 163.
54 'Stow Memorial Church', *Observer*, 11 February 1865.
55 Marsden et al. (eds), *Heritage of the City of Adelaide*, p. 27.
56 Ibid.
57 Ibid., p. 166.
58 Page, *Sculptors in space*, pp. 37, 76.
59 Letter from Mary to George Harris, 14 October 1838, SLSA PRG 1160/2.
60 'Town Hall opening banquet', *Observer*, 23 June 1866.

61   Marsden et al. (eds), *Heritage of the City of Adelaide*, p. 163.
62   Willington Family papers.
63   Hodder, *The History of South Australia*, pp. 222–223; Prest et al. (eds), *Wakefield companion to South Australian history*, p. 226.
64   'Stow Memorial Church', *Observer*, 20 April 1867.
65   Page, *Sculptors in space*, p. 36.
66   'Stow Memorial Church', *Observer*, 20 April 1867.
67   Marsden et al. (eds), *Heritage of the City of Adelaide*, pp. 159.
68   Page, *Sculptors in space*, pp. 34–38.
69   Sadly, today, this beautiful window is obscured by an organ imported in recent years from another church.
70   Page, *Sculptors in space*, p. 37.
71   Family Tree, Willington Family papers; Family Tree, Cook Family papers.
72   *Observer*, 25 April 1857 and 13 April 1867.
73   'The royal visit', *Observer*, 2 November 1867.
74   Ibid.
75   Marsden et al. (eds), *Heritage of the City of Adelaide*, p.166.
76   Hodder, *The History of South Australia*, p. 224.

Chapter 16

1   S. Marsden, P. Stark, P. Sumerling (eds), *Heritage of the City of Adelaide: An illustrated guide*, Corporation of the City of Adelaide, Adelaide, 1990, p.166.
2   'New General Post Office', *Observer*, 11 May 1872.
3   'Reminiscences' in E.K. Thomas (ed.) *The Diary and Letters of Mary Thomas*, W.K. Thomas and Co., Adelaide, 1925, p. 79.
4   M. Page, *Sculptors in space: South Australian architects 1836–1886*, Royal Australian Institute of Architects (South Australian Chapter), Adelaide, 1986, pp. 37–38.
5   Marsden et al. (eds), *Heritage of the City of Adelaide*, pp. 347–348.
6   Page, *Sculptors in space*, p. 37–38.
7   E. Hodder, *The History of South Australia from its Foundation Year to its Jubilee: With a Chronological Summary of all the Principal Events up to date*, vol. 2, Sampson Low, Marston and Co., London, 1893, p. 12.
8   Page, *Sculptors in space*, pp. 37–38; Alternatively 6 shillings and 5 pence per square metre.
9   During Robert George's earlier period in private practice in Adelaide, for example, he designed the home of Matthew Goode on the corner of Hutt and Wakefield streets in 1867. It later became the Wakefield Street Hospital but was demolished in 1933. (M. Burden, *Lost Adelaide*, Oxford University Press, Melbourne, 1983, p. 25.)
10   Probate Registry, Adelaide, Will of Mary Thomas, 27 February 1875.
11   'Mrs Mary Thomas and Others: Release by tenant for life and reversions of legacy', 15 July 1870, Willington Family papers.
12   Codicils to Will of Mary Thomas, March 1870, Willington Family papers.
13   Ibid.
14   Obituary, *Register*, 8 December 1883.
15   W. Prest, K. Round, and C. Fort (eds), *The Wakefield companion to South Australian history*, Wakefield Press, Adelaide, 2001, p. 336; Hodder, *The History of South Australia*, p. 231.
16   Codicils to Will of Mary Thomas, 28 August 1871, Willington Family papers.
17   Whilst the dividends paid when Mary inherited a life interest in them were £20 a share, their value slowly declined. The mine was almost worked out by the beginning of the 1870s.
18   Codicil to Will of Mary Thomas.
19   Letter from Mary to Robert George, 25 September 1872, Willington Family papers.
20   Letter from Mary to Helen Sawtell (nee Skipper), 3 March 1873, SLSA PRG 242.

21 Correspondence re Estate of Mary Thomas, August 1873, and January 1874, Willington Family papers.
22 Rate assessment records for town acre 56, (C5) Assessment Books (S54), 1874, ACA.
23 Correspondence re Estate of Mary Thomas, 23 August, November 1874, Willington Family papers.
24 Hodder, *The History of South Australia*, pp. 15, 24.
25 'The overland telegraph', *Observer*, 27 August and 3 September 1870.
26 Hodder, *The History of South Australia*, p. 230.
27 'Overland telegraph', *Observer*, 2 September 1871.
28 'Overland telegraph', *Observer*, 2 December 1871; Hodder, *The History of South Australia*, p. 234.
29 Hodder, *The History of South Australia*, pp. 25–26.
30 Ibid., p. 236.
31 'New general post office', *Observer*, 11 May 1872.
32 Hodder, *The History of South Australia*, pp. 26–27.
33 Hodder, 1893, *The History of South Australia*, pp. 24, 28.
34 Burden, *Lost Adelaide*, pp. 165–167.
35 'Reminiscences' in Thomas (ed.) *The Diary and Letters of Mary Thomas*, pp. 76–77.
36 Letter from Mary to Helen Mantegani (nee Thomas), 13 September 1856, SLSA PRG 106/1.
37 Hodder, *The History of South Australia*, pp. 37, 239.
38 'Proposal for an Adelaide University', *Observer*, 21 September 1872.
39 Prest et al. (eds), *The Wakefield companion to South Australian history*, pp. 252–253; Hodder, *The History of South Australia*, p. 243.
40 *Observer*, 9, 23 August 1873; Hodder, *The History of South Australia*, p. 70.
41 'Munificent gift to Adelaide University', *Observer*, 31 October 1874; Hodder, *The History of South Australia*, p. 70.
42 'The Adelaide University', *Observer*, 12 December 1874.
43 'Munificent gift to Adelaide University', Observer, 31 October 1874.
44 Marsden et al. (eds), *Heritage of the City of Adelaide*, p. 262; 'Proposed new institute', *Observer*, 3 January 1874.
45 Hodder, *The History of South Australia*, p .64.
46 Marsden et al. (eds), *Heritage of the City of Adelaide*, p. 262.
47 'The public health', *Observer*, 9 December 1871.
48 'The Public Health Act', *Observer*, 3 January 1874.
49 Ibid.
50 'Central Board of Health', *Observer*, 17 January 1874.
51 'The Public Health Act', *Observer*, 7 March 1874; Hodder, *The History of South Australia*, p. 254.
52 'The Adelaide Local Board of Health, *Observer*, 7 March 1874.
53 'The Public Health Act' and 'The Adelaide Local Board of Health', *Observer*, 7 March 1874. Work eventually started on a sewerage system in 1879 under the supervision of Robert George Thomas. Adelaide was the first of Australia's major cities to be sewered with the opening of the Islington sewerage farm and the completion of the main sewers in 1880–1881. (R. Gibbs, *A history of South Australia: from colonial days to the present*, Southern Heritage Press, Blackwood, South Australia, 1984, p. 162.)
54 'City drainage', *Observer*, 19 December 1874.
55 F.T. Whittington, *Augustus Short, First Bishop of Adelaide: The Story of a Thirty Four Years' Episcopate*, Wells Gardner, Darton and Co., London, 1888, pp. 116–117.
56 Hodder, *The History of South Australia*, p. 265.
57 'Fires', *Observer*, 23 January 1875.
58 'Those Women Pioneers' in Thomas (ed.) *The Diary and Letters of Mary Thomas*, pp. 93–94.

59 It has not been preserved in either the Reid papers or the Trinity Church papers held in the Archives of the State Library of South Australia and has probably not survived.
60 Sowden's unpublished 'History of the *Register*', SLSA PRG 41, p. 14.
61 Ibid., p. 47.
62 'William Kyffin Thomas' in D. Pike, *Australian Dictionary of Biography*, vol. 1851–1890, Melbourne University Press, Melbourne, 1966, pp. 264–265.
63 Two descendants, John Scales, Sir Robert's grandson, was an editor of the *Advertiser*, the paper with which the *Register* was incorporated in 1931; and Joan Willington, Evan's granddaughter, was also a journalist with the *Advertiser*.
64 D. Pike, *Paradise of dissent: South Australia, 1829–1857*, Melbourne University Press, Melbourne, 1967, p. 516.
65 Application to bring lands under the Real Property Act, book 193, no. 135, 7 September 1875, South Australian Land Titles Office.
66 Letter from Helen to W. Sowden, 6 August 1922, unpublished 'History of the *Register*', SLSA PRG 41
67 Family Tree, Cook Family papers; *Observer*, 5 January 1918.
68 Helen died at the home of her daughter Mrs Victoria Beevor on 17 August 1921 aged 96. For a time after Mary's death, it seems, she possibly operated lodging houses, in several locations in Adelaide and Semaphore, and then lived for some years before her death with her daughter. Helen's son, Alfred, known as Victor, worked for a number of years at the offices of the Register.

Appendix

1 M. Thomas, *Serious Poems*, Whittaker, Treacher and Co., London, 1832, preface.
2 Letter from Mary to George, 14 October 1838, SLSA PRG 1160/2.
3 K. Kyffin Thomas, Australian Broadcasting Corporation Broadcast, December 1960.
4 Ibid.
5 For example narrative ('The Pilgrim and the Cottager'), descriptive ('The Funeral at Sea'), didactic ('A Paraphrase on the 13th Chapter of the First Epistle to the Corinthians'), lyric poems ('Elergy on the Death of His Late Majesty George IV'; 'Epitaph on Mr Leonard Baugh'), occasional verse ('On Beholding the Demolition of the Ancient London Bridge') and light and humorous verse ('Celebs in Search of a Wife'; 'The Lame Man, the Blind Man and the Oyster').
6 *Register*, 15 February 1875.

Bibliography

Primary sources

Archival

State Library of South Australia (SLSA)
    Brown, John, Diary, PRG 1002/2
    Deane, Rachael, Diary, D 5711 (L)
    De Mole, Violet, PRG 39
    Everard Family, Letters, PRG 208 Special List 1/5–10
    Gliddon, A.W., Letter from the *Africaine*, D3227 1-2(L)
    Gouger, Robert, Diary, PRG 1012/1 and Correspondence, 1012/5
    Mantegani Papers, PRG 106
        Letters from Mary Thomas, 1856–1860, 106/1
        Letters from Frances Skipper (nee Thomas), 106/3
        Real estate transactions of Alfred Mantegani, 106/8/1-2
        O'Connor D., *A Home Away from Home*, Monograph on
        Alfred Mantegani, Flinders University, 106/10
    Mildred, Hiram, Diary of the Goldfields, 1852, Mildred Family, PRG 307
    Mortlock Pictorial Collection 1836–1877 (buildings and views of Adelaide)
    Research Notes, 'Pioneer Scientific and Literary Bodies'
    South Australian Historical Pictures Index, J.M. Skipper, vols 1 and 2
    Skipper Family, Letters, PRG 242
    Skipper, J.M., Papers 1841–1901, PRG 72
    Sowden, W., Papers, (History of the Register), PRG 41
    Survey of Adelaide's Buildings, G.S. Kingston's 1842 map
    Thomas Family, PRG 1160
        Diary of Mary Thomas, 1836, original and transcription, 1160/1
        Letters of Mary Thomas to George Harris, 1838–1841, 1160/2
        Robert Thomas's letter to the Colonial Office 1836, ms, 1160/4
        Journal of Mary Skipper (nee Thomas), 1839–1846, 1160/6
        Commonplace Book of Mary Thomas, 1160/7

Bibliography 293

State Records of South Australia
   Bankruptcy and Insolvency Documents, 1842 and 1843 (Robert Thomas, George Stevenson and R. Thomas and Co.)
   Gold Receipts from Gold Escort
   Government Gazette, 1842–1853
   Richard Horwood's Plan of the City of London and Westminster, 1813, reprinted by the London Topographical Society
   R. Thomas and Co. and colonial secretary, Correspondence, 1837–1848
   SA Almanacks (Adelaide Directories), 1939–1941, R. Thomas and Co., facsimile editions
   Skipper, J.M. and colonial secretary, correspondence 1847–1854
   Thomas, R. and colonial secretary, correspondence 1844–1853

Government Registry Office
   Envelope for Town Acre 56, containing Indentures and other documents relating to Acre 56 property transactions
   Indentures and Memorials concerning property transactions listed in:
      George Stevenson, Index of Memorials
      George Stevenson, Index of Deposits and Enrolments
      Robert Thomas, Index of Memorials
      Robert Thomas, Index of Deposits and Enrolments
   Map of Country Sections, District of Adelaide, from Colonel Light's survey, published in 1839 by J. Arrowsmith, London

Lands Titles Office
   Estate of Mary Thomas, book 193, no. 135, 7 September 1875, application to bring lands under the provisions of the *Real Property Act*

Adelaide City Council Archives
   Plan of the City of Adelaide from Colonel Light's survey, government photolithographer, M.G. Sherrah
   Rate Assessment Records, 1847–1874, Acre 56, Hindley Street and environs

Probate Registry, Adelaide
   Thomas Mary, Will, 1848 and codicil, 1871
   Thomas Robert, Will, 1860

City Of Norwood, Payneham And St Peters
   Discussion and correspondence with archivist Ms B. Brittle, January 2002

Southampton Archives, United Kingdom
   Correspondence, October 1997, April 1998
   Harris George, Counterpart Leases (extracts)
   Harris George, Will, 1831, Hampshire Records Office
   Poll Book, 1806 (extracts)
   Rate Books, 1787, 1801–1807 (extracts)
   Registers:
      All Saints Parish, Southampton (extracts)
      Holy Rood Parish, Southampton (extracts)
      Millbrook Parish (extracts)

Papers in the keeping of:
Victor Willington
> Addendums and Codicils to the Will of Mary Thomas
> Birth, marriage and death records of William Kyffin Thomas and his family
> Correspondence re the Estate of Mary Thomas
> Correspondence re the ancestry and family home of Robert Thomas
> Financial arrangements between Mary Thomas and Robert George Thomas
> Manuscript Book of Mary Thomas, poems and transcription of the voyage of the *Africaine*
> Newspaper cuttings re Mary and Robert Thomas
> Partnership Agreement between Robert Thomas and George Stevenson (R. Thomas and Co.)
> Real estate transactions of Robert and Mary Thomas, London and Adelaide
> Reversions of Legacy – disposal of the annuity of Mary Thomas
> William Kyffin Thomas – details of country section
> Other Thomas family papers

N. Cook
> Family tree of Skipper and Mantegani descendants

B. Rennie
> Letters and diary of E.W. Andrews (extracts)

South Australian Maritime Museum
Display of sleeping accommodation on emigrant vessels

Secondary sources
Books
Anderson, R.C. and Anderson, J.M., *Quicksilver: a hundred years of coaching 1750–1850*, David and Charles, Newton Abbott, 1973
Appleyard, A., Fargher, B. and Radford, R., *S.T. Gill 1839–1852: the South Australian years*, Art Gallery of South Australia, 1986
Auhl, I. and Marfleet, D., *Australia's earliest mining era: South Australia 1841–1851*, Axiom Press, Adelaide, 1975
Bell, W.G., *Fleet Street in Seven Centuries*, chaps 22–24, I. Pittman and Sons, London, 1912
Blagden C., *The stationers' company: a history*, Allen and Unwin, London, 1960
Bryant, A., *The age of elegance*, The Reprint Society, London, 1954
Bull, J.W., *Early Experiences of Life in South Australia and an Extended Colonial History*, E.S. Wigg and Son, Adelaide, 1884
Burden, M., *Lost Adelaide: a photographic record*, OUP, Melbourne, 1983
Carter, M., *No convicts there*, Trevaunance Pty Ltd, Adelaide, 1997
Chancellor, E.B., *The Annals of Fleet Street: Its Traditions and Associations*, chaps 1–7, Chapman and Hall, London, 1912
Chancellor, E.B., *The London of Thackeray*, chaps 4 and 5, Grant Richards, London, 1928
Clark, C.M.H., *A history of Australia*, vol. 3, Melbourne University Press, Melbourne, 1973
Clark, C.M.H., *A short history of Australia*, Heinemann, London, 1967
Cobbett, William, *Rural rides*, Penguin Books, Harmondsworth, 1967

Colwell, M. and Naylor, A., *Adelaide illustrated*, Lansdowne Press, 1974
Doubleday, Arthur, (ed.), *The Victoria history of Hampshire and the Isle of Wight*, A. Constable, Westminster, 1900–1914
Cruikshank, D. and Burton, N., *Life in the Georgian City*, Viking, London, 1990
Dickey, B., Martin, E. and Oxenbury, R., *Rations, residences, resources*, Wakefield Press, Adelaide, 1986
Dutton, F., *South Australia and its Mines with a Historical Sketch of the Colony*, State Library of South Australia, facsimile of the edition published by T. and W. Boote, London, 1846
Dutton, G., *Founder of a city*, F.W. Cheshire, Melbourne, 1960
Dutton, G., *A taste of history*, Rigby, Adelaide, 1978
Duthy, J., *Sketches of Hampshire*, Jacob and Johnson, Winchester, 1836
Elder, D. (ed.), *William Light's brief journal*, Wakefield Press, Adelaide, 1984
Elliott, J., *Our home in Australia: a description of cottage life in 1860*, Flannel Flower Press, Sydney, 1984
Fenner, C., Grenfell Price, A., et al. (eds), *The centenary history of South Australia*, Royal Geographical Society of Australasia (South Australian Branch), Adelaide, 1936
Fletcher, B., *A history of architecture*, chap. 28, Athlone Press, London, 1961
Gibbs, R.M., *A history of South Australia: from colonial days to the present*, Southern Heritage Press, Blackwood, 1984
Gibney, H.J. and Smith, A.G. (eds), *A biographical register 1788–1938*, vol. 2, Australian Dictionary of Biography, Canberra, 1987
Gouger, R., *South Australia in 1837*, Harvey and Darton, London, 1838
Harcus, W., *South Australia: Its History, Resources and Productions*, Sampson Low, Marston, Searle and Rivington, London, 1876
Hawker, J., *Early experiences*, W.E. Wigg and Son, Adelaide, 1899
Hindmarsh, F.S., *From powder monkey to governor*, Access Press, Western Australia, 1995
Hoad, J.L., *Hotels and publicans in South Australia 1836–1884*, Australian Hotels' Association and Gould Books, Adelaide, 1986
Hodder, E., *The History of South Australia from its Foundation to the Year of its Jubilee: With a Chronological Summary of all the Principal Events of Interest up to date*, vol. 2, Sampson Low, Marston and Co., London, 1893
Hodder, E. (ed.), The founding of South Australia as recorded in the *journals of Mr Robert Gouger*, Sampson Low, Marston and Co., London, 1898
Holt, A., *Vanishing sands*, City of Brighton, South Australia, 1991
Hope, P., *The voyage of the Africaine*, Heinemann, Melbourne, 1968
Hussey, H., *More than Half a Century of Colonial Life and Christian Experience: With notes of Travel, Lectures, Publications, etc*, Hussey and Gillingham, Adelaide, 1897
Jenkin, G., *Conquest of the Ngarrindjeri*, Raukkan Publishers, Point McLeay, 1985
Jones, H., *In her own name: a history of women in South Australia from 1836 including the story of women's suffrage*, Wakefield Press, Adelaide, 1986 (revised and updated 1994)
Kerr, C., *'A exelent coliney': the practical idealists of 1836–1846*, Rigby, Adelaide, 1978
Kerr, J. (ed.), *The dictionary of Australian artists*, Sydney: Power Institute, Sydney University, 1984
Langley, M., *Sturt of the Murray*, Robert Hale, London, 1969
Langmead, D., *Accidental architect: the life and times of George Strickland Kingston*, Crossing Press, Darlinghurst, 1994
Lloyd, E., *A visit to the Antipodes*, State Library of South Australia, facsimile of the 1846 edition
Magarey, S., *Unbridling the tongues of women: a biography of Catherine Helen Spence*, Hale and Iremonger, Sydney, 1985
Marsden, S., Stark, P. and Sumerling, P. (eds), *Heritage of the City of Adelaide: an illustrated guide*, Corporation of the City of Adelaide, Adelaide, 1990
Minchim, H., *The story of the Flinders Ranges*, Rigby, Adelaide, 1965

Morgan, E.J.R. and Gilbert, S.H., *Early Adelaide architecture 1836–1886*, Oxford University Press, Melbourne, 1969
Morton, P., *After Light*, Wakefield Press, Adelaide, 1996
Nicol, R. and Samuels, B. (eds), *Insights into South Australian history*, Historical Society of South Australia, Adelaide, 1992
Page, M., *Sculptors in space: South Australian architects 1836–1886*, Royal Australian Institute of Architects (South Australian Chapter), Adelaide, 1986
Parsons, R., *Migrant ships of South Australia, 1836–1860*, Gould Books, Gumeracha, South Australia, 1988
Peake, G.P., Sources for South Australian history, Gould Publishing Services, Adelaide, 1998
Peake Jones, K., *Recollections of Daniel George Brock*, Royal Geographical Society of Australasia (South Australian Branch), Adelaide, 1981
Perry D.M., *The place of the waters*, Adelaide: Glenelg Council and the National Trust of South Australia (Glenelg Branch), 1993
Perry D.M., *Sir John Morphett*, Cummins Society and the West Torrens Council, Adelaide, 1992
Pike, D., *Paradise of dissent: South Australia, 1829–1857*, Melbourne University Press, Melbourne, 1957
Pike, D., *Australian dictionary of biography*, vols 1–6, Melbourne University Press, Melbourne, 1966
Pikusa, S., *The Adelaide house 1836–1901*, Wakefield Press, Adelaide, 1986
Pitt, G.H., *The press in South Australia, 1836 to 1850*, The Wakefield Press, Adelaide, 1946
Porter, R., *London: a social history*, chaps 10 and 11, Hamish Hamilton, London, 1994
Pratt, B.W., *The Australian encyclopaedia*, Grolier Society, Sydney, 1983
Prest, W., Round, K. and Fort, C. (eds), *The Wakefield companion to South Australian history*, Wakefield Press, Adelaide, 2001
Price, A. Grenfell, *Founders and Pioneers of South Australia*, F.W. Preece and Sons, Adelaide, 1929
Radford, R. and Hylton, J., *Australian colonial art 1800–1900*, Art Gallery of South Australia, Adelaide, 1995
Reader, B., *Making costumes of the 1830s*, vols 1 and 3, bound typescript, State Library of South Australia, Adelaide, 1985
Ridgeway, A. (ed.), *Everyman's encyclopaedia*, vols 1 and 4, J.M. Dent and Sons, London, 1932
Ridley, A., *A backward glance: the story of John Ridley, Pioneer*, James Clark and Co., London, 1904
Spence, C.H., *Clara Morison*, Wakefield Press, Adelaide, facsimile of the 1854 edition
Statton, J., *Biographical index of South Australians*, South Australian Genealogy and Heraldry Society, Adelaide, 1986
Summerson, J., *Georgian London*, Penguin Books, Harmondsworth, 1978
Taylor, R., *Unearthed*, Wakefield Press, Adelaide, 2002
Tate, P., *The New Forest*, Macdonald and Janes, London, 1979
Temple Patterson, A., *Southampton: a biography*, Macmillan, London, 1970
Temple Patterson, A., *A history of Southampton, 1700–1914*, vols 1–3, Southampton University Press, 1971
Thomas, E.K. (ed.), *The Diary and Letters of Mary Thomas*, W.K. Thomas and Co., Adelaide, 1925
Thomas, M., *Serious Poems*, Whittaker, Treacher and Co., London, 1831
Tolmer, A., *Reminiscences of an Adventurous and Chequered Career at Home and at the Antipodes*, vol.1, Sampson Low, Marston, Searle and Rivington, London, 1882
Tomalin, C., *The invisible woman: the story of Nelly Ternan and Charles Dickens*, Penguin Books, London, 1990
Tomalin, C., *Jane Austen: a life*, Viking, London, 1997
Wakefield, E.G., *England and America (1834)*, Augustus M. Kelly (reprints of Economic Classics), New York, 1967
Wakefield, E.G., *The New British Province of South Australia*, C. Knight, London, 1835

Walker, D.M. (ed.), *The Oxford companion to the law*, Clarendon Press, Oxford, 1980
Wall, B., *Our own Matilda*, Wakefield Press, Adelaide, 1994
Warburton, J.W. (ed.), *Five metropolitan creeks of the River Torrens, South Australia*, Adult Education, University of Adelaide, Adelaide, 1977
Watt, J., *Family Life in South Australia Fifty Three Years Ago from October, 1837*, W.K. Thomas and Co., Adelaide, 1890
Whitelock, D., *Adelaide: a sense of difference*, Savvas Publishing, Melbourne, 1985
Whitington, F.T., *Augustus Short, First Bishop of Adelaide: The Story of a Thirty Four Years' Episcopate*, Wells Gardner, Darton and Co., London, 1888
Wilkinson, G.B., *South Australia*, State Library of South Australia, Adelaide, facsimile of the 1848 edition
Willington, J.K., *Maisie*, Wakefield Press, Adelaide, 1992
Wilson, S.C. and Borrow, K.T., *The bridge over the ocean*, Hyde Park Press, Adelaide, 1973
Woodruff, P., *Two million South Australians*, Peacock Publications, Adelaide, 1984
Worsnop T., *History of the City of Adelaide*, J. Williams, Adelaide, 1878

Newspapers

Hampshire Chronicle, United Kingdom, 6 July 1804
South Australian Gazette and Colonial Register, 18 June 1836–29 June 1839, all reviewed
South Australian Register, 6 July 1839–6 August 1842, all reviewed
South Australian Register then *The Register*, 1842–1848, reviewed re significant events
Observer, 1848–1875, reviewed re significant events
South Australian then *Southern Australian*, various issues

Pamphlets and periodicals

'A modern newspaper building', W.K. Thomas and Co., Adelaide, 1909
Borrow, K.T., 'The Hallett family', Pioneers Association of South Australia, Adelaide, 1946
Borrow, K.T., 'Government House (1837–1901)', Pioneers Association of South Australia, Adelaide, 1982
Ewens, L.J.T., 'The establishment of Trinity Church, Adelaide', Pioneers Association of South Australia, Adelaide, 1953
Fischer, G.L., 'The Queen's Theatre, Adelaide 1841–1842', Pioneers Association South Australia, Adelaide, 1957
'Glenelg illustrated 1836–1896', W.K. Thomas and Co., Adelaide, 1896
James, T.H., 'Six months in South Australia', in Tait's *Edinburgh Magazine*, Edinburgh, 1839
Journals and Newsletters, 1988–2004, Historical Society of South Australia, Adelaide
Mantegani, H., 'Recollections of the early days of South Australia from 1836', Royal Geographical Society of Australasia (South Australian Branch), vol. 5, Adelaide, 1902
McLellan, J., 'Adelaide's early inns and taverns', Pioneers' Association of South Australia, Adelaide, 1941
'Inflation: the value of the pound 1750–1998', Research Paper 99/20, House of Commons, United Kingdom
'Pamphlets of the press: Jubilee of South Australian journalism', State Library of South Australia, Adelaide
Skipper, O., 'Reminiscences of fifty-two years', Royal Geographical Society of Australasia (South Australian Branch), vol. 7, Adelaide, 1904
Stevenson, G., 'Extracts from his journal from the original in the papers of George Fife Angas', Royal Geographical Society of Australasia (South Australian Branch), vol. 30, Adelaide, 1933

'The Emigrant's friend or authentic guide to South Australia', J. Allen and D. Francis (pubs), 1848 fasimile edition by Reader's Digest Services Pty Ltd, Sydney, 1974
'The Register's 75th birthday', W.K. Thomas and Co., Adelaide, 1911

Electronic Sources

Early 19th Century London, Proceedings of the Old Bailey, http://www.oldbaileyonline.org
International Genealogical Index (IGI), http://www.familysearch.org
'Inflation: the Value of the Pound 1750–1998', Research Paper 99/20, House of Commons, http://www.parliament.uk/-parliamentary-and-archives/research
CPI Figures: Australia and Adelaide 1981–2007, Reserve Bank of Australia, http://www.rba.gov.au

Index

A
Aborigines 15, 19–20, 42–43, 48–52, 54–55, 75, 83–84, 100, 103–105, 108–109, 131–133, 137–138, 151, 167–168, 243, 248
first contact with 50–51
Maria massacre and summary executions 101–105, 108–110, 132–133
Rufus River massacre 137–138
Adelaide City Corporation 183, 204, 231, 246–247
Adelaide Hills 66, 158, 181
Adelaide Town Hall 225, 227–229, 232, 234
Adelphi rooms, London 15, 17, 85, 161
Alfred, Prince (Duke of Edinburgh) 231
Alice Springs 241
Allen, James 146, 153, 163
Andrews, Thomas and Clark 223, 242, 250
Angas, George Fife 16, 18–19, 41, 44, 64, 87, 179, 222
Ashfield Lodge 9

B
Bathgate, Jane 112
Baugh, Mr 72, 96–97
Beltana 241
Bennett, George 86, 88

Bennett, James 99, 120
Bennett Hayes, William 179, 204
Binney Reverend Thomas 212, 215
Birks, Rosetta (nee Thomas) (see Appendix A) 204–205, 216
British Parliament 16, 122, 127, 144, 178, 192
Brown, John 19, 22, 30–31, 63–64

C
Cape Jaffa 102
Cape of Good Hope 37
Central Board of Health 247
Central Telegraphic Office 234
Churches
Flinders Street Baptist 225
Freeman Street Congregational Chapel 89, 111, 212
Holy Rood, Southampton 8, 9
St Francis Xavier's Cathedral 211
St Mary's, Southampton 13, 22
St Peter's Cathedral 235
Stow Memorial 227
Trinity 86, 88–89, 91, 98, 218, 249
City Commission 177

Clements, Mr 12, 97
Colonial Office 19–20, 25, 51, 63, 69, 104, 122, 147
Coltman and Company 60, 67–68, 148, 152, 175
Coltman, James 60, 67–68, 148, 152, 175
Conversazione Club, London 15, 85
Coorong, The 101–102, 132
Cooper, Charles 84, 100, 145–146
copper 155, 163, 165, 177, 220–222, 244

D
Daly, Sir Dominick 225
Destitute Asylum 214
Dissenters 1, 18, 20, 169, 225
Dry Creek 157, 161, 170
Duff, Captain John 22, 29–30, 35, 48

E
Elder, Thomas (later Sir) 245
'electric' telegraph 197, 211, 220, 228
Encounter Bay 53, 69, 101, 131
Everard, Dr Charles 31, 35–36, 47
Everard, William 157
Executive Council 53, 61–62, 103, 122, 126
Eyre, Edward 138

299

F

Finniss, Boyle Travers 71, 198
Fisher, James Hurtle (later Sir) 54, 59, 62–64, 69–70, 81–82, 183
Fisher, Robert 41, 61, 65, 75
Fleet Street (London) 1, 9–11, 14, 17, 21, 149, 175
Flinders, Captain Matthew 16
Forster, Anthony 184, 223

G

Gawler, Colonel George 70–71, 81, 83–85, 103–108, 113, 119, 121–122, 125–127, 139, 183
General Post Office 228, 232, 234–235, 242
George IV, King 11
Gilles Arcade 66, 68, 87, 118
Gilles, Osmond 16, 49, 64, 184, 229
Glen Osmond 184, 200, 208–209, 217
Glenelg 54–55, 69, 139, 141, 149, 151, 185, 205–206, 231, 234, 236, 244
Glenelg, Lord (Charles Grant) 69, 103
Gliddon, Arthur 31
gold escort 181–182
gold rush 179–180, 195, 202, 214, 223
Gorton, John 24
Gorton, Mrs 92, 96, 124
Gouger, Harriet 27–28, 49
Gouger, Robert 14, 27–28, 30, 32–33, 35, 37, 41, 46–49, 51, 54, 63–64, 161, 206
Government House 66, 111, 126, 201, 231
Goyder's Line 223
Grey, Captain George 126, 136, 141, 163, 183
Grey, Sir George 19

H

Hallett, John 30, 38, 96
Hanson, Richard (later Sir) 245
Harris Snr, George 8, 12, 72

Harris, George 8, 12–13, 22, 67, 70–75, 77–78, 80, 82, 84, 90, 92–99, 101, 103–104, 109, 111–112, 114, 117, 121, 123, 125, 127–128, 152, 209
Harris, Mary (Thomas) *see* **Thomas, Mary (nee Harris)**
High Street, Southampton 8–9, 12
Hill, near Southampton 12
Hillier, Jane 87
Hillier, Mary 124, 141, 150
Hillier, William 145, 217
Hindley Street 3, 55, 59–60, 66–68, 74, 76, 87, 90–93, 112, 120, 141, 148–149, 151–152, 164, 173, 182, 193, 207, 210–211, 240, 244
Hindmarsh, Adelaide 66, 88
Hindmarsh, Captain John 21, 24–25, 49–50, 53–54, 59, 62, 64, 69–70, 103, 183, 207
Hobart Town 101
Holbrooke, Harriet (Turner) 86, 124
Holdfast Bay 45, 48, 51, 53, 60, 65, 70–71, 77, 107
Holmes, Ann 157–158, 165
Holmes, Captain John 157–159, 165–166, 168
Howard, Reverend Charles Beaumont 21, 91, 124
Hughes, Walter Watson (later Sir) 220, 223, 244

I

Inns and Hotels
  Adelaide Tavern 117
  Anchor Inn, Southampton 12
  Clarendon Hotel 177, 182, 200, 208, 237
  Fordham's Hotel 107
  John o' Groats Inn 76–77, 149, 153, 173–174, 176–177
  Southern Cross (Allen's) 37, 77
  The Dolphin 7–8
  The Royal George 8

J

Jickling, Henry 141

K

Kangaroo Island 41, 43–44, 46, 48, 53–54, 61, 96
Kensington, Adelaide 176, 185, 190, 208, 218, 222
King William Street 87, 111, 153, 164, 184, 220, 225, 227, 229, 231–232, 234
Kingston, George Strickland (later Sir) 2, 16–17, 21, 45, 48, 53, 71, 93–94, 166, 221

L

Lazar, John 117–118, 129, 135, 150
Lazar, Rachel 125, 135
Legislation
  Act for the Better Government of Australian Colonies 156, 178
  Act to Establish Standard Weights and Measures 155
  Adelaide University Incorporation Act 245
  Australian Colonial Government Act 178
  Bullion Act 181
  Corporations Act 204
  Deceased Wife's Sister Act 238–239
  Destitute Person's Act (Maintenance Act) 214
  Education Act 248
  Licensing Act 76
  Municipal Corporation Act 183
  Public Health Act 246–247
  Real Property Act 210
  Reform Act 18
  South Australia Act 16, 19, 113
  South Australian Constitution Act 203
  South Australian Institute Act 222
Legislative Council 156, 169, 173, 177–179, 202–204, 239
Light, Colonel William 2, 21, 41, 44–46, 53–54, 59, 62–63, 65–67, 70–71, 93, 211
Light Square 66

Lillywhite, Mary 22, 31, 75
London, England 1–2, 7, 9–11, 14, 16–17, 22–25, 27–29, 39, 45, 51, 59–64, 68, 70, 72, 78, 85, 87, 96, 111, 113, 117–118, 121–122, 127, 139, 141, 143, 146–147, 161, 167, 174–175, 190, 203, 215, 242, 250
Long Building 59–60, 65–66, 71, 92, 173, 177–178
Lunatic Asylum 152, 235

M

Macdougall, Archibald 79–81
Main North Road 154, 184, 186
Mann, Charles 54, 63, 69, 80, 91
Mantegani, Alfred 185–186, 189, 191, 194, 201–202, 207, 219
Mantegani, Alfred Victor 211, 219
Mantegani, Helen (nee Thomas) (see Appendix A) 10, 22–23, 26–29, 31, 36, 55, 84, 86–87, 89, 90–93, 95, 98, 100, 107–108, 123–124, 131, 138, 140, 143, 149–151, 157–158, 161, 164–165, 167–168, 182–196, 198–202, 205, 207–219, 221, 226, 231–232, 237–239, 251
Mantegani, Victoria Theresa 194, 201–202, 207
Maria massacre 101–102, 105, 110, 132, 133
McLaren, David 106–107
Millbrook, England 12
Mildred, Mr and Mrs Henry 142
Mildred, Hiram 142, 180
Montefiore Hill 87, 243
Montgomeryshire, Wales 9, 213
Moorhouse, Dr Matthew 87, 131, 137–138
Moorundee 161, 166
Morphett, John (later Sir) 161
Murphy, Francis 211
Murray River 16, 43, 132–133, 161, 166, 181

N

Nepean Bay 41–44, 48
New South Wales 15, 83, 125, 137
Newport, Wales 198, 213
Newspapers and publications
Adelaide Chronicle 99–100, 120, 143, 152, 228
Advertiser 2
Evening Telegraph 223, 228
Free Press 139
Herald and Weekly Times 2, 250
Independent 139
Observer 163, 184, 189, 203, 206, 211, 218, 222–223, 225, 229, 231–232, 242, 246–247, 249
South Australian Almanack 68, 77, 99, 119–120, 130, 139
South Australian Gazette 100, 104, 109, 119, 141, 145
South Australian Gazette and Colonial Register 2, 25, 60–64, 69, 77–81, 90–91
South Australian Register 100–110, 112–113, 120–122, 125–127, 130–133, 135, 137–140, 143, 144, 146–148, 152–154, 160, 162–164, 173, 177, 183–185, 189, 198, 210, 218–220, 223, 225, 228, 234, 242, 249–250
Southern Australian 69, 78–80, 105, 109, 146
Spectator 122
North Adelaide 113, 148, 197, 235, 243
North Terrace 87–88, 91, 117, 156, 189, 221, 227, 243, 245
Norwood 176, 185

O

O'Halloran, Major T.S. 102–103, 108
'Old Gum Tree' 46, 49, 206
Osborne, E. 31, 35, 41–42, 48, 60, 96
Overland Telegraph 224, 241–242

P

Patawalonga Creek 151
Penny, Dr Richard 131–134
Periwinkle Point 140, 150
Platts, Charles 86–88, 135, 239
Port Adelaide 77, 101, 105–106, 166, 185–186, 197, 235–236, 238
Port Darwin 241, 243
Port River 53, 106
Prince Alfred College 233
Princess Con 43, 48
Proclamation of South Australia 49–50, 61, 103, 107, 109, 205–207
Prospect, Adelaide 154
Pullen, Captain W. 101–102

Q

Queen Victoria 231
Queen's Theatre 117–119, 122–123, 125, 130–131, 133–135, 138, 140, 143, 150, 169
Queensland 241
Queenstown, Adelaide 186, 188, 193, 197, 208

R

Rapid Bay 44–45, 49, 51
Redbridge, England 12
Reid, Elizabeth (Primrose) 124, 140, 169
Rhantregwnwyn Cottage, Adelaide 92–95, 98, 128, 135, 142, 151, 159, 162, 166, 168, 173–174, 185, 188–189, 199, 202, 211, 216, 219, 229, 236–237, 248, 250
Rickmansworth, England 14
River Torrens 53, 66, 70, 74, 87, 92, 106, 148, 158, 167, 179, 221, 243
Robe, Frederick 169, 183
R. Thomas and Co. 2, 24–25, 61, 65, 68, 71, 76–78, 80–82, 84, 92, 99–100, 104–105, 109–113, 119–120, 124, 130, 138–139, 141, 143, 145–148, 151–153, 173, 175, 198, 200–201
Rundle Street 88, 90–91, 112, 148, 153, 164, 166, 244

S

St Leonards 151
St Peter's College 233
Schürmann, C.W. 100
Self, Benjamin 9, 12, 72
Ships
 Africaine 22, 26–31, 33, 37, 39, 41–48, 52, 54, 61, 64, 91, 94, 96, 229, 238, 251
 Buffalo (HMAS) 25, 30, 49–50, 52
 Cygnet 21, 53–54, 161
 Dorset 140, 145
 Duke of York 44
 Emma 44, 48
 Galatea 231, 233
 Investigator 241
 John Pirie 44
 Lady Fitzherbert 141, 143, 145–146
 Lady Mary Pelham 44
 Lalla Rhook 119, 139
 Omeo 241
 Pestonjee Bomanjee 70
 Rapid 53
 Tam o' Shanter 52–53
Short, Augustus 244–245
Sinnett, F. 223
Skipper, Frances Amelia (nee Thomas) (see Appendix A) 7, 10, 17, 22–23, 31, 60, 86, 89–93, 96–98, 100, 106, 112–113, 118, 123, 125, 127–128, 134–135, 138, 142, 149–150, 157–158, 165, 170, 174, 185–193, 195, 216, 218, 229, 231, 237–238, 240
Skipper, John Michael 31, 89, 91, 93, 98, 100, 108, 122, 140, 145–146, 157, 168, 179–180, 185–186, 191–192, 196, 199–200, 206, 209, 238–239, 251
Skipper, Mary Jnr (nee Thomas) (see Appendix A) 10, 22–23, 26–28, 31, 55, 84, 86–92, 95–98, 100, 107–108, 112, 117–118, 122–125, 131, 133, 135, 139–143, 145, 149–151, 156–159, 161–162, 164–170, 174, 186, 188, 190, 192–193, 195–198, 208–209, 212–213, 216, 218, 229, 231, 237, 239, 251

Skipper, Spencer John 185, 187, 189, 191, 208, 216, 237, 248
Slater, John 31, 35, 41–42, 48
slavery 12, 16, 18
Solomon, Emanuel and Mary 68, 86, 117–118, 123–123, 125, 129–131, 134–135, 140, 142, 145, 150
South Australian Association 14–16, 85
South Australian Commission/commissioners 14–19, 21, 25, 53–54, 62, 64–65, 69–70, 78, 83, 88, 90, 113, 121–122, 125–127, 136, 144, 177
South Australian Company 18, 41–42, 44, 48, 53, 64, 67, 100, 106, 165
South Australian Institute 221–222, 245
South Australian Parliament 202–205, 210
South Australian School Society 87
Southampton, England 1–2, 7–9, 12–13, 17, 21–23, 72, 123, 127–128, 149
Spence, Catherine Helen 4, 194
Spencer Gulf 40
Stephen, George Milner 70, 78–82
Stephens, John 163, 177
Stephens, Samuel 42, 44
Stevenson, George 2, 20, 24–25, 30, 50, 53–54, 59, 61–63, 69–70, 78–82, 84–85, 87, 91, 99–100, 102–103, 105, 108–111, 113, 119–123, 126, 131, 133, 136, 138, 144–148, 151–153, 173, 198–199
Stevenson, Margaret 24–25, 54, 63, 91, 96, 124
Stow, Thomas Quinton 85, 227
Strand, The, London 10, 14
Stuart, John McDouall 224, 241
Sturt, Captain Charles 16, 71, 87, 166, 224

Sutherland, Captain George 41, 43–44
Sydney, New South Wales 68, 75, 117–118, 145–147, 211, 220, 234–235, 244

T

Teichelmann, Dr G.C. 100, 131
Temple Bar, London 10
'Temple Bar', Adelaide 206
Test Valley, England 9–10
Thebarton, Adelaide 88
Thomas, Evan Kyffin 79, 229, 237, 250
Thomas, Frances Amelia (Skipper) (see Appendix A) *see* Skipper, Frances Amelia (nee Thomas)
Thomas, Helen (Mantegani) (see Appendix A) *see* Mantegani, Helen (nee Thomas)
Thomas, Mary (nee Harris) (see Appendix A)
 early life, marriage and children 7–11
 preparing to emigrate 13–26
 on board the *Africaine* 27–45
 Kangaroo Island 41–44
 at Glenelg camp 45–49, 51–55
 first encounter with Aborigines 51–52
 move to Adelaide 55, 59–60
 letters to her brother, George Harris 31, 47, 65, 67–68, 70–75, 77–78, 80, 82, 92–104, 109–112, 114, 117, 121, 123–125, 152
 letters to her daughter, Helen 182, 184, 190–193, 201, 207–218
 opinions
 of Governor Hindmarsh 49, 70
 of J.H. Fisher 63, 70, 82
 of J.M. Skipper 185, 192–193, 238–239
 of G.M. Stephen 80, 82
 of Governor Gawler 110–111

Index

Thomas, Mary cont'd
death of her daughter, Frances 189–190
relationship with her husband Robert 199–200, 208, 215–216, 217
death of her husband, Robert 217–219
poetry: *Serious Poems* (see Appendix B) 1, 12–13, 249
death and obituary 248–251
Thomas, Mary Jnr (Skipper) (see Appendix A) *see* Skipper, Mary Jnr (nee Thomas)
Thomas, Nathaniel 42
Thomas, Robert (see Appendix A) 1–2, 9–12, 14, 16, 19–20, 22–23, 28–34, 36–38, 41, 43, 48, 51, 59–62, 64–72, 77, 80–83, 87–89, 91–93, 95–96, 98–100, 104–105, 107, 112–113, 121, 124, 127, 136, 139, 141, 143, 151–153, 165–166, 168, 173–178, 182, 185, 190, 198–201, 204, 206, 208, 209, 212, 215–216, 220–222, 229, 239–240, 250
formation of R. Thomas and Co. 24–25
at Glenelg camp 45–46, 49, 53–54
move to Adelaide 54
loss of government printing and return to London for redress 110–111, 113, 117–119
return to Adelaide 145
last *Register* and insolvency of R. Thomas and Co. 146–149
Inspector of Weights and Measures 155, 164, 183–185
death and obituary 217–219

Thomas, Robert George (see Appendix A) 2, 96, 98, 124, 140, 143, 157, 167, 185, 190, 199, 218, 223, 237, 238, 239
in London 10, 14, 17
emigration, apprenticeship and surveying in South Australia 21, 45, 53, 59, 65, 70–71, 92–93, 161, 164, 166
return to England 168, 174, 198
marriage and children 198, 212–213, 222–223, 225, 231, 240
return to Adelaide and work as an architect and later in public service 222, 224–230, 232, 234–236, 245–247
death 251
Thomas, Robert Kyffin 208, 216
Thomas, Rosetta (Birks) (see Appendix A) *see* Birks, Rosetta (nee Thomas)
Thomas, William Kyffin (see Appendix A) 2, 18, 21, 61, 84, 86–87, 99, 111, 153, 157, 159–160, 166, 190–191, 194–196, 202, 204, 206–208, 212, 216–218, 221, 222, 225, 227, 229–232, 234–240, 244
in London and emigration 10, 14, 17, 22–23, 28–31
at Glenelg camp 48–49
in Adelaide 54, 59–60, 65, 77, 80, 92, 94, 96, 100, 118, 123–124, 140–141, 145
farming 154–155
at goldfields 179–180, 182
returns to *South Australian Register* and expansion 164, 184–185, 189, 220, 223, 228, 242, 250
Todd, Charles (later Sir) 241–243

Tolmer, Alexander 181
Torrens, Colonel Robert 16, 210

U
University of Adelaide 244–245

V
Van Diemen's Land 15, 65, 75
Victoria Square 111, 126, 211, 221, 227–228, 231–232

W
W.K. Thomas and Co. 229, 250
Wakefield, Edward Gibbon 1–2, 14–16, 41, 85, 144, 204, 250
Walkerville, Adelaide 88, 248
West Terrace 66
West Terrace Cemetery 218, 249
Whitington, F.T. 49
Wigley, Henry 141, 145, 149–150
Wilkinson, George B. 49, 167–168
William IV, King 207
Williams, Margaret 84, 86–87, 97, 135
Williams, William 92, 124
Women's Suffrage League 3
Woodforde, Dr John 97, 128, 149, 229
Wright, Charles 91, 124, 143, 149, 156–162, 165, 169–170, 195
Wright, Dr Edward 16, 97, 112, 124, 143, 149, 156, 160–162, 169
Wright, Edmund 225, 228
Wright, Mrs Edward 91, 158, 161, 166, 168
Wyatt, Dr William 84

Y
Young, Sir Henry 177

Wakefield Press is an independent publishing and
distribution company based in Adelaide, South Australia.
We love good stories and publish beautiful books.
To see our full range of books, please visit our website at
www.wakefieldpress.com.au
where all titles are available for purchase.
To keep up with our latest releases, news and events,
subscribe to our monthly newsletter.

Find us!

Facebook: www.facebook.com/wakefield.press
Twitter: www.twitter.com/wakefieldpress
Instagram: www.instagram.com/wakefieldpress

www.ingramcontent.com/pod-product-compliance
Lightning Source LLC
Chambersburg PA
CBHW070836160426
43192CB00012B/2210